The Legend of Charlie CHAPLIN

Sincerely Yours
Charles Chaplin

The Legend of Charlie CHAPLIN

Collected and introduced by

Peter Haining

W. H. ALLEN · LONDON
A Howard & Wyndham Company
1982

Copyright © 1982 by Peter Haining

Printed and bound in Great Britain
by Mackay's of Chatham Ltd,
for the Publishers, W.H. Allen & Co. Ltd,
44 Hill Street, London W1X 8LB

ISBN 0 491 02608 0

For
my children
Richard, Sean and Gemma
with love

By the same author

THE SHERLOCK HOLMES SCRAPBOOK
GHOSTS: THE ILLUSTRATED HISTORY
SUPERSTITIONS
THE MAN WHO WAS FRANKENSTEIN
MOVABLE BOOKS
SWEENEY TODD – THE DEMON BARBER OF FLEET STREET
THE FINAL ADVENTURES OF SHERLOCK HOLMES
THE SHERLOCK HOLMES COMPENDIUM

'It is given to few people to become a legend during their lifetime. Charles Chaplin has been a legend for the greater part of his life. His genius was apparent early, though not as early as with a child prodigy such as Mozart; his fame became worldwide soon after he came of age. It was chiefly with the aid of silent film that he attained this, for it was not essential to know English in order to understand and appreciate his antics. Indeed, while still in his early twenties, he was better known than any other man or woman has ever been in the world's history, known by Christians speaking a dozen tongues in two hemispheres, known by Hindoos, Moslems and Chinese, known even by Zulus and Bantus and more primitive people, who laughed at the shabby little man as he strove to overcome the buffetings and humiliations inflicted upon him by fate and his fellow creatures.'

R.J. Minney
Chaplin: The Immortal Tramp (1954)

CONTENTS

Peter Haining
INTRODUCTION

LIKE THE best moments in a Charlie Chaplin film, this book was conceived from an incident of unexpected embarrassment mingled with high comedy.

Publisher Bob Tanner and I were in Los Angeles visiting The Magic Castle, a famous private club for magicians which perches on a hillside overlooking Hollywood. The Castle is actually a restored 1909 mansion which has become the Mecca for celebrities from all over the world. To gain admission you must be a professional magician, but such was our determination we were prepared to use a little subterfuge to get in.

So Bob and I said we were members of the Magic Circle. It proved to be the open-sesame, and we couldn't help congratulating ourselves on so easily gaining entry to this wonderland of mystery. But our self-satisfaction was somewhat premature.

'Oh, by the way gentlemen,' the Master of Ceremonies who showed us to our table for dinner said. 'You'll be expected to perform a piece of magic for the other guests. It's a tradition you see – all our visitors do.'

The man turned his back and walked away. Bob and I looked at each other in the dimly-lit, ornately-furnished room. Our bluff had been called. Neither of us had ever performed a magic trick in our lives!

The next hour was sheer torture. Each time anyone approached our table we shifted nervously in our chairs and debated whether to plead inability, insanity or just beat a hasty retreat. Even the waiters began to eye us suspiciously. The anxiety didn't do much for our appetites, either.

Finally, the Master of Ceremonies came across to our table once more. The moment of truth had arrived. There was to be no escape.

'Oh,' said Bob before the man could speak, 'There's something –'

'Yes, there is,' I interjected just as quickly.

The man looked from one to the other of us. 'I'm sorry, gentlemen,' he said after a moment when he could see we were lost for words. 'I'm afraid there won't be time for you to perform. We've had to bring forward the exhibition of magic in the lounge. It's a shame. Perhaps another time?'

To this day, neither of us is quite sure exactly what we replied. But we both remember being thankful. *Very* thankful.

Later we both agreed: 'That was like something from a Charlie Chaplin film!'

Looking back now in hindsight, thoughts of the little genius of the silent screen had never been far from our minds during that stay in Hollywood, and to be sure his presence seems to pervade the atmosphere of the whole place. Yet, somehow, our interest in Chaplin was crystallized during that moment of comedy.

Both Bob and I had been admirers of Charlie since our childhoods and this fact made it all the more special to be spending some time in the very place where his art had developed and then taken the world by storm. We also found that we shared an interest in another aspect of Chaplin's life – the portrait of himself which he had presented through the pages of his autobiography which had then not long been published. We both concurred with the general opinion that what the star had revealed of himself and his career in *My Autobiography* was far from being the whole story. Indeed, the consensus of views was that Charlie had tailored the events of his life to suit his vision of himself as well as his effect on those who had been a part of the most dramatic rise to international stardom that any actor had ever know. There seemed little doubt that he had changed some facts, conveniently forgotten others and deliberately left out a good deal of fascinating and revealing material. It was an opinion that has perhaps been most emphatically stated by the critics

Raoul Sobel and David Francis in their book, *Chaplin: Genesis of a Clown* (1977):

'Unfortunately, his autobiography, which arrived in 1964, is more interesting for the manner of its telling than for the tale. Though the description of his early life makes interesting reading, there is no mention of some of the people who had the greatest influence on his career, and most of the rest is a catalogue of great names who paid him fashionable obeisance or who swept through his life dropping maxims like sugared plums. It does little justice to either the man or the artist.'

Through our long involvement in the world of books, Bob and I were very well aware that there had already been plenty of attempts to write biographies of Chaplin *in retrospect*. But what, we wondered in the harsh, bright light of a Los Angeles morning a day or so later when we were still laughing over our experience at The Magic Castle, what had been written about Chaplin by those who had known him intimately and actually worked with him? People who were close to the remarkable little actor and had committed their observations and impressions to paper while the memories were still clear and fresh in their minds? How did *their* accounts differ from Chaplin's own.

The existing studies of him gave plentiful evidence that fellow actors, members of his film company, even life-long friends and associates had all written pieces about him at some time, usually for newspapers or magazines. There was evidence, too, that Chaplin himself had penned various articles during the earlier stages of his career: articles that contained details he had omitted when he came to write his *Autobiograpy*.

So, surely, if a representative selection of these essays could be found there would be the raw material for a quite unique book on Charlie Chaplin. A book which would look at the man, his art and his impact from a highly personalized viewpoint.

Nearly a decade later, that idea has come to fruition in the form of this book. It has been a long, and at times extremely arduous task to locate the many rare items which appear here, as virtually every single one has not been reprinted since its original appearance. The contributions have been arranged in chronological order in virtually every instance, thereby leading the reader naturally from one stage of Charlie's career to the next, from the poverty of his childhood to the superabundance of his mature years and the international acclaim of the closing years of his life.

Two points should also perhaps just be made. Firstly, that Chaplin's habit of contradicting himself was not something he developed altogether in later life: even much earlier in his career he was changing facts about his life to suit his own purposes, I discovered, although at this time he was writing from a less pretentious and entrenched viewpoint, and consequently more of the real man shows through. Secondly, that the essays selected for this book lay greatest emphasis on the development of his art and the various phases of his *public* life. His private life has, of course, been a topic of endless debate – his various wives and love affairs the subject of scandalous and often totally untrue stories – and I feel it is not the purpose of a book such as this to become embroiled in still further speculation. The tales about this side of his life are without exception one-sided, and in what I hope is a balanced book, would be glaringly out of place.

The Legend of Charlie Chaplin is, then, a celebration of a great man who, despite the evident faults which are revealed in the following pages, still created a special place for himself in the consciousness of all mankind, giving all of us, whatever our situation, a view of romance, a view of comedy and a view of love that is unique.

My search for the real Chaplin through his own words and those of his friends has been a fascinating and rewarding one which has taken me from the glamour of modern day Hollywood back to the mean streets of London where he was born almost a century ago. All the time I have been involved, though, I have been spurred on by some of Charlie's own words: words that he addressed to his eldest son but which have relevance to everybody:

'You have to believe in yourself,' he said to the boy, 'that's the secret. Even when I was in the orphanage, when I was roaming the streets trying to find enough to keep alive, even then I thought of myself as the greatest actor in the world. I had to feel the exuberance that comes from utter confidence in yourself. Without it, you go down to defeat.'

Charlie, we salute you!

Peter Haining
December, 1981

CHAPLIN'S INSPIRATION

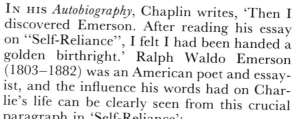

IN HIS *Autobiography*, Chaplin writes, 'Then I discovered Emerson. After reading his essay on "Self-Reliance", I felt I had been handed a golden birthright.' Ralph Waldo Emerson (1803–1882) was an American poet and essayist, and the influence his words had on Charlie's life can be clearly seen from this crucial paragraph in 'Self-Reliance':

'Insist on yourself; never imitate. Your own gift you can present every moment with the cumulative force of a whole life's cultivation; but of the adopted talent of another, you have only an extemporaneous, half possession. That which each can do best, none but his Maker can teach him. No man yet knows what it is, nor can, till that person has exhibited it. Where is the master who could have taught Shakespeare? Where is the master who could have instructed Franklin, or Washington, or Bacon or Newton? Every great man is unique. The Scipionism of Scipio is precisely that part he could not borrow. Shakespeare will never be made by the study of Shakespeare. Do that which is assigned you, and you cannot hope too much or dare too much.'

Chaplin on the pinnacle of sucess – and a rare picture
of 3, Pownall Terrace where he grew up and which
has now been demolished

16

Charlie Chaplin
MEMORIES OF MY CHILDHOOD

THE LEGEND of Charlie Chaplin begins in the heart of Victorian London in East Lane, Walworth where he was born on 16 April 1889, the son of Charles and Hannah Chaplin. Both his parents were actors, his father a comedian and his mother a singer and dancer. Talking to British journalist Stefan Lorant in 1936, Charlie graphically recalled those childhood days, 'I spent my youth in south-east London. It makes me sad to think back on this time. We were poor, very poor. My father had no engagements and was gradually taking to drink. We all but starved. My elder brother Sydney often queued up at the mission houses to fetch us some free soup. I should have liked to go with him – but that was impossible. We had only one pair of shoes between us, and had to take turns wearing them.'

After the sudden death of his father, aged thirty-seven, Charlie tried to earn money to help his impoverished family. 'As the child of an actor my first thought was naturally the stage. I was given some parts and earned a few shillings. I was just seven years old.'

Life continued to be a struggle for the three Chaplins, only relieved by the occasional job for one or the other of them. Charlie, though, persisted with his desire to act and as he grew towards manhood gradually learned his art in the tough school of the London and provincial theatres. As I mentioned in my Introduction, Charlie's vision of himself and his origins when written as an old man was shaped by various circumstances, and it therefore seems most appropriate to begin this book with an account of his youth written when he was still barely out of it. The article appeared in the British magazine, *Answers* in August 1915, and apart from filling in the details of his early career, shows us that Charlie saw himself not so much as a comic performer but a frustrated dramatic actor! It provides a fascinating insight into the young man's emotions at this time, and was in all probability written with the assistance of his secretary, Elsie Codd.

'A LOT OF people have given me shocks in my time, but, though "I says it as shouldn't", the most surprising fellow I've come across up to the present is – Charlie Chaplin.

'Why, it seems only yesterday that I was tramping round London dressed in my best clothes looking for any old play-acting job that would keep me in grub. Today I put on a collection of garments that would go begging in any doss-house – and I am a star! And that's why I find Charles Chaplin, Esq., such an extremely interesting fellow.

'Yesterday, so to speak, I was just an unknown individual fighting hard for his daily bread; today the picture is changed. Wherever I go I am recognized, and, yes, fêted. Girls who in the old days would have passed me by with not so much as a glance, today are only too willing to flatter "Charlie" with their attention.

'In a little States township only a short time ago the mayor actually turned out with the brass band to welcome me! I can see him doing that a couple of years ago, when I was "up against it" – I don't think!

'They say that a rolling stone gathers little or no moss, and that, if it does, the moss is only about as valuable as an Iron Cross to a German "hero". Be that as it may, I have rolled half round the world, and am still "reeling" – perhaps from the effects, but very effectively, as my producer wittily enough tells me.

'I think my sense of humour is becoming sadly shattered by all the humour that forms the greater part of my acting life. I begin to wonder at times whether or not I am really funny. My case, I think, is rather like that of the unhappy individual who went to consult a doctor. The medical man said:

'"Why, man, all you want is a hearty laugh; go and see Grimaldi at the ——"

'The patient turned sadly away. It was Grimaldi himself!

'Really, it is very difficult for an alleged comedian to realize that he is funny. In the old days, although I attempted mimicry and merry-making, I was never conscious of any success to my efforts. Even now I wonder at my popularity.

'It comes as a matter of course, somehow, to me now, when I walk along a greasy pole, carrying a bucket of pig's wash, and at the end of my journey, having tipped my load into my "hated rival's" face, to fall back, say, into a well or horse-trough. I now associate myself with experiences that to any ordinary individual would appear as horrible.

'For me to have a full-sized brick flung at my head is only the most ordinary, the most trivial incident in a day, and my first dislike for, after having thrown a bunch of roses at the heroine, picking up a brick and casting it at her, has now absolutely departed.

'I not only throw the brick, but I am maliciously careful in my aim, and that smile that you see flickering somewhere below my diminutive moustache is secretly one of triumph at the sureness of my aim.

'But I am digressing. My readers will have guessed all this by now. Having seen me plant my foot below the belt of my opponent, they will know that Charlie Chaplin, while gaining in cunning, has lost a lot of his youthful ideals.

'Speaking of my youth, shall I tell you a little about it?

'I can remember myself now as a particularly curious child – a creature of moods, and delicate in the extreme, a boy who had no knowledge that one day he was going to be in the great army of fun-makers.

'Coming from a theatrical family as I did, I naturally had thoughts of the stage; but it was not the lighter side that appealed to me. Rather did I dream of being Romeo, and playing to a Juliet, who, perfect in every way, was looking out over moon-kissed Verona into an Italian sky of serene beauty.

'Sometimes thinking of this, I laugh. Imagine Charlie Chaplin as Romeo, with, for doublet, a broken shirt-front, his sword a little cane held lovingly in the left hand, and for knightly cap a tiny bowler perched on a mop of black hair!

'But as I think, there comes the rub. In my heart of hearts I know that, although my feet betray me, my moustache is that of a perfect Romeo.

'How I wander from the path! Where was I? Oh, yes; back at my childhood days.

'I was too delicate, really as a boy, to have much education, but I believe that what little knowledge I gained I picked up very quickly. I had a way of concentrating on anything that influenced me, and making myself familiar with it very speedily.

'My boyhood passed like a flash, and the day came when I was to choose for myself the line of life that I was to take. Was my serious side to come uppermost, or was my precociousness to lead me either to bitter ill-success or the fame that I had hoped for in the serious drama?

'It did neither. It flung me into the whirlpool of mirth. It made me a "Merry Andrew" of the film – the flickering creature of fun that flitters across the screen at a shambling run, to make you laugh, and to bring me perhaps not quite that fame that I had dreamed of, but a popularity above the expression of words.

'You may be surprised, but my boyhood finished at the age of seven, for a little after that time I was busily working on the music halls, not for much, it must be admitted, but, like "Meredith", I was "in"!

'At that time I was one of the Eight Lancashire Lads.

'My work on that tour was arduous in the extreme; young as I was, I was an adept at dancing and acrobatics. It was excellent training for film-work, for I learned many little tricks on the dusty stages of music halls that no doubt now have passed, to be but a memory to those who once formed their audiences.

'It was later on in 1901 that I "reeled" forward again to a new experience in acting – my first legitimate engagement in drama. Mr William Gillette engaged me to play Billy, the page-boy in *Sherlock Holmes*, at Daly's Theatre

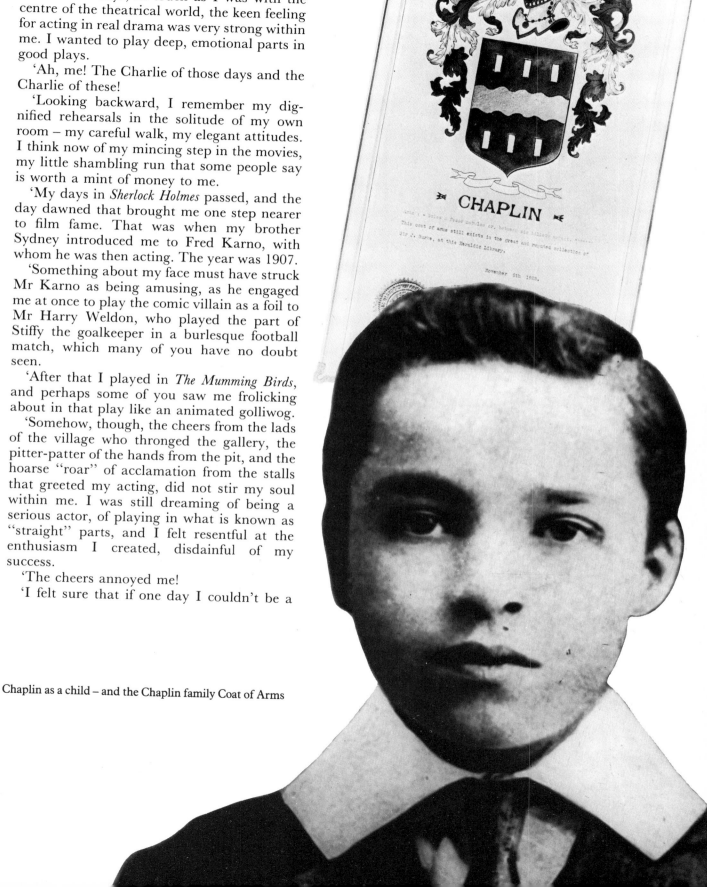

– and Billy I played. It was Billy night after night, for what seemed an interminable time (until 1905, in fact) but I must say I never wearied of the part.

'In those days, in touch as I was with the centre of the theatrical world, the keen feeling for acting in real drama was very strong within me. I wanted to play deep, emotional parts in good plays.

'Ah, me! The Charlie of those days and the Charlie of these!

'Looking backward, I remember my dignified rehearsals in the solitude of my own room – my careful walk, my elegant attitudes. I think now of my mincing step in the movies, my little shambling run that some people say is worth a mint of money to me.

'My days in *Sherlock Holmes* passed, and the day dawned that brought me one step nearer to film fame. That was when my brother Sydney introduced me to Fred Karno, with whom he was then acting. The year was 1907.

'Something about my face must have struck Mr Karno as being amusing, as he engaged me at once to play the comic villain as a foil to Mr Harry Weldon, who played the part of Stiffy the goalkeeper in a burlesque football match, which many of you have no doubt seen.

'After that I played in *The Mumming Birds*, and perhaps some of you saw me frolicking about in that play like an animated golliwog.

'Somehow, though, the cheers from the lads of the village who thronged the gallery, the pitter-patter of the hands from the pit, and the hoarse "roar" of acclamation from the stalls that greeted my acting, did not stir my soul within me. I was still dreaming of being a serious actor, of playing in what is known as "straight" parts, and I felt resentful at the enthusiasm I created, disdainful of my success.

'The cheers annoyed me!

'I felt sure that if one day I couldn't be a

Chaplin as a child – and the Chaplin family Coat of Arms

CHAPLIN

Tree,* I might at least be a Charlie "Sapling"! But my boughs were cut. To use a mixed metaphor, I was not allowed to wing away in search of the higher art. I was already marked down for a creature of humour.

'My comedy antics were successful – those bad lads of the village were making me quite a well-known person.

'One day, sick at heart, I approached a manager, and, flinging my chest out and making my eye luminous, I said:

'"I am tir-r-red of humour. I want to play in the real dr-r-rama."

'I leaned forward and raised my hand.

'"I want to make audiences thr-r-rill. I want to lift them up as Harvey, Alexander, Henry Ainley. I want to hold the serious people in the hollow of my hand."

'"Have a Woodbine?" said the manager coldly.

'With all the dramatic tenseness in my power, I drew back and looked at him. Was he taking me seriously?

'He came closer, and patted me on the shoulder.

'"Buck up, Charlie," he said; "you'll soon be better!" Then he came closer. "Look here, old man," he went on, "you're a born comedian. Why waste your thoughts on wanting to be a great tragedian? Make the world laugh, man. It will be better for it."

'I can tell you that it was a gloomy Charlie Chaplin who, looking deeply into a glass of barleywater, pondered over the inviolability of Fate. I was sure my powers were great as a big actor, and that evening, on my way home, I tested them on a servant-girl who was sitting at a window all covered in wistaria.

'Looking up, I played Romeo to her. But all she did was laugh, too!

'It was the last great act of my life, for when I got back to the company, a boy came forward with a letter. I took it, and, opening it, read something that gave me new hope for an added interest in life.

'It was from my brother Syd, who was then film acting, telling me what opportunities he had discovered in this new art form. The greatest moment in my life had come: although little did I realize the fact or that fame was waiting for me just across the Atlantic!'

* The 'Tree' that Charlie refers to was the great actor-manager, Sir Herbert Beerbohm Tree (1853–1917). Charlie later appeared with Sir Herbert in a single stage performance of *Oliver Twist* at the Mason Opera House, Los Angles, on 10 February 1916, in aid of a fund for Los Angeles News Boys. Charlie played The Artful Dodger to Sir Herbert's Fagin.

Dreaming of the past – Charlie in *The Gold Rush* (1925)

Elsie Codd
CHARLIE CHAPLIN'S FIRST SCRAPBOOK

ONE OF THE people closest to Chaplin during his early years in the film business was Elsie Codd, his English secretary and confidant, who saw him as intimately and objectively as anyone at that time. Although working for Chaplin was a demanding and hectic occupation, Elsie found time to write a fascinating book about his working techniques, *Charlie Chaplin's Methods* (1920) as well as this informative article which was also published the same year. In it, she looks back at some of her employer's earliest achievements on the English stage prior to his entering the world of films.

'The other day I was looking through Charlie Chaplin's press cutting albums, a most interesting record of his amazing rise to fame and fortune. In the huge cumbersome volumes that form this unique collection you can follow through every variety of journalism, good, bad and indifferent, the impressive phases of Charlie Chaplin's career, from the perilous period of his reign as a hilarious and fashionable cult to his final acceptance as a national institution.

'Human nature is very accommodating, and even under extreme provocation will gradually accustom itself to any and everything. Personally, it is a bit steep for me to figure out how, in Charlie Chaplin's place, I could ever come to regard the bulk and number of press cuttings with anything approaching poise and equanimity. But it appears it can be achieved in time, if the Press is obliging enough to persevere with the treatment and the subject during the early stages shows no symptoms of developing the insidious and distressing malady "caput inflatus" – vulgarly known as "swelled head".

'Whilst looking through the bulky tomes covered, be it owned, by the dust of many seasons – for Charlie as a rule prefers other forms of literature – I came across a volume which at some period of his career had evidently enjoyed the privilege of being cherished even as the apple of his eye.

'This was Charlie's very first album of press clippings, the sort of thing for which we used to save up our pocket money as children, and in which we used to stick our scraps and transfers on a wet Saturday afternoon. The outer cover is of that same neat and chaste design as those of the bigger volumes, but when you open it you find that inside is carefully preserved the original gaudy red and gold binding with the picture of the old mill in faded colours that we all used to find so beautiful as little girls and boys.

'The old book must date back some twenty years, for it was purchased in all the glow and pride of sudden fame, when little Charlie Chaplin made his first hit as Billy the page-boy in the Gillett production of *Sherlock Holmes*. Anyhow, I found on its opening page, much creased and soiled by constant fingering, two printed records of this early triumph.

'The one critic, blissfully unconscious that he is for the first time presenting to public notice the boy who was destined to become the most famous man in the world, comments that, "Mr Charles Chaplin," who, incidentally, at that period must have been about twelve years old, "is unusually bright and natural as Billy."

'The other even goes so far as to assert boldly that "one of the brightest bits of acting in the play was given by Mr Charles Chaplin, who, as Billy, displayed immense activity as well as dramatic appreciation."

'And, delightfully human touch!, the Mr Charles Chaplin of that period had been unable to resist the temptation of thickly underscoring these lines.

'"Turning the accomplishment of many years in an hour glass", the next notice in the scrapbook dates some seven years later, when Charlie was playing the name part in a clever little sketch entitled, *Jimmy The Fearless*. The production was intended to be a skit on the staple literature of the average errand boy.

'Jimmy is addicted to heavy suppers and penny dreadfuls and he has a dream in which he figures as a kind of youthful movie hero and rescues the customary beauteous heroine from the usual band of American roughs.

'Then, of course, he wakes up.

'Referring once more to the book in the red and gold binding, I learn that the "strong company included a comedian of strikingly original talents in the role of the hero." Another critic also felt that "a word is due to the very capable comedian who played the dreamer, but whose modesty kept his name off the programme."

'In later clippings I note that this omission has been rectified, and one paper even goes so far as to give a portrait of "Mr Charles Chaplin" then about nineteen, with a very stiff collar and sleekly plastered hair. Mr Charles Chaplin at nineteen looks considerably older than he now does at thirty-two. Also, incidentally, considerably plumper.

'A note of prophecy is struck by a writer in the *Yorkshire Evening Post* of 23 July 1910.

Under the heading "A Rising Actor", he comments thusly on Charlie's appearance with the Fred Karno Company at the Leeds Empire:

'"To assume roles made famous by Fred Kitchen is no small task for a stripling of twenty-one, yet Mr Chas. Chaplin, who has caused so much laughter this week as Jimmy the Fearless, has done so with vast credit to himself. Mr Chaplin has not been more than three years with Mr Karno, yet he has played all the principal parts, and he fully realizes the responsibility of following so consummate an artiste as Fred Kitchen. He is ambitious and painstaking, and is bound to get on. Young as he is, he has done some good work on the stage, and his entrance alone in *Jimmy The Fearless* sets the house in a roar and stamps him as a born comedian."

'It was that same year that Mr Alfred Reeves, who was managing Karno's interests in the United States, came to England in search of a new comedian for the American company, and, knowing a good thing when he saw it, drew the big prize of the lottery in the person of Charlie Chaplin.

'Now there is a general belief that Charlie was an entirely unknown quantity before he broke into pictures. I myself laboured under this popular delusion – until I dipped into that red and gilt scrapbook.

'From the very first, America realized that Charlie was "somehow different". I even find on a close perusal of those clippings that just those aspects of his genius were appreciated which have made his methods so unique on the screen.

'From these years also dates the portrait of the rather prim-looking young man in the high black "choker" with whom his fellow-countryman only became really familiar when the sudden fame of the picture Chaplin swept his native England with the force of a cyclone.

'The last cutting in this most interesting album combines a notice of Charlie's final appearance on the vaudeville stage with the following announcement:

'"Charlie Chaplin, who numbers his friends by the thousands, is going to desert the stage to become a movie actor and play the chief comedy roles with the Keystone Company. As a film actor Charlie should surely make good, for during the five years he has been with the Karno Company, and on all his visits to this city, he has not spoken a dozen lines, and has depended on facial expression and pantomime, the two secrets of success in the silent drama, to gain him the laughs. We shall all be anxiously awaiting the Keystone films in which he appears, and it goes without saying they will be just as funny as he has been in the various Karno offerings."

'Which final remark, as you must own, showed fairly good judgment!'

Fred Karno
THE BIRTH OF A STAR

THE MAN WHO gave Chaplin his first leg up the ladder of success was Fred Karno, the 'King' of Music Hall sketches, an astute businessmen who is said to have 'brought pantomime slapstick to the region of high art'. A former acrobat, he virtually invented the burlesque sketch and on this success built an empire of touring companies which travelled not only in Britain, but throughout Europe, across the Atlantic in America and Canada, and even as far afield as Africa and South America. As the productions were a mixture of music and mime, their 'language' was universal, a fact quickly appreciated by the young Chaplin. Charlie joined Fred Karno in 1907 when he was fifteen as a result of an introduction by his elder brother, Sydney, who had already followed in his parents' footsteps and gone onto the stage in one of Karno's companies, and was then a leading man. How Sydney used his influence to get his young brother a job is described here by Karno himself, in an essay published in April 1931. To his dying day, Charlie always acknowledged the great debt he owed to Fred Karno.

'ONE DAY, Sydney Chaplin who had belonged to my company for some time came to see me in my Camberwell studio in London.

'"Guv'nor," he said, "I wonder if you could do anything for my young brother, Charlie? He has more talent than I have, although he is only a kid. He has been appearing with a little troupe, "The Eight Lancashire Lads".'

'I thought for a minute. So Charlie had already played on the stage. And he was a dancer.

'Sydney then went on to tell me that his brother had also appeared in the provinces in *Sherlock Holmes*, although only in a very small part.

'"Bring me your brother," I said, "so that I can see him."

'A while later Syd arrived, accompanied by a young lad, very puny, pale and sad looking. He seemed undernourished and frightened, as though he expected me to raise my hand to hit him. Even his clothes were too small for him!

'I must say that at that first moment he seemed to me to be much too timid to do anything good on stage, especially in the

Rare photograph of Chaplin (middle, centre) rehearsing with a Fred Karno company

knockabout comedy shows that were my speciality. Still, I didn't want to disappoint Sydney, so I took him on.

'Charlie had only been in the troupe a week or two when I decided to give him a part. It was in a sketch called "The Football Match" and he played the part of a cheeky young boy who followed the goalkeeper in order to drug him before the match. It was a semi-dramatic part, and I soon realized that not only could Charlie play the clown, but he could also act.

'From that he became the drunkard in the famous sketch called "The Mumming Birds". He earned three pounds a week.

'Charlie took part in one after another of my companies, thus getting a first-rate schooling. It was easy to see that he was more eloquent with his hands than most people are with their vocal chords. He also showed himself a good, reliable performer.

'We all thought him more than a little eccentric, however. He was very untidy in his person. Even when he was a leading man, he would often turn up at train-call in a pair of old carpet slippers, his collar only partly buttoned, and his tie hanging loose round his neck.

'He could also be very unlikeable. I've known him go whole weeks without saying a word to anyone in the company. Occasionally he would be quite chatty, but on the whole he was dour and unsociable. He lived like a monk, had a horror of drink, and put most of his salary in the bank as soon as he got it.

'At last it was decided to send him on a tour of America. The repertoire included three sketches into which Charlie had put a good deal of his amusing personality. One of the sketches was "The Wow-Wows", a skit on secret societies. Charlie was initiated into the Secret Society of the Wows-Wows. You can imagine the farcical nature of the business! The other pieces were the popular "Mumming Birds" and "The Smoking Concert".

'The company went all round the Sullivan & Considine circuit twice, visiting all the principal cities east and west, including Salt Lake City, and travelling as far north as Winnipeg and south as far as New Orleans.

'It was while he was in one of these cities

Fred Karno

that the offers for cinema work came in and were too tempting for Charlie to resist. So he left and joined the Keystone Film Company.

'It had been obvious to me for a long time that Charlie was destined for the cinema. Between acts in the theatre, he would sometimes go to the cinema. He would stand at the back of the seats and follow the action on the screen, improvising in his own way. This would delight his friends and often caused the audience to stop following the film and watch his clowning!

'Some years after Charlie had left me, C B Cochran and I decided to put on a revue at the London Opera (now Stoll Pictures). It was to be a spectacular affair which would include a complete circus, a boxing match each evening, and several other numbers.

'One day, Cochran said to me: "What if we could get Chaplin as the star? You could use your influence on him. What would he say to £1,000 per week?"

'So I called Charlie in America. I have kept his reply to this day:

'"Dear Guv'nor,

The figure you mention to appear in London would have given me a heart attack once upon a time! But I am tied up now for some years and I don't see any possibility of being able to come to London.

But if I am able to do so one day, be sure I would let you know before anybody.

Wishing you all luck, I am, Guv'nor,
Your Charlie Chaplin."'

Stan Laurel
MY ECCENTRIC ROOM-MATE

IT IS IN connection with Chaplin's tour of North America with Fred Karno's company that one of the most glaring omissions occurs in his *Autobiography*. For nowhere in the book does he make any mention of Stan Laurel, later to be half of the famous film partnership of Laurel and Hardy, who was also a member of the party. Although Chaplin may have considered the quietly-spoken Stanley Jefferson (he had not yet changed his surname) who was his understudy, an unimportant member of the group at that time, the two men did share the same rooms on the tour and came to know each other well. Stan, for his part, obviously learned something of Chaplin's stage techniques, for when Charlie left the company to join Mack Sennett and later established the screen persona of the Little Tramp, he created a twelve-minute vaudeville sketch which was a direct imitation of his former room-mate. However, he did not have to remain as an imitator for long – his partnership with Oliver Hardy was just around the corner and along with it the fame which was to make him as well-known as Chaplin. In this brief essay, Stan Laurel recalls the days he and Charlie spent in Fred Karno's touring company in America. . .

Stan Laurel

'AMERICA WAS A whole new world for us. We were thrilled at the excitement of New York, but seeing the whole country, mile after mile, was really the way to see it.

'I was Charlie's room-mate on that tour and he was fascinating to watch. People through the years have talked about how eccentric he became. He was a very eccentric person even then. He was very moody and often very shabby in appearance. Then suddenly he would astonish us all by getting dressed to kill. It seemed that every once in a while he would get an urge to look very smart. At these times he would wear a derby hat (an expensive one), gloves, smart suit, fancy vest, two-tone side button shoes and carry a cane. I have a lot of quick, little memories of him like that.

'For instance, I remember that he drank only once in a while and then it was always port. He read books incessantly. One time he was trying to study Greek, but he gave it up after a few days and started into study yoga. A part of this yoga business was what was called the "water cure" – so for a few days after that, he ate nothing, just drank water for his meals. He carried his violin whenever he could. Had the strings reversed so he could play left-handed, and he would practice for hours. He bought a cello once and used to carry it around with him. At these times he would always dress like a musician, a long, fawn-coloured overcoat with green velvet cuffs and a collar and a slouch hat. And he'd let his hair grow long in back. We never knew what he was going to do next. He was unpredictable.

'We had a lot of fun in those days. Charlie and I roomed together and I can still see him playing the violin or cello to cover the noise of the cooking of bacon I was doing on the gas ring (forbidden, of course). Then we'd both take towels and try to blow the smoke out of the window. I remember one funny incident in those early days just after we landed in the States. I suppose you know that in England hotels guests leave their shoes outside the door when they retire so that the porter can give them a polish during the night. I did that as a matter of course the first night we landed in the States in our New York hotel. The next morning I got up, went to the door, looked out – and no shoes. I went down to the desk clerk mad as hell and demanded to know what had become of my shoes. When I had explained where I had put them, the man wanted to know why in the hell I had done *that*. I explained but it didn't do any good. My shoes were stolen – and to show you my financial situation at the time, they were the only shoes that I owned! So – and this is true – I actually walked over to the theatre fully dressed, wearing my slippers. I'll never forget those slippers. They each had a single candle painted on them, and running around the glow of light from the candles were the words, *Good Night*. Good night is right!

'We must have been funny-looking chaps what with our English style of dress and speech. I remember one time Charlie and I were walking over to the theatre all dressed up, hanky up the sleeve, spats, double-breasted coat, carrying canes – and on the way there we became aware of Nature's urgent call. Now, public conveniences are a regular part of English life, but they certainly aren't in America. We searched high and low and couldn't find accommodation. Finally, in desperation, we asked a cop where the nearest public convenience was.

'"The nearest what?" yelled the cop.

'We asked again, very politely.

'He finally got our drift and said very loudly, "Aw, hell, you'll have to go to a saloon, mister!"

'Mind you, we were now in a pretty anxious state. We got to a saloon and started down the aisle, as it were, when we realized that we hadn't purchased anything to warrant our use of the facilities. These polite Englishmen. So, tortured as we were, we marched up to the bar very bravely, ordered a beer and sipped it for a few seconds before we flew away!'

Mack Sennett
HOW I DISCOVERED CHARLIE

MACK SENNETT, an unsuccessful Canadian musical comedy actor who turned film maker, is the man who must take credit for introducing Charlie Chaplin to the screen. He had quite by chance seen one of Charlie's stage performances in New York, and was so impressed that when a vacancy arose in his company in 1913 he sent for the young English comedian. Sennett himself had been brought into films in 1911 by the director D W Griffith, then working for the Biograph Company. (Griffith was later, of course, to form the independent film company, United Artists, with Chaplin, Mary Pickford and Douglas Fairbanks.) Griffith assigned Sennett to direct a number of comedies for Biograph, and it was during the making of these that he evolved the fast-moving burlesque style which became his trademark. In 1912 he set up his own company, Keystone, a name which soon became synonymous with slapstick comedy, and a year later he added Chaplin to his roster of actors – as he describes in the following article from *Photoplay Magazine* of August 1928. Sennett's famous maxim, 'You have to spill soup on dignity to get a real laugh' was as deeply influential on Chaplin as were the lessons he learned in his film studio.

'MY ASSOCIATION with Chaplin began in 1913 when I had a comedian in my Keystone Comedy Company named Ford Sterling. This Sterling was going to quit because, as he expressed it, "he could get more money than I could pay him". I tried to coax him to stay, but there was nothing doing.

'Then I remembered a little Englishman I'd seen one night at William Morris' three-a-day vaudeville show, the American Music Hall in New York. So I sent round and hired him. It was only then I learned his name was Charlie Chaplin.

'I had been impressed that night I first saw him, more than impressed. Stunned might be a good word.

'I think I was so struck by him because he was everything I wasn't: a little fellow who could move like a ballet dancer. The next week I couldn't remember his name, but I sure as hell never forgot that wonderful easy grace of movement. I had seen nothing like it. I've seen nothing like it since, except in Chaplin films.

'And to think it was luck, pure chance, that I saw Chaplin the first time! I had an appointment with a friend that night on Eighth Avenue. I waited, he didn't show up, so I thought I'd kill time by wandering into the nearby music hall. So, bless my friend for missing our engagement!

'Chaplin was not so different then to today. He didn't have that clothes make-up he uses now. His costume was actually assembled on my lot out there in Los Angeles. He tried out several different make-ups before he found the right one.

'The first he used was that of a drunk – a man in evening clothes, with a red nose – the old stuff, you see. It didn't go very well, in fact it wasn't different enough to give it originality.

'Then he tried other things – I forget just what. In those day we used to get on new make-ups and run around the stage to see if we could get a laugh from the rest of the gang.

'One day Chaplin took a pair of Chester Conklin's baggy trousers, the small derby that Roscoe Arbuckle always wore, and the big shoes which were part of Ford Sterling's old make-up. The cane was one of Charlie's own props – he always used a cane.

'Well, as soon as I saw the get-up, I knew that was it!

'I remember one thing particularly about Chaplin. He was the most interested person where he himself, his future, the kind of thing he was trying to do, was concerned, that I ever

knew. He wanted to work – and nearly all the time. We went to work at eight o'clock and he was there at seven. We quit at five, say, or later, but he'd still be around at six and wanting to talk about his work to me all the time.

'The average actor, as maybe you know, is just an actor. When it's quitting time, he's through. His job is done. He's thinking of something else – maybe even when he's working! – and he wants to get away so he can attend to it. But these personality people are different.

'Why, this fellow Chaplin used to fairly sweat if he thought he hadn't done a thing as well as he should have! And he was always complaining of this, that and the other – the kind of director he had, the kind of actors that worked with him, that his part wasn't big enough, that he ought to have more stage room to do the thing the way he wanted to do it.

'And when the time came that he could see the film of the day's work, he was always there, whereas most of the others in the picture would never come around. And if anything in the run didn't please him, he'd click his tongue or snap his fingers and twist and squirm.

'"Now why did I do that, that way?" he'd say. "What was the matter with me, anyhow? So and so (the director) should have caught that! Heavens, it's terrible! There's always something wrong!"

'Chaplin was one fellow who had to work alone – and alone he now works!'

Charlie with Mack Sennett beside him and D.W. Griffith (right)

31

THE TRAMP'S COSTUME

'HIS LITTLE MOUSTACHE? That is a symbol of vanity. His skimpy coat, his trousers so ridiculously baggy and shapeless? They are the caricature of our eccentricity, our stupidities, our clumsiness. The idea of the walking stick was perhaps my happiest inspiration, for the cane was what made me speedily known. Moreover, I developed business with it to such a point that it took on a comic character of its own. Often, I found it hooked round someone's leg, or catching him by the shoulder, and in these ways I got a laugh from the public while I was myself scarcely aware of the gesture. I don't think I had fully understood in the beginning how much, among millions of individuals, a walking stick puts a label marked "dandy" on a man. So that when I waddled on to the stage with my little walking stick and a serious air, I gave the impression of an attempt at dignity, which was exactly my aim.'

Charlie Chaplin

Alfred Reeves
CHARLIE'S FILM DEBUT

A GENIAL Englishman named Alfred Reeves was the man who had been the manager of the Fred Karno company in which Chaplin traversed America and it is to his eternal credit that he unhesitatingly advised Charlie (who was, after all, his star performer) to accept Mack Sennett's invitation to go into films. A firm friendship had apparently already grown up between the two men (it is said that Reeves had actually known Charlie since he was fifteen and had seen Chaplin senior on the London stage), but the young comedian never forgot Reeves' good advice. Indeed, when Chaplin decided to set up his own film studios in 1917, the first person he asked to join him was 'Alf' Reeves, whom he made a Vice President of the Corporation as well as his personal manager. Reeves' dedicated work behind the scenes and his organizational ability left Charlie free to utilize his creative talents, and it is no surprise that their association lasted unbroken until Reeves' death in 1946. In this rare item from *Photoplay*, July 1921, Reeves turns back the clock to 1910 to recount the little-known story of Charlie's very first appearance before a camera...

'WHILE WE PLAYED in New York Charlie conceived the idea of utilizing his spare time away from the theatre in the making of picture comedies. He outlined his idea to all the members of the company, thinking then that all we needed was a camera.

'Charlie and myself, always the best of friends, agreed at the time to put up one thousand dollars each for the purchase of a camera. We thought then that all we had to do was to play as in our vaudeville act, in the open air, and it would register on the screen. The idea of scenes made in short lengths, long shots and close-ups, and inserts being taken separately and later assembled was never

WHEN CHARLIE FAILED.

THE STORY OF HIS VERY FIRST FILM AND WHY IT WAS A FAILURE.

CHARLIE CHAPLIN.

WE are so accustomed to associate Charlie Chaplin with the American film world, that it is astonishing to learn that his first appearance on the " creeping celluloids " was recorded by a British camera-man on British soil, and, still more astonishing, the said camera-man was so disgusted with the result that he presumably destroyed it as so much negative run to waste.

It happened thus :

In August, 1912, Chaplin, then a member of Karno's variety company, happened to be performing in Jersey at the time of the annual Carnival of Flowers. A camera-man had been sent down from London to film the proceedings for a " Topical Gazette," and eventually set up his machine on the racecourse, where a big crowd had gathered to watch the procession.

A movie camera was a bit of a novelty in those days, and after experiencing a good deal of difficulty in keeping the curious at bay, the camera-man at last succeeded in getting a clear " shot " and started grinding his machine with his eye fixed to the " finder."

C.C. Walk Got Its First Laugh.

Whilst he was thus occupied, a little boyish-looking man quietly detached himself from the crowd, and, to the latter's huge delight, started a curious shambling walk straight in the camera's direct line of vision.

For a time the assembly watched the comedy in silent rapture, till at last a particularly funny bit of " business " evoked a storm of laughter and applause.

It was only then that the preoccupied man behind the machine realised that something had gone wrong with his calculations, and discovered that some twenty feet of his great floral picture had merged into a record of Charlie Chaplin's first efforts as a moving picture star.

Charlie Knew He'd Make Good.

Needless to say, Charlie's evaporation on discovery was in keeping with the best Chaplin screen traditions. He relates that the last words he heard as he unobtrusively melted into the crowd were those of a little boy protesting at the abrupt conclusion of the impromptu comedy.

" Oh, mamma," the child complained in a shrill treble, " why has he gone away ? I did want to see the funny man again ! "

Charlie declares that that child's laughter was his guarantee that one day he would make good in the movie world. Moreover, that little boy has got his wish. He has probably laughed many times since then at his funny man, but how many times has that camera-man cursed the day when he scrapped the historic strip of celluloid that recorded Charlie Chaplin's first appearance before a moving picture camera ?

—∞—

Pearson's Magazine, May 1917

dreamed of by us. The cutting of the film, in which Charlie has no equal, was never dreamed of by him then.

'We entered into this agreement in all seriousness, but because our work took us away from New York, it was abandoned. But Charlie always carried the idea in his mind. Since then we have often wondered what the outcome would have been had we carried out the original agreement.

'On returning to England in the summer of 1912 we combined business with pleasure by playing the theatres of the Channel Islands. While playing the theatre on the Island of Jersey, there was a street parade and carnival in progress and a news weekly cameraman recorded the event.

'He was here, there and everywhere, but wherever he went a very pompous gentleman, who was apparently in charge of affairs, would always be found in front of the camera lens. He would shake hands with the local dignitaries and always turn away from them and face the camera as he did so. He might be termed the first "camera hog". Always would he bow and register his greetings to the camera while his guests stood in the background, or off to one side.

'Charlie was completely fascinated by this bit of business and told me then that some day he would put it in a picture. In an early picture of his – *Kids Auto Races* you will find the fulfilment of his resolve.

'We returned to America shortly afterward on our second tour and while playing in Philadelphia, upon response to a wire from Mack Sennett, Charlie went to New York and there signed his first picture contract.

'And so, contrary to the general idea that Charlie was discovered for pictures while playing in Los Angeles, Charlie arrived in California with a one-year picture contract in his pocket. The rest of Charlie's history is written by the children and himself.'

Charlie with his manager, Billy Reeves

Two amusing moments from *Kid Auto Races at Venice* (1914)

Charlie Chaplin
HOW I BROKE INTO THE PICTURES

In addition to the accounts of Fred Karno, Stan Laurel and Mack Sennett about Charlie's progress from music hall comedian to the verge of film stardom, we also have the following report by Chaplin himself. This unique item appeared in the popular British magazine, *The Strand* in January 1918.

'When I began work in the motion-picture field I did not expect to become permanently connected with the industry. In fact, motion-picture production at that time was regarded by even the boldest operators as a rather hazardous investment – the sort of enterprise that might only be briefly profitable. Nobody had the foresight to recognize that the world's greatest baby had been born and was being boarded round in one house and another like any common foundling.

'I launched my first picture efforts in Los Angeles, which from the very beginnings of the picture industry has been a sort of production centre. Motion-picture people call Los Angeles "headquarters", just as men and women of the stage do London or New York. The Keystone Company offered me an opportunity to go on, and I was glad of the chance to acquire experience because of certain plans that I had in mind. My companion, when I applied for the job at the Keystone studio, was Albert Austin, who is still a member of my company and who came over with me from England at the time I made my first vaudeville tour of the United States during the previous season. Our second tour of the United States occurred in 1911, and it was in that year that my first picture engagement was secured.

'Austin and I had been appearing in Fred Karno's musical vaudeville skit called "A Night in a London Music-Hall". My salary with that concern was ten pounds a week "and pay your own hotel bills".

'One of my stunts in Karno's show was to play a drunken man. In the course of that skit

36

I had to do a good deal of staggering about, and that was the first time I found out that footwork – hopping backward on one leg and acting like a man with locomotor ataxia – was funny to the onlooker. The fellows in our company thought it was great stuff, and certainly it always got a laugh.

'I put on the big shoes at the suggestion of Austin, who thought they would emphasize the shuffling walk I used in my first production. There was no particular name to that show, if I recall. It was just a mess of motion. I hooked a string of sausages with my cane, and the sausage-man chased me out of the picture. There were some girls in the story, but I don't recall what it was all about.

'That was the first picture I ever saw myself in. It gave me ideas. For more than a week I observed all sorts of audiences viewing that picture. They all seemed to laugh at my feet and the hookey cane. The little low-crowned Derby hat I was wearing seemed to be popular too. It's good policy never to throw away a laugh, so I saved all those I had and set about inventing some more. The loose trousers followed, and the too-small cutaway coat. The present Chaplin make-up was assembled by degrees, but it hasn't been changed much for a year or two because the public resents any change.

'My friends won't have me in any sort of character but the one in which they first adopted me. Once I appeared in my own person – a dress-suit and all that. There was such a frost that I shall never forget it.

'My first week's pay with the Keystone, which at that time released through the Mutual, was twenty-five pounds, but the pay envelope contained thirty pounds a week after that. They began to like me.

'Nobody knew very much about picturization in the early days. People were pretty well satisfied if they saw plenty of motion on the screen. It was a novelty to see dogs, cats, roosters, and geese moving about in a picture. For a brief season nearly anything on the screen was good enough, but it wasn't long before there came a demand for plot and story. I consider that there is more real art now involved in motion-pictures than there is in

staging plays for the speaking stage. Enormous difficulties have been overcome, and more are being overcome every day. There is no limit to the ultimate possibilities.

'After two and a half years with the Keystone Company I became associated with the Essanay for a period, and then signed up with President John R Freuler, of the Mutual Film Corporation, on a contract to produce twelve pictures in a year at a salary of £134,000.

'Of course, I may have appeared calm and collected to Mr Freuler when I signed the contract. I know the money is earned through the success of my productions, but it was difficult to accustom myself to the idea of being responsible for so much money. I remember I used to try to recall the names of worthy philanthropic societies to which I might send part of the wealth that promised to overwhelm me. I soon discovered that I had been needlessly alarmed. The philanthropic societies all had my address!

'I have stuck to comedy because I am convinced that my public is better satisfied with that than with any other kind of production. I essayed the "straight drama" once or twice, and cannot say that my efforts in that direction were very highly appreciated. Any time that I appear without my original make-up there is discontent. It originates with the children, who are my best friends; is endorsed by the women, who are my second best friends; and so far as the men are concerned, they talk as though I had been sentenced for life to the same suit of clothes, and howl their heads off if there's a button changed.

'The odd thing about my success in the pictures is that it developed out of unvalued assets. I learned that big-foot shuffle and the ataxic walk from an old cab-horse tout in London, who used to hold horses outside the Elephant and Castle while drivers were inside getting a drink. The old man was a physical wreck, but he had that comic walk and it used to amuse me, so I imitated it for the amusement of a few of my friends. I'm glad I did. If it hadn't been for poor old Bill and his funny shuffle I should probably be knocking out twenty pounds a week or so as a vaudeville performer "doing the provinces", as we say in

England; or perhaps I might have hooked up with light opera in the United States. As it is I think I shall remain in the motion-picture field indefinitely. It is good enough for me.'

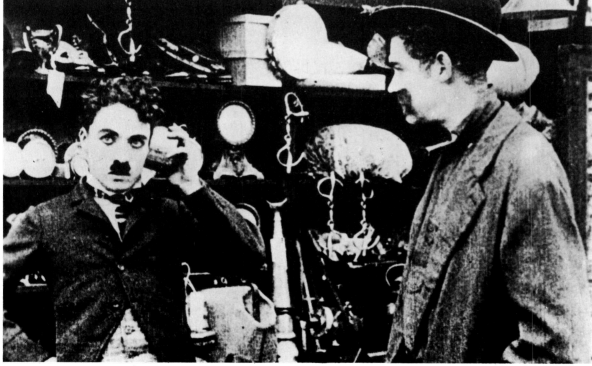

Charlie with his friend Albert Austin in *The Pawn Shop* (1916); and Chaplin's Hollywood studio

Roland Totheroh
CHAPLIN THROUGH THE EYE OF THE CAMERA

THE TWO YEARS which Chaplin spent with Mack Sennett helped him develop the skills of film acting and his remarkable total of thirty-five films for Keystone during this period took him from obscurity to a degree of fame. Making these short movies also convinced him that to achieve real success he needed to be his own master when creating pictures. In January 1915 he was offered this chance by a rival firm, The Essanay Film Company, who had been watching his progress. While working for them, he met another man who was to play an important role in his rise to fame, Roland H. Totheroh, who became his cameraman and worked with him for a total of thirty-seven years! Although not always given the credit for his work that he deserves, Totheroh was the man who interpreted and fulfilled Chaplin's exacting demands and undoubtedly contributed in no small degree to the style and quality of the finished pictures. A former professional baseball player and novice cartoonist, he had joined Essanay in 1911 to act in Westerns with the joint owner, G. M. 'Bronco Billy' Anderson. (Anderson had been the star of the first real film story *The Great Train Robbery* in 1903, and had formed Essanay with George K. Spoor: their initials giving the company its name.) When Totheroh grew tired of the rough and tumble of acting he opted to change places and work behind the camera. He soon found he had a natural aptitude with the camera, and when Chaplin joined Essanay he was shortly afterwards assigned as Charlie's personal cameraman. Thereafter they worked on all the little comedian's pictures until 1952 when Chaplin was forced into exile. In the following article, completed in 1967 shortly before his death, Totheroh offers an intimate picture of life on the set with the budding genius.

'WE GOT WORD that the studio had signed up

Mr Chaplin. We all thought he was a little Frenchman, and of course we'd seen the films he was making for Sennett. So Joe Flynn – he was G. M. Anderson's chauffeur – asked me to ride down to San Francisco to pick up Chaplin.

'When we got back, Joe and I took Charlie over to Anderson's bungalow.

'We all had bungalows at the studio. I had a corner one; later on Ben Turpin had the next one. All the different actors and heads of departments had these little bungalows, and Anderson had one about a block down the road. It was anything but a palace; he had an old wood stove in the kitchen. So, Charlie had one handbag with him, just a little old thing, one of these canvas-like handbags. So we got the old wood stove going in the kitchen. Knowing Charlie was an Englishman, someone heated up some tea. We opened up his bag to take some things out. All that he had in it was a pair of socks with the heels worn out and an old worn out toothbrush – and that's all. Joe said, "Jesus, he hasn't got much in this bag, has he?" Later Charlie started talking about he's going to make all this and that, and he was going through motions, and Anderson was sitting there. Finally, it was time to leave and we left. Then the next morning the crew came in – Ben Turpin, Leo White and a few that they had sent from the Chicago studios.

'But Charlie wasn't real satisfied with the bungalow. Later on, he didn't stay there. They got him a room in a little hotel that was across the tracks, so he didn't stay at Anderson's. They set him up in a better place. Charlie a lot of times talked about it, "I'll never forget down there. No bed and no ..." this and that. I felt like saying, "Yeah, but what the hell did you have?" Nothing in his handbag! Of course, Charlie was getting along on $150 a week from Sennett. Then to get this $1250 – he didn't have very much money. His manager,

40

Alfred Reeves, had advised him to get into pictures. Charlie didn't know anything about motion pictures, and he had gotten this offer from Sennett. So Mr Reeves heard about it and talked him into it. Charlie was dubious; he didn't know whether he wanted to or not. "You go ahead," Reeves said. "That's the coming entertainment. You get into it by all means – and that money – you never earned that money here – $150 a week. By all means, Charlie."

'Well, he finally accepted. But he had a rough time at Sennett's. They wouldn't let him do his kind of comedy. And when Charlie came up to Niles, he had nothing. But he talked like he was used to luxury, commanding this and commanding that. It wasn't like him; later I could see that he was very shy.

'Charlie had done a picture or two for Spoor and Anderson at Essanay's Chicago studio. When he came to Niles, I was photographing for Broncho Billy. He took quite a liking to me. He used to come over to me and say, "I can hear Rollie's camera cranking out there." It was a huge box and you could hear every movement of the gears. When we went on location, he used to come out and watch us. Finally, we shot his first picture. At that time I used to help G. M. Anderson cut the pictures. The way he would cut was he came right up to

a big close-up and roll his eyes around. There was no expression and he could use it anywhere. He just measured off the tip of his nose to the length of his arm and tore it off. That was Anderson's way of editing in a close-up!

'After Charlie finished his first picture, he wanted to rest and go to San Francisco for a couple of days over the weekend. He was getting $1250 a week and he'd been on this one picture close to a month and the picture wasn't out yet. Anderson decided he was going to cut it so he got hold of me and we went in and we started to cut on the first reel of Charlie's picture. Lo and behold! Chaplin didn't go to San Francisco. He decided not to at the last minute and came walking in on us. We were cutting the first reel, and Charlie said, "Take your hands off that." At that time we never had a print made; we used to do the cutting on negative. If we scratched it, it was just too bad. So Charlie said, "And furthermore, I want a print." At that time we had our own little laboratory, but we never had a printing-machine because we never used it. Our laboratory man didn't know anything about a printing-machine. So they had to send all the way back to Chicago to get one.

'By the time we sent for it with express, it was two weeks before we got it. Then they went to make the print and they had forgotten

Scene from the shooting of *The Gold Rush* (1925)

41

to send the blower for the machine. The blower would contact each frame on the aperture when it went through the printing machine; it held the film firm. So this laboratory man made the print with everything going in and out of focus. So Charlie said, "How am I going to cut with that thing? What's the matter with it?" So they had to send all the way back to Chicago and get that other part.

'They were going into the second month and the first film still wasn't out yet. So finally they got everything on schedule, and Charlie started getting his films done.

'Later we heard that Spoor and Anderson were fighting about money and that things were going to change. When I was working with Lloyd Ingraham on the Snakeville Comedies, he invited me to go down to Los Angeles to work with him for Griffith. I didn't want to leave Niles; I had begun to feel at home there. But when Snakeville closed down, I decided to leave for Los Angeles. I had worked with Anderson but not for Chaplin yet.

'When I got to Los Angeles, I took a bus out to Universal to see Roy Clements. He had just hired a cameraman a week earlier, so I went over to see Chaplin at his new studio.

'Charlie was in New York but when he finally arrived back in town, I went to see him. Charlie said, "Sure, we can use you." He said we'd get started the next week. The cameraman was Bill Foster, later head cameraman at Universal. I met Bill and told him I'd been shooting comedies and everything else, and I knew about the speed. At that time they had no motors on the cameras and we changed speeds for chases. Foster had always shot dramas and things like that. We started together, Bill and I, as camera 1 and 2. When it came to selecting scenes and that, pretty near all of my scenes were selected. When Charlie would do something like kick his feet, we had to be all prepared and crank.

'Bill Foster had heard about some new director who was going to do a film at Fox, so he left to work over there. Now I was on my own. I did all the Mutuals, the First Nationals, and all the rest. The funny thing was when I joined the Essanay, it was 6 March 1911.

And I joined Mr Chaplin on the same day – 6 March 1916.'

ON THE SET WITH CHAPLIN

The Ideas

'When Charlie was working on an idea, often he would call me in. There were always a lot of his own people around. He'd hit on a certain situation where there was something he was building on and he'd want conversation more or less. If somebody came up with an idea that sounded as if he could dovetail it and it would build up his situation, it would sink back in his head and he'd chew it over. And there'd always be someone there to write things down. Everytime he'd speak, "put it down. Don't lose it. We'll go back to that, I'll lose my train of thought", he'd have someone like Danny James, one of the assistants on *Dictator*, someone like that taking dictation. He'd dictate so darn many things that, unless you're pretty clever and keep them in sequence, you could lose it easily.

'I remember one time Charlie really chewed out Danny James. He said, "What we were talking about three days ago, remember that? Now read it all." Well, first of all you have to be a mind reader with Charlie. I could pretty well tell what he was thinking about, what he was going to do. So he said, "Danny, what we were talking about? This isn't it here. What I really want is what I did three days ago."

'And Danny said, "Well, which one do you mean?"

'"Ah, for goodness sakes. We worked on it three days ago. You took it down and everything."

'"I know, but what part?"

'"Well, you've got it down there. Find it!"

'Most of the time Charlie pretty much had a basic idea when we started filming. The first idea he had for *The Gold Rush*, for instance, was Chilkoot Pass where they had such hardships and everything, going over this treacherous grade, this mountain called Chilkoot Pass. He had that in mind first. But the basic idea on all his films would often change; it did on pretty near everything we took. After running with the dailies, then he'd be inspired and it would

44

Previous page: Charlie with Roland Totheroh on location for *The Gold Rush* (1925)

give him another idea, another thought. If not, he'd throw it out and do it from another angle. On the early features we only had sort of a synopsis. The first script we had with a breakdown was *The Great Dictator*. Of course, with sound Charlie had a greater overhead and everything else. He had to plan further. But he didn't always go to the budget that was set up for a picture. Sometimes after a set had been torn down, he'd get a new idea and we'd have to reconstruct the whole set exactly as it was before so that he could reshoot some shots for a scene.'

Script

'Pretty near everything prior to *The Great Dictator* was *ad lib*. He didn't have a script at the time, didn't have a script girl or anything like that, and he never checked whether the scene was in its right place or that continuity was followed. The script would develop as it went along. A lot of times after we saw the dailies the next morning, if it didn't warrant what he thought the expectation was, he'd put in some other sort of a sequence and work on that instead of going through with what he had started out to do. We never had a continuity. He'd have an idea and he'd build up. He had a sort of a synopsis laid out in his mind but nothing on paper. He'd talk it over and come in and do a sequence. In a lot of his old pictures, he'd make that separation by using titles about the time: "next day" or "the following day" or "that night" – these would cover the script gaps in between.

'Every picture that he made always had one particular highlight, a good built-up spot to rock the house with it. Of course, everyone would contribute a little bit to the ideas and the script. But no one'd dare butt in and say, "Oh, you should do this and you should do that." I would never leave the camera when they were rehearsing, always right behind them watching every move, everything that he did. When the scene was taken, if I saw something in there, I was around that camera in a wink. In a nice way I'd say, "Gee, Charlie, you could do this", or "are you going to do that?" and he'd agree to it. But you couldn't go out and say to him, things like some of them did, like Albert Austin who'd say

something to Charlie and then tell everybody all around the lot: "I gave Charlie that gag."

'Charlie would rehearse them. He'd rehearse everybody and even in silents, we had dialogue. It came to a little woman's part and he'd get out there and he'd play it. He'd change his voice and he'd be the character that he wanted the little old woman to play. He'd build their lines up and rehearse them, even before he rehearsed himself in it. He rehearsed so many darn different ways with them that when he came in there, it'd be changed all around with what he put down. You had to be on the alert for him.

'I never got away from that camera, looking through that lens. And all those rehearsals, I sat right there, watching every move he made. Then if he came along and something spontaneous hit him, you had to be ready there to take it and get it.'

The Director

'As a director, Mr Chaplin didn't have anything to say as far as exposures, things like that. Otherwise, I used to say, "Take a look through here." The idea of that was that if he was directing, he'd have to know the field that I was taking in. Of course, in the early days, the role of the cameraman was much bigger than it is now. It was up to the cameraman to decide what angle to shoot for lighting; or outside, which is the best angle on a building or whatever it is. Then you figure what time of the day it would be better to shoot that shot, whether you want back-light or cross-light or whatever on your set.

'On a filming day, I would go to the studio early. I had to see to it that my cameraman had all the film loaded and all the equipment brought on the stage. I generally knew where we would be shooting and I'd tell them where to put the camera. When Charlie came in, I'd see if he was going to alter some scene or whatever he's going to do and tell him the equipment was all ready. I'd check all the lamps to be sure they were working. The lamps we had in those days were carbon lamps and of course a lot of times the carbon would get lower and they'd bounce up and down and flicker all over the place. Then when we went into Cooper-Hewitt, which is the Murphy lamp; you'd have to milk them like a cow in the morning when it was cold. The Murphy wouldn't go through the tubes and you'd have to warm them up. And we had to change with that lighting system all the make-up. It was terrible looking, turning reds into purple. It worked on the blue end of the spectrum. Then when we got into incandescent lighting, everything was reversed; more or less it was high on the reds while before it was high on the blues. I had to keep the set pretty well-lit. You couldn't underlight and get some nice shadows. No, Charlie wanted to look like a clown. He wanted that pretty near white face. And you had to watch out; you couldn't have shadow over here or back of you because you never knew where he was going to work. You had to watch out and keep your eye out all the time.

'On a typical day, we'd shoot from around eight or nine in the morning right straight through till lunch. Of course, this was before unions. And a lot of times he'd want to shoot two hours after dinner. After we'd break for lunch or for dinner, we'd start up again. I could always tell my set-ups because I was smoking *Bull Durham* and I used so many matches. You could see all these matches all over the floor.

'While Charlie was working, rehearsing or filming or whatever, lots of his people would stand around and watch. He used to use their reactions to see how his stuff was going over. But later on he got so that if they stood there gawking at him, he'd stop and say, "Get out of here! What are you standing there glaring at me for?" But prior to that, anything he'd do on location or anything, crowds around, they'd laugh their heads off at his antics.

'A lot of times we'd get through a sequence and run it maybe three or four days later. And he'd figure, "No, that's not it." So he'd go on to something else. Then if that was worthy of carrying on and adding and building to it, then he'd go and do it. He finished a lot of times a sequence and then he'd blame it on somebody else. He didn't want people to think that he didn't know what he was doing. He'd turn around and think overnight. "Jesus Criminy, this is what I should have done. I

didn't do it." Now he'd dismissed all the people and had sets torn down. But, it was his own money, so what the devil – "Call the people back." He'd look for some excuse, something wrong, somebody else to be at fault for it; he'd have to call them down. You'd break any company the way he'd shoot. Of course, it was his own money but he'd take scenes over and over and over and then run them and if it wasn't right, then he'd add to it and make it. When he finished, he really had something. But the way he shot the scene over and over he'd wear out all the actors and actresses. But he was patient with everyone who was acting. Even though, he'd confuse them by doing something so many times and so many different ways, they got so they didn't know which way they'd done it at any one time. Lydia Knott in *Woman of Paris*: he wore her out. Finally she said, "Oh, Mr Chaplin, please tell me what I'm doing wrong and what you want! I'm worn out. I just don't know what to do."

'He said, "You're doing all right, it's just some little thing I want you to do."

'But if he was entertaining royalty, some out-of-towners, it might be just after lunch and we're all ready to go. But Charlie would sit there and talk to them for two hours. Then all of a sudden, maybe a light would go out or somebody would pass out or maybe a glass on the table would break; he'd say, "For goodness sakes, that costs money! You know that! Be careful what you're doing!" He just didn't have much patience with the technical side of it.

'Lots of times he'd really start building sets before he was really set on his story. Once, they double-crossed him after he pulled this once or twice. He'd have an idea but it wasn't really set. Then for a stall he'd say, "I don't want the window in the back there or the door in this side. I want the door on the back and the window on this side." So it would take a few couple of days to make that changeover. So he'd go over to his hotel or go home and wait. Then they got tired of that, and they put casters on the set!

'Charlie never really got involved with running the cameras. 'Course, the cameras were so different from today. First breaking in, my trouble was in cranking the camera. As a rule for comedy it was fourteen frames a second and sometimes you drop to twelve frames a second, for instance if somebody's running away from the camera and you wanted to speed it up. The cameraman regulated everything! We didn't have change of focus apparatus on the camera; we'd have to reach over while still cranking and turn this apparatus we had on the mount that held the lens. Say we're on a twelve-foot focus and it comes to a six-foot focus; we'd have to reach over there while still cranking and turn to six feet. So both hands were really operating different things at one time. You get used to it. It comes to you naturally; after a while, you can get it pretty well on the nose. Charlie used to say, "Rollie, let's see: we'll make this a happy twelve." He left it up to me; I would then find what I thought was a happy twelve, or a good fourteen. At that time I was using what I called "the bullet", a Bell and Howell with the magazine on top. It was a compact thing with only a 200-foot magazine. Later on we had 1,000-foot magazines for that camera.

'Before I joined Mr Chaplin, they were more or less using the Pathé. On the Pathé, instead of having the crank on the side, you cranked from the rear. And the loading of the camera was different, too; you had to make loops. In the Bell and Howell you made a loop but it didn't have the drag; you were pretty sure to go through without buckling. When the film buckled up in your camera, you'd have to open up and pull it out and clean your aperture. Everything I learned about running those cameras I got from Jess Robbins, Broncho Billy's head cameraman. When sound came in, we'd use the Mitchell, which was quite a bit different. Before that, I used Bell and Howell; first the box, then the bullet. And about 1918, they came out with motors so you could set your speed and not worry about cranking. And at that time we'd do our dissolves right in the camera. I'd fade out, check the frame number, then wind back that many frames and fade in.

'When Charlie built his new studio, he built a lab there, too. We had a lab for quite a while and then it got to be so long in between pictures, you couldn't very well hold over a crew. Then some of the men would come and learn experience, and they made a lot of errors. So Charlie eventually sent the lab work out. I don't know if somebody told him that it was cheaper to send it out than have your own lab, but that's what he did.

'Charlie was always so proud when he was building a set. We had the lousiest looking sets I ever saw, a side wall and a back wall. He'd build something with a little balcony or something and he'd get ahold of Doug Fairbanks or somebody and say, "I want you to see this set I'm building." He'd make his little sketches for the set crew. Later on where we required big sets, it was different. In the early days, our sets consisted of a wall on the right and a wall in the back with a window in it. If he built a set – for instance in *The Gold Rush*, a borrowed set – he had all the crowds there and he brought Doug over to look at it. To give atmosphere to the set, I had a lot of smoke in the place and the highlights would pick up the smoke and gave atmosphere to it. Anytime he built a set like that he'd call Doug, which was silly because Fairbanks had the most spectacular sets of anybody. And Doug used to say, "Oh gee, that's swell, Charlie." He always wanted to encourage Charlie in whatever he did.

'When we were filming on the set, everybody was there until the picture was finished, because with *ad libs*, Charlie didn't know what he would use in another scene. A lot of times a person would change his make-up and play three or four different characters in the picture before it was through. You'd see a fellow with a beard on; the next thing you know, you'd see him in a different kind of make-up. Perhaps the public wouldn't know it was the same character, but he'd be in one scene then you'd see another scene and he'd be in that scene, too. Charlie'd use the prop men and anybody around; there was no guild where it was compulsory that you had to use extras – you could use anybody.

'Some of the make-ups were terrible, especially Henry Bergman. He always thought he was a great make-up artist. He'd put on a beard and you'd see the glue sticking through

47

it. He thought he was the greatest make-up man in the world. He used to brag about it. And Charlie would go around rehearsing everyone's part regardless of who it was. He'd take every scene over and over again and he'd work and work and work. He had no make-up man; he used to make himself up first thing in the morning. By the time he got through rehearsing and was ready to shoot a scene, he'd be wringing wet with perspiration and the make-up on his face would be all pocked and marked. I'd say "Charlie, you'd better fix up your make-up a bit."

'He'd say, "Oh, we got no time." Once he was set so that he didn't get out of rhythm or forget it, he'd say, "Give me a little powder," and he'd put a little powder on. Half the time there would be a big chunk of powder sticking on his face, not smoothed off or anything. He'd say, "It's okay now." He always wanted his face to look like a clown with no highlights of shadows or anything.

'Later on when we started making dialogue, it was compulsory that you had to have on every set a make-up man and a hairdresser. Prior to that, Charlie took care of everything, including the wardrobe for his leading lady. He'd comb their hair so that he could get exactly what he wanted his actresses, especially, to look like. In *Modern Times*, Paulette Goddard wanted to look like a glamour girl. And she said, "Charlie, isn't there anything where I can put on some clothes to look glamorous."

'He said, "I'll take care of that."

'In the picture she wore the same costume all the way through; he got a little hat and put some little roses in it. He loved even doing the actor's hair. He loved to cut hair and trim. In fact, he used to cut his own hair at home; he didn't want to sit around in a barbershop.'

Raymond Lee
I WAS A CHAPLIN KID

AN INSIDER'S VIEW of Chaplin the film maker in his early days has also been recorded by someone who actually worked alongside him on the set. He was Raymond Lee, who is best remembered for his part as the tough young bruiser in the Chaplin classic, *The Kid* (1920), although he also appeared in *A Day's Pleasure* (1919) and *The Pilgrim* (1923). Lee was one of several youngsters whom Chaplin discovered and coaxed into giving memorable performances in this picture – the most famous, of course, being Jackie Coogan, his co-star. Coogan has already given his impressions of working with Chaplin on the film in his *Memoirs* published in 1938, but the following account by Raymond Lee is perhaps more informative and certainly much rarer. Its only previous publication was in *The Classic Film Collector* of Winter–Spring 1966–67 from which it is reprinted.

'"CUT!"

'Hopping out of the director's chair wedged against the camera legs, Charlie Chaplin suddenly shortened his leap, straightened up and scowled at the two small boys who had been playing the scene. And the two small boys stared back as if Chaplin had turned into a giant. Jackie Coogan was one of the boys and I was the other.

'The Time: 1920

'The Place: Hollywood

'The Picture: *The Kid*

'Chaplin spoke like a school teacher. "You know, we've shot this scene exactly fifty times."

'Squelching any possible doubters among the rest of the company, Chaplin continued: "I've been keeping count!"

'After listening to his voice echo down the tenement street set, he walked slowly around in a circle, his hands flapping under his coat-

Charlie and Jackie Coogan in *The Kid* (1921)

49

tails, his hair looking like a cat had just jumped out of it, his shoes belonging more to a duck than man. Twice he slowly walked the circle. Then a stop. A thought. A smile with every tooth in it. And doing his best to look simple, Charlie Chaplin closed in on us with confessional intimacy.

'"Boys this is a very simple scene. Very simple. Two boys fighting. All boys fight. Must be a million boys fighting all over the world this very minute. It's born in you – like tonsils. But boys, you aren't fighting. You're dancing with each other."

'Hypnotized by Charlie's moustache, I had scarcely heard a word. It reminded me of a cigar stump my Dad occasionally left in an ashtray. One time the moustache feathered his lip. Another time it resembled a cricket tweaking his nose, cleaning one nostril. Sometimes it would jump up and down like a Jack-in-the-box. Digging into first one side of his mouth and then the other, it changed into a toothbrush. I wondered what it would do next.

'"The whole scene is awkward!"

'Chaplin turned to Jackie.

'"Jackie, I realize that Raymond is twice your size and it is hard for you to hit him but if you will just follow my directions everything will be fine. You see, Jackie, fighting with a bigger boy creates sympathy for you. Understand?"

'Jackie nodded. Chaplin smiled, his coattails flapping again.

'"Just remember David and Goliath."

'Chaplin pulled at his nose as if it were putty.

'"Lillian, you have told Jackie the story of David and Goliath?"

'When Jackie heard his mother's hesistant "no" his lower lip quivered, his bobbed head sagged and his big brown eyes got bigger and looking first at his parents, then Alfred Austin, an assistant, then Chaplin, he tried hard but failed to hold back two large tears that plopped on his cheeks.

'Quickly gathering Jackie up in his arms, Chaplin dragged out a handkerchief from his trouser pocket and blotted out the tears. Finishing the tears, he worked on Jackie's nose making him blow it twice. Twisting one end of the handkerchief, he pretended to clean first one ear and then the other ear.

'Jackie sniffed, trembled a little, but helped by the tickling in his ears, pulled a smile across his lips and side-longing a glance at his "Daddy Dear" who had a hard time smiling through his own tears, gave Charlie Chaplin the hug of his life.

'Chaplin slid Jackie to the sidewalk, motioning to Mr Coogan.

'"Better fix his make-up, Jack."

'Taking my arm, Chaplin squatted us both on the curbing.

'"Raymond, in rehearsal the pattern I had you follow worked out fine. Your footwork and body movements almost gave the illusion that Jackie was putting up a good fight. But every time we shoot it, the scene looks faked."

'I felt my lip quivering so I bit it and watched a red ant slide down into a crack in the cardboard sidewalk. But I looked at Chaplin when I spoke.

'"I know, Mr Chaplin. But I feel like I'm fighting with my feet when I should be fighting with my fists." Chaplin said: "And since you aren't a kangaroo, it is a bit awkward."

'Chaplin stood up. I stood up. Time stood up.

'Perched on a stool behind the camera, Austin put a finger to his lips. And Mr Coogan, sitting beside the organ and violin players, shook his head from side to side. I found my mother's face in the crowd and felt better for her thin smile.

'As Jackie rejoined us, Chaplin fingerbrushed some excess powder on his right cheek.

'"We must remember, Raymond, that this is Jackie's first picture while you've been acting for almost five years."

'I have never felt so old then or since.

'"Maybe the scene doesn't mean anything to you. Maybe that's it."

'Chaplin extended his left hand to the director's chair as if he expected it to walk over to him. Plump Henry Bergman, his lifelong friend, brought the chair forward. Chaplin slouched into it. Suddenly his costume slouched too. He didn't look like a giant now. More like a real little tramp. A frown pleated his forehead. As though he had been thinking a long time about what he was gong to say, Chaplin's voice rose sharply against the hot afternoon quiet.

'"Hunger. Hideous word. Most hideous of all tortures. Of course neither of you boys have ever been hungry. God forbid! Your stomach like a balloon without air. Your heart in your eyes and your eyes without a friend."

'Despite his heavy make-up, Chaplin's skin whitened, the lines around his eyes, stitches in a wound.

'"There is hunger in this scene. A boyish hunger makes Raymond steal Jackie's toy. And Jackie fights for his hunger for it. It's not an ordinary fight. It's been going on for thousands of years but it still isn't an ordinary fight." His hands visored the down-draught of sunlight.

'"I've been so hungry I could eat a shoe!"

'Cracking his knuckles, Chaplin leaned back in his chair, and cupping his mouth, whispered to Austin. "I must sound like a damn fool talking to these kids like this."

'Austin sliding off his perch still tall. "Maybe if we took a breather, Charlie . . ."

'My stomach suddenly felt like a balloon without air.

'"Mr Chaplin, I think I know what's wrong with the scene."

'Chaplin's head turned my way and drawing his knees up to his chin, he glared at me. I took a deep breath and said.

'"You see, Mr Chaplin, Jackie and I are little boys. But you want us to fight like you fight. It may not seem like that to you but it does to me. How about you, Jackie?"

'Jackie nodded. No stopping now.

'"If you'll just let us do it once for ourselves, maybe you'll see."

'Like a ducal butler, Chaplin unwound from the chair.

'"Very well, Mr Raymond, you direct the scene. I won't even sit in my chair while you shoot it."

'Jackie and I rehearsed our own fight a couple of times and then told Mr Chaplin we were ready for the take. At the finish Chaplin shouted: "Print it!" He grabbed Jackie in his arms and kissed him because he was only five

years old, and he shook my hand because I was nine. As Charles Spencer Chaplin shook my hand, I came of age as an actor.

'The next scenes showed Chaplin entering and coaching Jackie how to hit and kick me. Suddenly my Bully Brother, Chuck Reisner, lumbers into the scene and warns Charlie. "If your kid beats mine, I'll beat you." Chaplin quickly grabs Jackie and throws him to the street, puts his foot on the little boy's chest, raises my hand as the winner. But Jackie jumps up and knocks me down. My brother rushes Charlie, stops to knock a hole in a brick wall and bend a lamppost to show his strength. Chaplin resembles a tramp Nijinksy while Reisner is a fist-flinging windmill. At the peak of the quixotic fight Edna Purviance, the leading lady, enters and pleads with the men to stop fighting. They shake hands. But Charlie, taking advantage of the intercession, coyly bats Reisner over the head with a brick, ducking and bobbing he dervishes around him until Reisner is a reeling dummy.

'During the mirthful melée there were close-ups of Jackie and me rooting for our favourites. My close-up was shot first. Charlie called for Jackie. No Jackie. Mrs Coogan called him. Mr Coogan. Mr Austin. No Jackie.

'Chaplin slumped in his chair, out of breath from the fight-scene and out-of-sorts about Jackie's disappearance. Raking his greying black curls he let his temper out on Mrs Coogan.

'"Lillian, you should at least keep an eye on the child. Besides his own personal safety he might be worth a million dollars if this picture is a success!"

'Mrs Coogan's cheeks reddened. She wiped her damp face and arms with a handkerchief, slowly knotting it.

'Chaplin cracked his knuckles. "For God's sake! Look for Jackie!"

'The company spread out quickly. I stood by mother waiting for her to do something. Chaplin, small in his chair, head in his hands. Bergman, Austin and Alfred Reeves, the studio manager, flanked him. The quiet made breathing seem loud.

'"I'll get the office force out, too," Reeves finally said.

A tearful young Raymond Lee, with Chaplin, on the set
of *The Kid* (1921); Charlie and Jackie Coogan, stars of the
Funny Wonder comic strip, 1932

'Reeves started down the street but Chaplin's yell checked him. "My God, Alf, why don't you wear rubber heels?"

'Reeves tiptoed out of sight. Ten minutes passed. Fifteen. Chaplin jumped to his feet screaming. "Christ! The swimming pool!"

'The large swimming pool reflected the greenness of the grass bordering the offices at the entrance to the studio. The long shadow of the big stage wavered on the right edge of the water. Chaplin's bungalow headed the row of dressing rooms on the opposite side.

'We all stood back afraid to look. It was Chaplin who looked. I never thought so funny a face could look so sad. The sun burned all the colour out of even his yellow make-up. Slowly he got down on his knees, stared into the rippling water, shouted. "Jack!"

'Coogan rushed to him.

'"That dark spot –"

'Reeves stood beside Chaplin.

'"That's only the drain, Charlie –".

'"I don't give a damn what it is! Send someone down!"

'And someone went down. And the seconds went down too, as if anchored with granite. The swimmer's head pierced the rippling surface. Chaplin almost fell into the pool grabbing him before he could catch a breath.

'"Speak man! Speak."

'The swimmer shook his head negatively.

'Chaplin sighed weakly, and let Reeves help him to his feet.

'"Alf, have the pool drained immediately. It'll stay empty till *The Kid* is finished."

'Chaplin jerked his moustache off and everyone knew that ended work for the day. Mrs Coogan began to cry a little and Chaplin crossed to her and put his arm around her tenderly.

'"He can't have gone far, Lillian. We'll search every inch of the lot. Just have patience."

'"But maybe he's been kidnapped."

'Cautiously, a baby giggle tickled the quiet. Like a mischievous elf, Jackie poked his head out from behind an empty dressing room door. Grinning from ear to ear, he skipped down the steps to the red-bricked walk.

'Jackie's father let out a tearful shout, and I thought he would leap across the pool.

'"Where have you been?" he demanded, grasping the boy by the arm.

'Dangling like a puppet, Jackie gulped, but held his grin.

'"I been playing hide and seek. It was fun – everybody calling my name. And nobody found me. Not even you, Daddy Dear. You're it!"

'Mr Coogan had a struggle between a smile and a tear, but he turned his son over his knee and spanked his little bottom, million dollars worth and all.

'An interesting sidelight to *The Kid* – Jack Coogan Sr played without pay, in four episodes – as a bystander in the fight scene – as a member of a socialite party for Edna Purviance, as the octopus-handed pickpocket in the flop house – and a devil in the dream sequence.

'When my agents, Lichtig and Englander, sent Mother and me out to the Chaplin Studios for an interview, they said the part would probably last a week. It lasted ten. One of Chaplin's many whimsies kept people he liked on the payroll long after they had finished in the picture. He had a passion for familiar faces. A strange face would upset him like a tainted oyster. Death made the only changes in his crew and office force.

'Chaplin even extended this frantic familiarity to his use of old sets. For years he shot and re-shot some of his greatest comedies in the same old settings. I once heard him say that the frame around the Mona Lisa didn't make it a masterpiece.

'The loyalty and spirit of the people who worked for Chaplin were outstanding. Working for a genius wasn't always pleasant, but at least provocative and sometimes inspirational.

'Money meant absolutely nothing to him. If an idea struck him, he would halt production, retire to his bungalow and write the rest of the day. Or if a musical inspiration hit him, he would change places with his organist and sit musing for hours. Out of many of these musical wanderings, Chaplin found background themes for the scores of his films which he personally wrote.

'He lived his role of director as deeply as his

role as actor. He could portray any part of the picture, including the female roles. And yet he raised hell if you tried to mimic him. Reflect the conception, but don't mirror the conceiver.

'Though Chaplin dominated even the camera man and every nerve in the throbbing body of his cinematic creation, he would listen to suggestions as I have mentioned before. But heaven help you if what you suggested didn't almost reach perfection.

'Chaplin's greatest gift to me was his restraint. He approached the most ridiculous situation in the world with kid gloves. He never mauled or manhandled his material. He underplayed even the use of a custard pie. He fondled his laugh with the care of a miser and yet with the delicacy of a child who loves the colour of his ice cream, but still must eat it.

'The plot of *The Kid* is really a modern fairy tale. A mother abandons her child, hoping it will be found by a rich person. A tramp finds and raises him. Through their struggles for survival a policeman haunts them and finally discovers the truth and the mother, now a famous opera singer. In the end, the tramp, a guardian angel in rags, becomes the kid's father.

'Scenes from *The Kid* for example:

'The setting was Chaplin's hole-in-the-wall room. The camera first shows Jackie beating up some batter for pancakes, then shifts to Chaplin lying on a rickety old bed that sways like a hammock every time he breathes. But despite the moth-eaten blanket thrown over him, the worn and stained wallpaper surrounding him, and the impending danger of the near collapsing bed, Chaplin lies back with the relaxation of a millionaire counting his last killing.

'He yawns and stretches. His nose nibbles the smell of the pancakes as they sizzle in the frying pan. He studies his nails nonchalantly. As Jackie calls him for breakfast, he rises elegantly out of the bed which nearly hurls him to the floor and then for the pathetic touch, the moment of search for suitable clothing to breakfast in. Chaplin quickly upends the moth-eaten blanket, his head darting bird-like through a gaping hole. With the smoothness of molasses, he manages to slip

out of the rocking bed and cross to the table wearing a morning robe only the human heart could buy.

'Another shot shows Chaplin leisurely strolling down the slum street twirling his cane, wearing rags as if they were robes. Wearing fingerless gloves he removes them with the deftness of a baron, reaches in his pocket for his cigarette case, a sardine box, studies the contents, they are all butts, carefully selects the longest, taps it, lights it, inhales with slow elegance.

'Another wonderful piece of business shows Jackie throwing rocks through windows. Chaplin appears on the scene and mends them to earn money to keep them both alive.

'A scene never shot before or since shows Chaplin's puzzlement regarding the foundling infant's sex. While the little tyke sleeps, Chaplin shyly peeps under the blankets.

'Chaplin shot almost half a million feet of film on *The Kid*. He shot sometimes with complete abandon in the hope of catching a smile or half-tear that had never been laughed or cried over before. Out of this mass of frames he had to cut a feature picture that would run around 6,000 feet. It was a brain-exploding job. But brain-exploding jobs were always Chaplin exploits.

'The movie camera seemed to be Chaplin's conscience, forcing him to film only perfection. At times he captured the unqualified moment. In the four reeler *The Pilgrim*, he worked this celluloid miracle.

'Chaplin played an escaped convict who stole a clergyman's clothes for a disguise and slipping off a train, bumped into a surprise welcome for the new minister. The townspeople rushed him off to the church, where he had to deliver a sermon.

'The situation was in true Chaplin tradition – any minute the cops might appear – but he felt obligated to give a good sermon, since he wore the cloth. His crisis – his hide or his ideals.

'Taking David and Goliath as his theme, Chaplin acted out one of his funniest pantomimes. He squatted for David. He stretched almost to the ceiling for Goliath. David stalked Goliath. Goliath stalked David. Chaplin even impersonated the slingshot. Suddenly the rock flew through the air. Goliath grunted as if a flea had bitten him, and then toppled over.

'Chaplin topped this by smilingly sliding to his feet and gently dusting off the clerical frock with the due respect.

'There must have been thirty takes of this sequence though the actor was Charlie Chaplin. But Chaplin, the director, had no favourites, including himself. What amazed me was how Chaplin judged himself. A wall of mirrors in front of him couldn't have been more critical.

'At the finish of the sermon, a dead silence from the confused congregation. Then suddenly I jumped up and applauded much to everyone's consternation, and more specifically – my make-believe mother's. Chaplin quickly led off with the singing of "Onward Christian Soldiers" to brush aside the embarrassment, keeping one eye on the door for any cops.

'Though it was not in the script, Chaplin decided on a close-up of me singing, and to illustrate my daydreaming, he had me absentmindedly scratch the back of my head. My mother frowned. I scratched with the other hand. She clamped both my hands on the hymn book. I scratched with the end of the book. A sound boxing of my ears climaxed the close-up.

'For some unknown reason, this bit delighted Chaplin. It delighted him so much, he kept shooting and reshooting it all afternoon until I felt I had worn a bald spot on the back of my head which a photo I saw twenty years later presaged.

'To me Chaplin had no apparent devices, no tricks or even technique. He recognized simplicity as the governing force in everything. And of course his most disarming use of simplicity was a simple look. A look. Have you ever realized that Chaplin always looked at you from the screen – no matter what the action – he looked at you, the audience, as if he knew you – was about to tell you a secret? Made you wonder if he were a neighbour you'd neglected, the new groceryman, or a magazine salesman. He established an intimate contact with you in the look which relaxed you in your seat, prepared you to

Another escapade successfully completed for Charlie and Jackie in their *Funny Wonder* comic strip

believe anything he wanted to show you. And with an inimitable wink, profiled glance, or eyebrow-raised stare, he tapped your heart for an extra beat. That look – that simple gaze of familiarity first pulled the margins away from the silent comedy screen and laid the fantasy right in your heart as well as your lap.

'His use of props was fantastic yet every one had its bit. If it weren't in the routine it was thrown out. Remember what he wore on his uniform in what many believe his greatest funfest *Shoulder Arms*? A coffee pot, an egg beater, a mousetrap, a vegetable grater, a safety razor, a small bathtub, all these props along with his army equipment, the little soldier won World War I singlehanded – in his dreams.

'Charlie Chaplin was dragged into flickers like a trapped rabbit. Contract in his pocket but fear in his heart he lingered outside the Mack Sennett Studio wondering whether he shouldn't hop the next train back to New York.

'Here are Charlie's own words about that fateful day: '"When I got the contract I immediately began to attend every picture show where Keystone Comedies were being shown. I was terror struck! I saw Mabel Normand leaping about on the edges of high buildings, jumping from bridges, doing all manner of falls – if they expected that of a woman, what would they expect of me?"

'The gateman didn't recognize Chaplin as he wavered whether to enter or not to enter. Sennett in his crow's nest office that allowed him to watch out of the back of his head everything within a mile, recognized Charlie just as fear almost cancelled out the contract. Sennett rushed down and grabbed the little guy by the collar and hustled him into the studio and explained the use of the film "Double" when Charlie told him his fear of high places. Thus the silent screen's greatest comedian was rescued from oblivion.

'I worked in three Chaplin films *A Day's Pleasure*, *The Pilgrim*, and *The Kid*.

'I remember five Chaplins: Chaplin the writer, Chaplin the director, Chaplin the composer, Chaplin the actor, and Chaplin the producer.

'The world has wondered about Chaplin the man.

'I always remember Chaplin, the man, as a frightened little guy ordering his swimming pool drained the morning Jackie Coogan disappeared.'

Sidney Drew
CHARLIE CHAPLIN'S SCHOOLDAYS

BY THE END of 1915, with the thirty-five Keystone films and twelve movies for Essanay behind him, Chaplin had become world famous. He was also the centre of a remarkable 'craze' on both sides of the Atlantic. The Little Tramp figure was to be found in all manner of books and magazines, in cartoons and comic strips, on postcards and in advertising. Toys and statuettes were produced in his likeness, as were cups, mugs, vases and even candles. People began to imitate his clothes, his walk and his moustache. Popular songs were written about him such as 'The Chaplin Strut', 'The Chaplin Waddle' and 'Those Charlie Chaplin Feet', and he was widely impersonated on the stage and screen. People everywhere, children in particular, made up verses about him. He was now truly a cult figure, as the items on the next few pages from the period will demonstrate. The story here, 'Charlie Chaplin's Schooldays' written by the popular English author of juvenile serials, Sidney Drew, appeared in the *Boys' Friend Library* and was the first serial to fictionalize his life. The particular episode which I have selected offers a hilarious idea as to how Charlie might originally have got his baggy trousers!

'CHARLIE'S NEW SUIT had arrived. He tried it on in the dormitory. The Eton jacket fitted perfectly, but the trousers were not such a success. They did not crease nicely. From the knees downwards they fell in graceful folds that put the wearer in mind of a couple of concertinas of large size that had been badly damaged in a railway smash. Master Chaplin smiled as he surveyed himself in the mirror.

'"Don't mensh, but they are stylish!" he murmured; "stylish and roomy, absolutely ball-roomy. I like them very much."

'He surveyed himself in the wardrobe mirror and then went down to the study.

'"Hold your breff and mind your eyesight, chaps," he said; "and tell me what you think of my new reach-me-downs. Classy – what? All made to measure, and none of your slop-shop trash. I think the tailor must have cut 'em out with a knife and fork, don't you?"

'Fane, Bindley, Pye, and Manners went down on their hands and knees to get a better view, and crawled round him, howling with laughter.

'They had not much time for mirth for the class bell was ringing.

'"I'm going to let Pycroft have a good view of them," said the proud owner of the new suit. "Don't mensh, but I know they will glad his artistic eye. He'll want to write a few poems about 'em, and get Chules to paint his portrait and exhibit it at the Royal Academy, or the Dogs' Home, or wherever he sends his daubs."

'Master Chaplin sat next to Beelby. It was not exactly a post of honour, but Charlie had not been long enough at Calcroft to display any dazzling scholarly ability. He had a nice rosy apple in his desk, and he opened his desk when greedy Beelby was looking that way. Of course, Beelby could not resist it. He made a snatch at the tempting apple, and squealed with pain when the new boy let the lid fall smartly on his fingers.

'"Silence! What are you doing, Beelby? How dare you, sir? Write a hundred lines!" cried Mr Pycroft.

'"Please, s-sir, I-I couldn't help it!" whined Beelby, with his fingers in his mouth. "I-I trapped my hand, sir."

'"Oh-er-did you indeed?" said Mr Pycroft. "Even that is no excuse for making such a barbarous noise. I-er-notice, Chaplin, that you appear to be highly-hum!-amused at Beelby's accident, if I-er-am to judge by the wide and idiotic grin on your face. Such a grin ought not to be wasted on the desert air. Bring that chair forward, Chaplin; stand on it, my dear boy, and continue to grin for the benefit of-er-the class until you receive instruction from me to-ha!-to discontinue your facial grimaces and labial contortions.''

'The new boy picked up the chair and placed it in front of Mr Pycroft's desk. Then he climbed on the chair and grinned his best. It was a delightful grin, but it was not the grin that evoked the howl of mirth that almost deafened Mr Pycroft, but Charlie's new trousers.

'''Silence! Silence!'' pleaded Mr Pycroft. "Turn this way, Chaplin, as your – er – bewitching smile seems to exercise – ha! – such risible influence on the class. You may smile on me, my dear boy, without imperilling my sanity.''

'The yell of laughter that went up when Charlie turned was louder and longer than the first. Mr Pycroft rose and took up his cane.

'''I will not have this uproar!'' he cried. "Silence, or I shall detain the whole class! Chaplin, you may go back to – you may – Good gracious! What in the name of –''

'''Ha, ha, ha, ha, ha!'' laughed the boys of the Third Form. "Oh! Wow! Help! Ha, ha, ha, ha, ha, ha!''

'Mr Pycroft smote his learned brow so hard that he knocked off his mortar-board. He stooped and peered at Charlie's new trousers. He removed his glasses, polished them, replaced them on his nose, and peered again.

'''What in the name of – Good gracious! Where in the – Dear me! Who in the – Wha-what are th-those?'' stammered Mr Pycroft.

'''Which are what, please, sir?'' asked Chaplin.

'As Mr Pycroft gingerly stretched out his hand and took a pull at the neat black cloth out of which Mr Slapp had built the new boy's amazing lower garment, Fane put his head on Bindley's bosom and wept.

'''Those – those – those, boy!'' cried Mr Pycroft. "Wh-what – In the name of all absurdity, what are they?''

'''Please, sir, they've only just come, sir,'' said Charlie. "They're my new trousers, sir. Here's the bill, sir, I think.''

'Mr Pycroft reeled. He looked at Mr Slapp's bill that had been enclosed with the suit.

'''Ha!''

'Mr Pycroft tore open the envelope. It contained the bill, and at the bottom Mr Slapp had written something:

'''Honoured Sir, – I trust the suit of clothes will prove satisfactory. I have tailored for the young gentlemen of Calcroft for many years, but I never before knew a young gent go such an awful lot round the knee. He is about as much round the knee as round the waist. Cutting out those trousers has nearly broke my heart. Honoured sir, I remain to command – Your humble and obedient servant,   EBENEZER RUFUS SLAPP.''

'''Good gracious!'' said My Pycroft. "Silence! I sent someone with this wretched boy. It was you – er – Bindley!''

'''Yes, sir,'' answered Bindley, in a strangled voice. "Get off me chest, Fane, or I'll bite a piece out of your ear. Yes, sir.''

'''Just because they didn't like his trousers, they chased him round and round and round the houses,'' said Fane.

'''Was – was the boy – er – was he measured, Bindley? Was – er – did Slapp show – er – any symptoms of over-indulgence in alcoholic beverages? Did – er – the tailor display any signs of intoxication, Bindley?''

'''Not at all, sir,'' said Bindley, with a gulp. "He got it badly in the neck – I mean, he seemed rather surprised, sir, when he barged the tape – er – when he measured Chaplin's knees, sir. It staggered him a bit.''

'''Good gracious!'' said Mr Pycroft. "Pull up your trousers, Chaplin, as high as you can, my boy.''

'Charlie did not want to. He had not bargained for this.

'''Please, sir,'' he began, "I –''

'''As you are so amazingly modest, Fane will do it for you,'' said Mr Pycroft. "Come here, Fane!''

'''Sorry, Chappie, but it must be done,'' whispered Fane. "Do it yourself, you idiot!''

'The boys of Mr Pycroft's junior class craned their necks, expecting, most of them, to

THE MAGNET LIBRARY.

No. 660.

IF CHARLIE CHAPLIN WERE A FORM-MASTER

The First of a Screamingly Funny Set of Comic Pictures. Drawn by J. MACWILSON.

WONT YOU SIT DOWN SIR

2. "Woof!" gasped Charlie, as he subsided into about a gallon of watery wetness. "Ha, ha, ha! What a priceless old prune you are, to be sure, sir," chirruped the infants. "You absolutely take the bath-bun—'specially the bath, indeed you do, sir!" "Oh, throw me a lifebuoy, someone!" gurgled the Form-master.

lads and lassies! Charlie Chaplin, as struck a fine job as Form-for the Sons of Cabinet "What joy!" chortled ruffled Willie Wagg

1. Tee the scr master Minis the pol

he took his seat on the hand-straightway arose with exceed-he howled. "I've been attacked But when he saw that tack—

6. Biff! Over went the jar of blue-black on to the of the naughty little nippers. "Toodle-oo, boys! Charlie. "The class is dismissed!" *But look out* THE MAGNET LIBRARY.—

THE BOYS' FRIEND COMPLETE LIBRARY

No. 334

3^D

CHARLIE CHAPLIN'S SCHOOLDAYS

Two more examples of Charlie's fame in juvenil publications – as pupil and master!

see some terrible deformity.

'Charlie Chaplin was still standing on the chair. He raised one leg of his ample trousers. The first thing that came into view was a white sock, and then quite a shapely calf, clad in some striped material of white and blue.

'There was nothing visibly wrong with his knee. It was just an ordinary knee, neither smaller nor larger than it ought to have been.

'Mr Pycroft peered at it in utter bewilderment, and again glanced at the bill.

'"How – how – how do you explain this? How do you – er – explain this monstrous, this incredible blunder, Chaplin?"

'"Please, I had – I'd hurt my knees, sir, and had them bandaged, and I – I think I forgot to mention the bandages to the tailor, sir," answered Charie Chaplin, and the class shivered. "It – it was an oversight, sir."

'Mr Pycroft picked up his mortar-board, fanned himself with it, and put it on his head with the back to the front.

'"An – er – oversight, Chaplin," he said. "Dear me, those things would fit an elephant! Your other trousers, Chaplin, are preposterous enough, but these are suicidal monstrosities! Go at once and put on the other pair."

'"Please, I can't, sir!"

'"'Can't, sir!' You 'can't, sir'! Don't – er – you anger me, Chaplin!" thundered Mr Pycroft. "Go at once and do what I bid you!"

'"But please, sir, I've torn them, sir," said Charlie wearily. "I fell down on a slide, sir, and made a big hole in them."

'Once more the juniors roared with laughter. Master Chaplin caught Bindley's eye, and gave the ghost of a wink.

'"Very good," said Mr Pycroft. "Excellent! Good gracious!"

'Mr Pycroft took up the cane, bent it a few times, as if meditating a fierce assault on Master Charlie, and then threw it down. He took another glare at the terrible trousers and shuddered. Then he opened his desk and searched for something. With his hands behind him he scowled at the new boy.

'"Take them off!" he suddenly shouted.

'This was quite the last thing in the world that Master Chaplin had bargained for.

'"Wha-wha-wha-what for, sir?" he stammered.

'"Not 'wha-wha-wha-what, sir,' but take them off, sir," said Mr Pycroft.

'"Yes, sir," replied Charlie meekly.

'He could not guess what was going to happen. There was no need to remove his boots, but to gain time he did so.

'He placed the boots neatly side by side, temptingly close to Haik, who immediately uttered a chuckle, and emptied the contents of an inkpot into them. Charlie was making for the door to undress in privacy.

'"Here, sir – here!" shouted Mr Pycroft. "Where are you going, sir? Take them off! Silence – silence! Get on that chair, boy!"

'Mr Pycroft might as well have attempted to impose silence on a thunderstorm. As Charlie pulled off the trousers, and stood revealed in his socks, shirt, and striped pants, the juniors shivered. Mr Pycroft seized the trousers, and in dumb show beckoned to Fane. Then Mr Pycroft drew his right hand from behind his back, and revealed a pair of scissors. Then, with a few skilful snips, Mr Pycroft converted Master Chaplin's new trousers into knickers cut well above the knee.

'The whole form was in hysterics.

'"Oh, carry me out – carry us all out!" moaned Bindley. "With a weak heart like mine, this is a bit too much."

'Mr Pycroft tossed the abbreviated garments to their owner, and commanded him to put them on with a gesture, for he could not make himself heard. He rushed to the blackboard and wrote on it:

'"Unless you are silent immediately, Saturday afternoon will not be a half-holiday!"

'The threat was fairly effective. There were spasms of snorting and sniggering, but Mr Pycroft could make himself heard. Master Chaplin was beginning to think it was the Housemaster's jape, not his.

'"Very – er – becoming, Chaplin," said Mr Pycroft. "Light and airy, and – er – calculated to give you perfect freedom of limb. You will wear them until we can provide you with others, my dear boy. Your boots, now. Fane, give Chaplin his boots."

'"Catch, Chappie," said Fane.

'He tossed up one of the boots, and as Master Chaplin caught it a black fluid shot out and covered the new boy's collar and features with ebony-hued blotches and streaks.

'The class writhed and groaned and snorted and grunted. The juniors were purple, and their eyes were strained and glassy with their efforts to restrain their laughter. But it was of no avail. They could not help themselves. Even if Mr Pycroft deprived them of every half-holiday for the remainder of the term, it had to be. They exploded with mirth, one prolonged, crashing, ecstatic peal of it that shook the windows.

'"Go-go – This is intolerable! It is – er – maddening! It is – ha! – monstrous!" said Mr Pycroft, holding his head. "Good gracious!"

'He looked wearily at Fane, who was dancing on one leg. Charlie Chaplin, in his shocked surprise, had at once flung the bewitched boot away. Fane's mouth was wide open, emitting shrieks of laughter, and his eyes were shut, when the boot alighted on his toe. Fane shut his mouth, opened his eyes, and danced.

'Haik was almost in a state of collapse. He rolled about the form, tears trickling down his cheeks, and leaned against Reffel for support. Reffel was in need of support himself, and not at all inclined to render first aid to his leader. He pushed Haik rudely away, and Haik fell to the floor in a condition bordering on imbecility.

'"Silence! Silence, for pity's sake!" pleaded Mr Pycroft. "My patience is – er – utterly exhausted. I can bear no more."

'This time, stern measures being necessary, Mr Pycroft meant business. Again he snatched up the cane. A few stinging cuts put a sudden end to Fane's dance. Then Haik got it and howled. Mr Pycroft pranced along between the desks, laying about him right and left without fear or favour.

'"There! Phew!" he panted. "It was not my – er – wish to do anything so drastic, but you – phew! – your disgraceful and unruly conduct has compelled it. I am almost demented – almost crazy. I warn you to be – er – careful, that is all – to be extremely careful. I don't know what is the matter with your face,

Chaplin, wretched youth, and I do not care. Put on your boots, and go and wash yourself. Good gracious!"

'"Wow!" moaned Haik.

'Master Charlie Chaplin, streaked like a zebra, and spotted like a leopard, descended from his post of honour. He grinned rather feebly and forlornly. He was aware that somebody had poured ink into his boot, for he had tasted some of it, and he recognized the flavour. He picked up the boot that had caused Fane so much anguish, and peered into it. Haik, although he was in pain himself, sniggered.

'"Please, sir, I – Don't mensh, sir, but I think someone has spilled ink in my boots, sir!" said the new boy.

'"Ink!" said Reffel, in an undertone. "What a jolly waste to go and black 'em inside! Why don't the kid use 'em as coal-boxes?"

'"Ha!" exclaimed Mr Pycroft. "Is that so? Dear – er – me! Bring them – er – here, Chaplin, and we will investigate!"

'Mr Pycroft inspected the interior of one of Master Chaplin's ample boots. Then he twisted up a piece of white paper, and made a tree. As the end of the paper came out moist and black, it was quite apparent that there was more in the boot than laces and leather. Mr Pycroft laid a finger on his learned forehead, and knitted his brows, as if pondering over some weighty and extremely difficult problem.

'"Wretched boy!" he murmured. "Wretched boy!"

'Mr Pycroft's amazing brain was at work. He took up a duster and a lead pencil. The next moment Haik shuddered. Very deliberately Mr Pycroft approached the front row of desks. With the gaze of his fascinated scholars upon him, he thrust the pencil into Bindley's inkpot, and withdrew it. The result was quite satisfactory, from Bindley's point of view, for there was a good half an inch of ink on the pencil. Mr Pycroft wiped the pencil with the duster, and Haik quailed.

'"Marvellous!" grinned Brindley. "We must write to Sexton Blake about it, and warn him that our Mr Pycroft will collar his job, if he doesn't look out! My word, what a brainy brain!''

'Fane, Pye, and Reffel passed the test with flying colours. Then it was Haik's turn.

'"Aha!" cried Mr Pycroft triumphantly. "Oho!"

'There was not enough ink on the pencil to make a small blot. Like a grim and remorseless sleuthhound that would not be shaken off the scent, Mr Pycroft had tracked the culprit down.

'"Pounced on by Pycroft; or, the Clue of the Empty Inkpot!"' whispered Fane. "Write it up, Bindy, and have it printed in the school magazine. It would make a ripping detective story. Wow! He's got the right man, I'll wager!"

'Mr Pycroft tossed the duster away, and gazed fixedly at Haik after this triumphant exhibition of skilled detective work.

'"Ahem!" Mr Pycroft cleared his throat, and took up the cane. "I am not going to be – er – hasty, Haik," he said, "as I am perfectly aware that – ha! – it is a highly dangerous thing to rely too much upon circumstantial evidence. Circumstantial evidence has hanged many innocent people ere to-day. Let us examine this affair, my dear Haik, and place the facts in their logical sequence. It should interest you, Haik. Come to the blackboard, my boy!"

'Haik went forward limply.

'Taking the chalk, Mr Pycroft made a sketch of what might have been a pair of boots or a couple of legless and trunkless elephants, and another sketch that his admiring and interested scholars took to be an inkpot.

'"Pay the greatest attention, my dear Haik!" said Mr Pycroft, with a terrible smile. "Endeavour to stir your – er – puny intellect sufficiently to grasp the – ha! – elements of this simple problem. Let X be a pair of boots, and Y an inkpot, and Z the ink. Let it be granted, Haik, that the – er – inkpot originally contained ink, and the boots none. Therefore, Haik, Y and Z equals the inkpot filled with ink. But the inkpot is now empty. What follows? Y and Z equals the boots with the ink in them. The problem is – er – is, Haik, to discover by what extraordinary process Y and Z became X and Z. That is – er – to say how the ink left the inkpot and entered the boots.''

'Mr Pycroft might have gone on in this strain for quite a long time, and the unhappy Haik knew it. It was only drawing out the agony, and Haik thought it better to get it over and done with.

'"Please, I poured it in," he said. "I – I couldn't help it, sir! I can't stand those trotter cases – those boots – sir, at any price! They're just too awful!"

'"Ah, I thought so, Haik, when I found your empty inkpot," said Mr Pycroft. "I – er – think you had better write a thousand lines, and – er – of course you are gated for Saturday, and – dear me! – I think you had better pay a visit to my room after tea, when I shall be able to give you a very suitable reward for your enterprise!"

'"Yes, sir," said Haik meekly.

'"And – er – Chaplin, your appearance is not conducive to that spirit of study and diligence which I must have in the class, so – er – you had better take steps to remove your peculiar – er – trousers, and immediately procure some nether garments which will fit you to mix with civilized people."

'"Yes, sir," said Charlie, as he moved to the door; "and please, sir, will you save the pieces you cut off? They will do very nicely to patch my new ones!"'

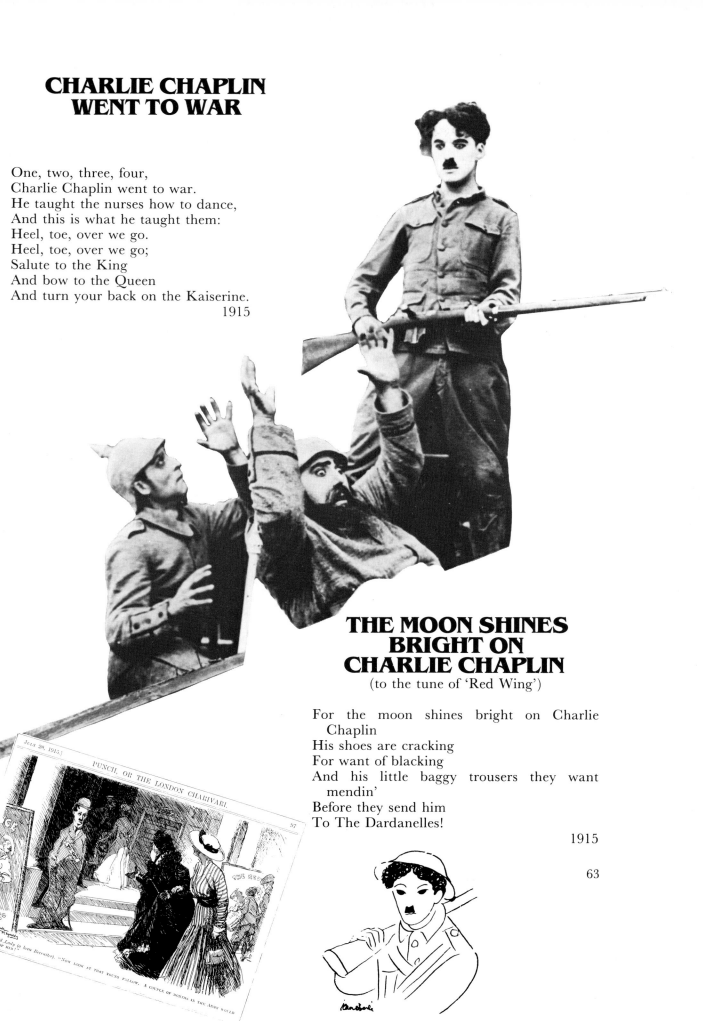

CHARLIE CHAPLIN WENT TO WAR

One, two, three, four,
Charlie Chaplin went to war.
He taught the nurses how to dance,
And this is what he taught them:
Heel, toe, over we go.
Heel, toe, over we go;
Salute to the King
And bow to the Queen
And turn your back on the Kaiserine.

1915

THE MOON SHINES BRIGHT ON CHARLIE CHAPLIN
(to the tune of 'Red Wing')

For the moon shines bright on Charlie
    Chaplin
His shoes are cracking
For want of blacking
And his little baggy trousers they want
    mendin'
Before they send him
To The Dardanelles!

1915

63

CHARLIE'S FAME

This is a very curious world
So many things are happ'nin;
For all the girls
Wear Pickford curls,
And boys play Charlie Chaplin.

Motion Picture Magazine
May, 1916

CHARLIE CHAPLIN MEEK AND MILD

(To the tune of 'Gentle Jesus')

Charlie Chaplin, meek and mild,
Took a sausage from a child.
When the child began to cry,
Charlie slapped him in the eye.

1931

THE CHAPLIN ABC

A is for Anderson, Charlie's best pal,
B is for Boots that fit Charlie quite well.
C is for Charlie, the Chaplin of fame,
D is for Doings that have made his name.
E is for Essanay, the firm that produce,
F Frolics of Charlie that sorrows reduce.
G is for Gambols, Gyrations and Gusts,
H Humour – one sees Charlie and busts.
I for Individuality, Charlie I'm told,
J Jibes with a wit worth its weight in good
    gold.
K is his Kultur, a curious thing,
L Laughter to give us, would make the dead
    sing.
M Mincing step, when he shambles his way,
N Natty – right to the heart of the play.
O for the Only great cinema star.
P is for Pantomime actions that are
Q Queer they say, but take it from me,
R Rich is the humour of our old Charlie.
S for the Simpering way that he moves,
T for Trousers that everyone loves.
U for the Unction his brick-bat bestows,
V for Vivacity, Charlie e'er shows.
W for the Wonder he reveals in his plays,
XYZ – hopeless, I should be here for days!

Charlie Chaplin's Scream Book
1916

65

Charlie in strip cartoons in France, Britain and America
The artist of *Charlie Chaplin's Comic Capers* was E.C.
Segar later to become world famous as the creator of
Popeye

Langford Reed
THE CHAMPION

WITH CHAPLIN firmly established as the world's greatest screen draw – in Hollywood he was being referred to as 'the biggest single fact in the motion-picture industry' – it was not long before his films were being novelized for newspapers and magazines: becoming, in effect, the forerunners of today's enormously popular 'film tie-ins'. Perhaps the best of the novelizers of Chaplin material was Langford Reed, a British writer who came from a similarly humble background to Charlie, and who managed to capture the Little Tramp's special brand of humour as well as introducing fascinating passages about his screen characteristics. This spirited short version of *The Champion* was one of a series of *Charlie Chaplin's Humorous Adventures on the Films* which he wrote for *The Family Journal* in the autumn of 1915. In 1917, Reed was responsible for the 'compilation' film, *Chase Me Charlie* made up of extracts from Chaplin's Essanay comedies. It seems particularly appropriate to include this story because Chaplin was very interested in boxing during his early days in Hollywood and spent many an evening watching prize-fights in the saloons – occasionally even acting as a second to one or other of the boxers!

Charlie the boxer from *The Champion* (1915)

'CHARLIE WAS A wanderer, a happy-go-lucky young fellow who took life philosophically. He believed in luck, and he was convinced that one day Dame Fortune would favour him.

'Accompanied by his faithful bull-dog, Winston, he was strolling about trying to evolve some scheme whereby he and a good dinner might become intimately acquainted. Suddenly his foot knocked against a piece of metal, and looking down he saw a horseshoe! He put the find carefully in his pocket, and then, on the door of a gymnasium opposite to where he stood, he noticed a placard stating that "Battling Bill, the Battersea Bruiser", required another sparring partner to practise on for his forthcoming battle for the championship of the world with Ikey Cohen, heavy-weight champion of Lundy Island. Charlie applied for the vacant position and was at once engaged.

'Charlie found Battling Bill rather different from what he expected. True, he did not look at all refined, but, despite his unpleasant appearance, he seemed quite a humourist, for directly he saw our hero he went into a violent fit of laughter, and roared out "Hullo, earwig, so you're my new sparring partner, are you? Be gentle with me, 'cos I'm delicate!"

'At this point he threw up his hands and went into such a fit of mirth that his huge frame shook like a cheap jelly. Charlie felt distinctly annoyed at the pugilist's lack of breeding, and so he suddenly let drive, hard, at well, just in the region of "the equator".

'The noise of Bill's laughter abruptly ceased, but apparently he was still convulsed with mirth, for he doubled up and held his sides, while his face became even more contorted than before. To straighten him up Charlie got behind him, and administered a cheery kick, putting all his strength into this little service. The big fellow at once resumed the perpendicular, in which position, he made horrible grimaces at our hero, though he said nothing.

'Rather surprised at his employer's manner of announcing that the practice should commence, Charlie, nevertheless, rose to the occasion. Stepping back a pace, he delivered a "straight left" at the grimacing countenance in front of him. Strange to say, Battling Bill made no effort to guard the blow, and a moment later, when the stretcher-men entered, they found Charlie, without a mark on him, energetically sparring at an imaginary opponent, while the fistic pride of Battersea lay unconscious on the floor. Charlie was forthwith hailed as a champion, and prevailed upon to go into training to fight Ikey Cohen himself.

'Charlie quite enjoyed his training, despite the many mistakes which occurred because of his lack of experience, for there were many compensations.

'One of these was the trainer's daughter, Seraphina Squinch.

'Seraphina was "some" girl. Eighteen years old, as dainty as a dandelion, and as sweet as sugar, she was remarkably intelligent. In fact, she knew a thing or three.

'"I grew very fond of Serry," said Charlie afterwards, when recalling his friendship with her. "She was not one of your milk-and-water lassies, with eyes like a love-sick angel's, and feet the size of an ant's. And she was so thorough, too. If you threw a brick at her, she would reply with a wall, brick by brick. Oh, she was a nice girl!"

'The day of the great fight arrived, and a vast crowd of true-blue sportsmen assembled to watch the historic event. They came to London from great cities all over the world, from New York, from Paris, and from Mugglesea.

'Charlie's opponent, Ikey Cohen, was exactly like Battling Bill, only very much more so. He was, in fact, a most ungentlemanly-looking fellow, and Charlie took an instinctive dislike to him at once. His lucky horseshoe, pressed against his knuckles inside his glove, and the sight of Seraphina sucking a melon in a side-box, inspired him with the determination to die rather than yield.

'Round one was distinctly in our young friend's favour. Ikey never touched him once; in fact, he couldn't catch him. The active Charlie raced round the ring at full speed, and the lumbering heavy-weight was a poor second all the time. After making twenty circuits of the ring, Mr Cohen became so dizzy that he reeled like a drunken man. This was

Charlie's opportunity. He himself was not in the least giddy, for he had taken the precaution of running round the ring with his eyes shut!

'He dashed in, and planted a couple of sweet uppercuts on the pugilist's jaw. His giant opponent staggered and fell, and only the call of "time" prevented him from being counted out, then and there.

'Round two saw Ikey wary and watchful. He stood still and waited for his youthful antagonist. Charlie, nothing loth, dashed in, and in a second the two men were locked in a clinch.

'"Break away there!" yelled the referee. "You've not come here to cuddle one another." But the boxers had unconsciously got into the steps of a Tango, at which they might have given a very clever exhibition, had not the referee suddenly dashed between them.

'"Break away there!" he yelled. "Break away, you silly cuckoos!" The two pugilists this time obeyed him, and the Lundy Islander aimed a terrific blow at Charlie. But, luckily for our hero, it accidentally caught the referee instead, and knocked that functionary right into the audience!

'A fresh referee was procured, and the fight continued. Round three went distinctly against Charlie at first. He was knocked about like an india-rubber ball, and Ikey finished up seizing him by the neck, and bumping him violently up and down on the floor.

'The audience yelled "Shame!" and the referee cried "Foul!" Suddenly there was a loud bark, followed by a commotion among the audience. The next instant Charlie's faithful bull-dog dashed upon the stage. Springing on his antagonist from behind, he took a good hold, about a foot below the belt, and hung on like a leech. Ikey roared, and so did the crowd.

'The luckless pugilist tried in vain to free himself of his encumbrance, and swung round and round so violently that it was all Winston could do to maintain his hold, while Charlie found it almost impossible to hit his opponent. At last, however, the whirling man stopped, exhausted, and this was our young friend's chance. Dashing in quickly, he shot a couple of crooked lefts to the jaw, following these up with a fancy kind of uppercut. The huge form tottered, and then fell headlong.

'And that's how Charlie Chaplin won the championship of the world. Today he believes more than ever in luck, and the horseshoe which brought him his good fortune he has had mounted on a ring, which he wears on his watch-chain on every anniversary of the great battle.

'In conclusion I should add, in proof that my story of Charlie's prowess is not exaggerated, that the Essanay Film Company secured a splendid exclusive film of the fight, in which every move is clearly seen. Under the title of *Champion Charlie*, this picture is now showing all over the country.'

BILLY WEST
in the
KING BEE COMEDIES

is an asset which you cannot afford to ignore. To make your audience really jovial—to assist them in forgetting the strain and stress of life to-day—is essential to success. Billy West will do this—make them roar—will create in fact a regular barrage of laughter.

But you must book now, for the demand is great.

These are twelve two-reelers :
DOUGH NUTS—BACK STAGE—THE HERO—THE MILLIONAIRE—CUPID'S RIVAL—THE MODISTE—THE VILLAIN—THE GOAT—THE GENIUS—

and three more to follow.

SUN EXCLUSIVES

In "Cupid's Rival."

THE Family Journal
A WEEKLY PAPER FOR THE HOUSEHOLD
PRICE 1D. EVERY WEDNESDAY

£4 in Cash P' EVERY WE 'Topical Ta' Competition

CHAPLIN APPEARS IN THIS NUMBER

The Champion Mirth-Maker in his Own Home!
SEE PAGE 509.

The "F.J." is EVERYBODY'S PAPER.

No. 332. Vol. XIII.

Sept. 11, 1915.

DICKY DOENUT
THE CHAP TO MAKE YOU CH

TEE! HEE!!

HAW! HAW !!! HAW !!!

HOW'S THAT!

HELP!

NOW LAUGH!

1. It was a lovely day, and Dicky Doenut was toddling across the park, too busy with the paper to know or care much whither he was bound. And it was just that which caused Percy Pushoff to cackle. "He, he!" he wheezed. "He's making straight for the fountain!"

2. Sure enough, that's just what Dicky Doenut was doing, and a word of warning would have saved him. But Percy thought it too good a joke to spoil. "Ho, ho, ho! Hold me, somebody!" he howled. "What did I say? Didn't I tell you as much!" Yes, he thought it a funny joke.

3. But Dicky did not, needless to say. "Very funny, is it not?" he warbled. "Well, perhaps you'll appreciate that joke, too! It's even wetter than the other one!" And, flopping forward across the basin of the fountain, he caught his stick round the stem and bent it down.

4. So that the stream was directed straight at Percy Pushoff, soaking him to the skin in less than two twos. "Now I laugh!" wuffled Dicky, with a grin on his face from ear to there. "You don't seem to be smiling very loudly, though, I notice! Toodle-oo!" And away he toddled.

Charlie not only had to compete on the screen – but also with comic strip rivals like 'Dicky Doenut' and look-alike actors such as Billy West

69

Draycot M. Dell
A QUICK MOMENT
WITH THE QUICKEST MAN ON EARTH

THE PHENOMENAL popularity of the Chaplin films naturally prompted an ever-increasing interest in the man behind the screen image. Charlie was, of course, well aware of the importance of publicity, but already had a distracting habit of telling interviewers different facts about himself and his background. He compounded this habit in 1916 by publishing an 'autobiography', *Charlie Chaplin's Own Story*, in which he claimed, among other things, to have been born in France and raised in a Dickensian London under the 'guardianship' of a Mr Hawkins, to all intents and purposes a carbon-copy of Fagin! Perhaps this over-fictionalizing of his life accounts for the failure of the book, but certainly Chaplin became embarrassed by it and quickly had it withdrawn from sale. One side-effect of the book was that it encouraged others to romanticize the life of the Little Tramp – a typical example being the 'interview' here, published in *Charlie Chaplin's Scream Book*, issued in Britain in 1916. It was written by Draycot M. Dell, a prolific English writer of the period who was also editor of a number of magazines including *Chums* and *Young Britain*. His invented ideas about Chaplin will be contrasted next by the genuine article.

'I OPENED THE ominous little envelope from a well-known editor as though it had been the outer covering of a sentence to death. The worst had happened! I was destined to interview Charlie Chaplin, the funniest man on the "movies".

'Visions of flying brickbats and the sharp prongs of a hay fork came to my tortured eyes. I felt sure I should find Charlie hedged about by barbed wire entanglements, and, at the end of his expressive feet, little needlepoints that somehow or other I knew would find my most vulnerable point and puncture my romance!

'I had seen Charlie, and laughed – had seen his well-directed foot leap like a flash of light into the bay window of his enemy. I knew his tricks by heart, but I feared that it would be almost impossible to counter them.

'Nevertheless, I determined to interview Charlie, for I knew that fame would follow success, so having made my will, having kissed my wife for the last time, picked up a Remington repeater, grabbed my little typewriter case and a bottle of arsenic, I sallied from home in search of the headquarters of the Essanay Film Company, where I knew Charlie to be in laager – no, not the now banned beverage, but an entrenched camp of Charlie's own conceiving.

'Night had fallen when, through the hazy mist from the fields, I perceived my destination. The studios were plunged in darkness. It was the very opportunity I sought. I would catch Charlie napping! With my neat little Colt revolver pressed to his frolicsome forehead, I would find out the whole truth, and nothing but the truth, of his success as a cinema "star".

'I crept past the sentry, Broncho Billy, who, leaning against a bucking broncho, was finding fine targets by shooting at the stars. At the same time he was dreaming of saving damsels in distress and destroying all the sheriffs in the United States at one shot. His reverie saved my life. The noise of his barking revolver drowned the bark of the watch-dog, and let me pass unperceived.

'Creeping up to the door of the studio, I looked within. My heart rose, for there, lying amid a camp of disused baggy trousers, and surrounded by hosts of diminutive bowlers, was the man I sought. In his hand was a little cane, and in his eye – sleep. I told myself that he had just finished reeling off half a dozen plays that day, and, worn out, was sleeping the sleep of the just – the just finished.

'I unhitched my typewriter, and, finding a convenient little table, placed it thereon, un-

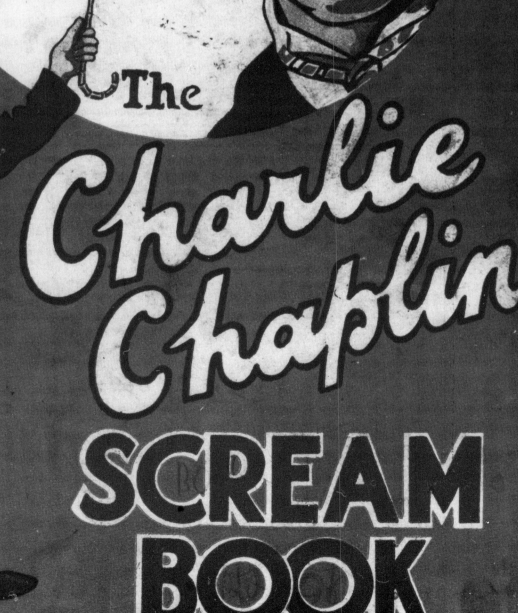

2d.
ONE
LONG
LAUGH

The
Charlie
Chaplin
SCREAM
BOOK

loosened my Remington repeater, and, finding a good-sized megaphone near by, placed it to my lips.

'"Charlie Chaplin, I believe?" I bellowed, the notes of my voice booming through this place of hitherto silence.

'Charlie Chaplin looked up, at first with a look of amazement. His little moustache twitched, a bright light came into his tired eye, and he felt for his cane. Next he sat up, and, turning his head ever so carefully, looked down the barrel of my rifle – looked in a pathetic manner, as though to say: "This *is* a rude awakening!" Then slowly he rose to his feet, and, hitching his trousers, flicked a little dust off the end of his boot, an act performed with great difficulty, as there is nothing in the world so far off from Charlie as his feet. He can achieve success for the asking, but if he wants to polish his boots – my word!

'Charlie drew a Woodbine from behind his ear, and, having lit it, threw the match very discreetly into my face. It was a pleasing little compliment which I greatly appreciated as I cocked my rifle. Next he looked about him. Was there a brick, he wondered, or perhaps a cobblestone that he might make me a gift of? But no! He gave up the quest as a bad job, and turning his back on me, with his feet splayed out, plunged his head on his breast and thought deeply and darkly.

'I was not prepared for the next happening. He turned with a quick, jerky movement, and the next thing I knew was that a boot – oh, that boot! – had hit me right in the belt. Charlie was looking at me as though to say: "Oh, you saucy puss!"

'I brushed this mark of affection aside, and, having regained my breath, murmured: "Is it true that you are deaf and dumb, Mr Chaplin?"

'Charlie looked softly at me. "Yes, both," he said blandly. "But you won't tell the world, will you, Mr Interviewer – nor that I suffer from corns, or that my left eye is glass and my feet false? These are little secrets I wouldn't like to leak out."

'"And your favourite hobby, Charlie?" I said. I was calling him "Charlie" now in the most affectionate manner.

'He hung his head. "It's a toss-up", he said quietly, "between walking a mile of greasy tight-rope and boxing with horseshoe gloves."

'"Horseshoe gloves?" I said, surprised. "What kind of boxing is that?"

'A little simpering look came into Charlie Chaplin's face; then he hung his head like a shy girl. "Well, to tell you the truth," he said, "it is a little unfair, but it's very amusing. You challenge a man smaller than yourself to fight you, and when he is not looking you find the largest horseshoe you can, insert it carefully into the glove, and, swinging your arm round at a rate of 3,000 miles a minute, you give him a blow beneath the chin that makes him wonder whether he is in New York or Thursday. That's boxing with horseshoe gloves, and that's what they mean when they say I've got a punch like the kick of a horse."

'I was puzzled. It struck me as being unfair competition, and I told Charlie so; but he only laughed.

'"I had to get the championship," he said proudly, "and, you know, a knock-out in time saves nine. The horseshoe is a proper sleep-producer."

'I now understood what a genius he was as a pugilist.

'"Yes," said Charlie meditatively, "a horseshoe has always brought me good luck."

'It was a sore point but I had to touch on it. "Your feet, Mr Chaplin. I have heard many rumours about them."

'Charlie held up his hand. "They are all untrue," he said quickly. "Don't you believe anything you hear. They have done some dirty work in their time, I admit; but, as for being faked, that's perfectly untrue. As Broncho Billy, with whom I act occasionally, says, 'They are my greatest feat!'"

'"Two feet one yard," I said dreamily under my breath, thinking of my schooldays, but Charlie heard, and, quickly stepping out past his barricade, came up to me, and, laughing in my face, knocked me down with an uppercut.

'"Fine joke," he said brightly, and as I got up, dazed, he jabbed me from behind with one of the members we had just been discussing. It was like the kick of a horse, and it contained all the poetry of motion that you can get into the cylinder of a

Jack Johnson shell.

'"You are a marvel," I said, sitting up and rubbing my head.

'He bowed, and shook his head playfully at me, as though to say, "Not at all – not at all!" and then, giving a hasty glance behind him, he threw open the door of the studio and shambled away into the darkness. I could hear him laughing in the distance behind a dust cloud.'

Two feet of fun in a hayfield

PLONK!
PLONK!

CHARLIE'S SERENADE

The garden is full of worms, dear.
'The cowslip has slipped off the hedge;
The cat on the tiles,
A creature of wiles,
Has put all my nerves on the edge.
By the cabbages growing near me,
By the moon and the stars in the sky,
No lover can love as I love—
No lover can love as I.

The bricks of your house are hard, dear.
The scent of the onions brings tears;
And the fruit you just threw
Lends soft memories of you,
That will live in my cranium for years.
By the bottles that lie broken near me,
By the water flung down from on high,
No lover can love as I love—
No lover can love as I.

The moon has departed with groans, dear.
The cat lyeth dead by the fence;
All the flowers round about
Are beginning to sprout;
The success of my song is immense.
By the fire brigade quickly coming,
By the iron-bar near where I lie,
No lover can love as I love—
No lover can love as I.

No! No lover can love as I lie,
And lucky no lover who can.
For my head is a reel, with the pains that I feel,
And somebody just threw a tram.
Good-bye, oh! beloved I leave thee
For the day—and the public draw nigh:
And the ominous beat of a P.C.'s broad feet
Are urging me, dearest to fly.
Good-bye.

73

Konrad Bercovici
A DAY WITH CHARLIE CHAPLIN

WHEN AN observant writer managed to get close to Chaplin for any length of time, he found a man vastly different from the comical figure described in the last item. The real Chaplin beneath the masquerade of the Little Tramp was a complex personality clearly obsessed with his art. One writer who gained an insight into the star, and soon became his friend, was Konrad Bercovici, who contributed to some of the most prestigious magazines in America. The friendship of the two men was also partly founded on the fact that both had Gypsy blood in their veins. Bercovici wrote several perceptive essays on Chaplin, including the following item which throws considerable light on the enigma of his personality. It appeared in *Harper's Magazine* of December 1928. It is sad to have to report that the two men fell out in 1947 when Bercovici suddenly instituted a lawsuit against Chaplin. The writer claimed that Charlie had used some of his ideas in the making of *The Great Dictator* and demanded over six million dollars in compensation! Although Chaplin initially wanted to contest the suit, it came at a troubled period in his life (as we shall see later) and instead he settled out of court for $95,000. The dispute naturally brought about the end of their friendship.

'I ARRIVED in Hollywood one afternoon when the sun was blazing its white-hot rays upon the multi-shaped roofs of the fairy-like cottages of the city of film fame. From a distance, from the heights of the Cahuenga Pass, Hollywood presented itself not like a city but like a monster exhibition of Spanish architecture. Every form and every variation was exhibited in colours grading from a glaring yellow to a shining blue that rivalled the blue of the sky. I had come by car through the Utah deserts. The sudden transition from the cold to the pleasant, almost enervating warmth made me conscious of the fine road sand which had filmed my face and body.

'I drove up to the front of Chaplin's studio (having made a telegraphic appointment with the comedian whom I hadn't seen in more than a year). Half a dozen cars whose license plates showed they had come from that number of states, were parked there. In the Chaplin office, on a bench by the wall, weather-beaten, sun-browned men and women were waiting patiently for a glimpse of the great little man who had made them laugh.

'"Why do you let them wait inside? And why doesn't Mr Chaplin come out to see them? It would only take a minute," I asked one of the secretaries. She only raised her shoulders eloquently in answer.

'After shaking hands with Tom – Tom Harrington, who had been Chaplin's secretary, bodyguard, valet, and protector for many years – I asked: "Where's Charlie?"

'"Haven't seen him in two days. He hasn't been down to the studio at all."

'Chaplin was making one of his pictures but he could not always resist the temptation to run away and to try to forget that he was working. A hundred men and women were walking about impatiently on the "lot", all dressed up for their respective parts. The cameramen had trained their apparatuses and were waiting at their posts; for no one knew when Charlie would suddenly appear and begin to work as if nothing had happened, as if he had left off just a few minutes before.

'Taking possession of one of the dressing rooms, I plunged into the large swimming pool where a few mermaids were already disporting themselves – snatching a swim while the boss was away.

'I had not been in the water more than a few minutes when a loud yell announced Charlie's arrival. The mermaids clambered out, leaving me alone in the pool, and rushed to the dressing rooms to get into their clothes.

Two shots of Charlie with Mabel Normand in *Mabel's at the Wheel* (1914)

'Charlie, a little thinner, a little older than I had left him the year before, sat down on the edge of the pool and, taking his shoes off, began to wiggle his small, beautiful, feminine feet in the cool water. To the inevitable Tom who approached to whisper something in his ears, he motioned over his shoulders: "That's all for the day. Tomorrow at seven o'clock."

'Standing up to my neck in water, we talked of this and that for a while. Then Charlie suddenly suggested: "Let's go and see Doug."

'We talked while I was dressing. I wondered what had gone out of the man. He was much quieter than usual. He was making a great effort to keep up his spirits. There was something indescribably sad in his face. His nervous fingers twitched continually.

'"What on earth is the matter with you?" I asked.

'But I had struck the wrong note, for instantly he began to cut capers, jump, sing Jewish dialect songs, and show me a new trick he had learned to do with his hat. He was defending himself, shutting himself in. I responded to his mood. A few minutes later we were ready to go. As we were about to pass the door I remembered the waiting admirers and the automobiles in which children were broiling in the sun for a glimpse of the man they adored. The memory of the eyes of a little boy of about eight who had been looking steadily at the door, afraid if he should turn his head for a second he would miss the great chance, made me stop Charlie and say: "I have joined the Boy Scouts."

'"You?" Charlie laughed.

'"Yes. And I have sworn to do a good deed every day. It's getting dark and I haven't done one yet."

'"You will soon do one," Charlie said. "Traffic in Hollywood has become impossible, and you know how afraid I am to cross the street."

'"Charlie," I suggested, "there are forty people waiting outside who have come thousands of miles to see you. There are little boys and little girls who could be made happy. When they return home they will tell the world – their little world – that they have seen you with their own eyes."

'Charlie grew pale. "I have been away for two days because of that. There is an old man with a terrible face, and he has been camping in front of my door for a week now. I can't do it."

'Knowing Chaplin's sensitiveness to faces, I understood his reactions. But I had already passed an arm around his and was dragging him almost bodily into his office.

'"Here's Mr Chaplin!" I said to the assembly while the comedian was grinning and showing his teeth and trying to appear unconcerned. A man arose from the bench and instead of approaching Chaplin and looking at him with the same curiosity the others were doing, he called out from the door, "Come in, everybody!"

'What an indescribable tumult! What cries of joy and delight during the next few moments! Chaplin had dropped his shyness and was shaking hands all around and telling everyone how glad he was they had come. He was distributing autographed photographs of himself to everybody – autographed photographs that bore no resemblance to the twitching, gesticulating, clumsy, nimble figure of the screen.

'An old man, whose beady eyes danced shrewdly and whose swollen lower lip hung flabbily above a long chin, came in leaning on a knotted stick. Instantly Charlie lost his composure and gaiety. He looked at me appealingly, like a child in danger demanding protection of a stronger person. It was *the* man! He approached within a few feet of the comedian and examined him closely; as if he were looking at a new kind of potato bug. Then making a wry face, he turned around and said to the others: "That ain't he!"

'Man, woman, and child became silent. Had they been panning for gold and been told that the nuggets were only brass, they could not have been more disappointed.

'"Throw him out!" Charlie cried. "Throw him out!"

'But even before Tom had invited the man to leave the office, the crowd had pressed the old man out of the door, and I could see in the faces of the children how eager they were to throw things at his head.

'I took the quivering comedian to his dressing room and looked out of the window to see what was going to happen. One by one the cars were started, some going to the right and others to the left. And though they wouldn't believe what the old man had said, he had robbed them of absolute certainty. They were as willing to believe as they were willing to doubt. The old man walked away and, though he was hooted and cursed by the youngsters in the car, he shook his head and screamed at them: "It ain't he!"

'"You did your good deed?" Charlie jeered at me.

'"If I did nothing else, I got rid of the old man," I rejoined.

'A veil fell from the face of Chaplin. He was his old self again. He was no longer worried, no longer depressed. He looked well, his eyes were sparkling, his fingers had stopped twitching, and when he called Tom and his administrator, Reeves, his voice rang as gaily and as familiarly as of old.

'When Chaplin is in a good mood he is called "Charlie" by everybody. When he is in a bad mood he is never addressed, even by his most intimate friends, otherwise than as "Mr Chaplin". Reeves talked to him with just a tinge of reproach in his voice.

'"The appearance of that old man cost me ten thousand dollars," Charlie said laughingly.

'"Why didn't you tell Tom or Reeves to get rid of him?" I asked.

'"Hadn't thought of that. Heavens! I hadn't thought of that!" Then turning to his employees, "Well, tomorrow, eight o'clock."

'Tully, Chaplin's secretary, put in an appearance. He asked for something or other. But Chaplin did not take the trouble to answer him.

'We were soon at Doug's. The square mile of land was crowded with turrets and bridges and walls of Oriental design. Men and women dressed in Oriental garb were loafing singly and in couples. Seated before a piano, a charming young girl, dressed in nothing much, was pounding out Oriental melodies, creating atmosphere. Doug was in shorts. His brown, muscled body glistened under the mellow light of the setting sun. Unconcerned with everything about him, the acrobat-actor was keeping fit physically by jumping from one spanned net into another one, doing the trick much better than a number of other actors. But when I watched more closely, I saw how the others were "pulling their punches", deliberately not doing as well as they were able, to flatter by their physical inferiority the pride of the great man. A second later the competition narrowed down to Chaplin and Douglas; and though the husband of Mary did his best, he was easily outclassed by the nimbler, lighter man. The hangers-on and yes-men turned their faces away not to see the defeat of their idol. If anyone had expected to ask a favour or a good word from Doug that evening, the opportunity was lost. A little later, while we – Doug, Mary, Charlie, and myself – were having some coffee Charlie said:

'"I have been the 'old man' for him tonight. He, too, will lose two days."

'While we were talking of old things, I thought of the old spontaneity in the slapstick comedy of Chaplin and the naïve heroisms of Fairbanks. No one could have hurt them more than those who told them they were artists and had made them self-conscious.

'I told Charlie the old story of the centipede. Taking a morning stroll, the centipede was met by another insect who asked: "In the morning which foot do you put down first and which do you put down afterwards?" The centipede didn't know; but the following morning he couldn't walk, because *he did not know* which foot to put down first and which afterwards.

'Doug was curious, Mary was pensive, Charlie was happy. He had overcome his self-consciousness for that day. When we walked out, he said: "You were the second 'old man' tonight. I bet you a nickel Doug won't work tomorrow. Last week when he showed me the drawbridge of his castle for the picture he is doing, I said, 'This is a nice thing to lift in the morning and take in the milk bottle.' He wasn't able to work afterwards for two days. He was angry because I had ridiculed his

fantasy."

'On Sunset Boulevard garish automobiles were taking home the stars of first magnitude. Less garish cars took home those of the second rank, and those who hadn't yet reached the firmament were walking on the hot pavement. Most of the men and women were still in their make-up and some even wore the costumes in which they had worked during the day. False beards. False moustaches. Wigs. Faces painted blue and red. Ladies in Louis the Fourteenth dresses walked side by side with primitive men, Indians, cowboys, and Chinese mandarins. A celebrated dog attended by two keepers was being taken home in a luxurious limousine. Soon another limousine passed. An equally celebrated canine was being whisked home to his comforts. Hollywood disputed the respective merits of these two stars and gossiped about their affairs with the same malice with which Hollywood gossips about its two-footed stars.

'Seated behind a table in one of the restaurants, a number of acquaintances came to shake hands with me. To my surprise I discovered that several celebrities had never before met Chaplin officially. Ridiculous! but the rules of etiquette in Hollywood are enforced more rigidly than anywhere else. Strange that actors, who not many years ago experienced the snobbishness of Society, should now live according to the formalities which once oppressed them so!

'We were soon alone.

'"Spend the evening with me," Charlie suggested.

'I had some business to attend to, but his voice was so appealing; the great loneliness of the man was packed into those few words. There was a look of gratitude in his eyes when I told him that I hadn't intended otherwise.

'We had hardly begun to eat when the old man with the beady eyes and swollen lip appeared in the door of the coffee house. Charlie's spoon dropped out of his hand. The old man remained at the door, looked around, but his eyes rested only for a second on the comedian and then roved from one table to another. I got up and approached him.

'"Tell me," I asked, "why did you say it wasn't he when you looked at Mr Chaplin? What made you say such a thing?"

'"Of course it isn't he," the old man replied. "Don't I know him? I would recognize him in a hundred."

'"Him? Who?" I asked.

'"My son!" the old man replied. "I have been looking for him now for five years. He disappeared from home. People told me he got into the movies. When I came here last week someone told me that Mr Chaplin was my son. And it ain't true. Don't I know him? He was a head taller five years ago than Chaplin is now."

'Charlie was trembling from head to toe when I took the old man to our table. When I told him the story he wanted to know everything. An hour later, when Charlie and I walked out, he asked: "What is it, father love?" And then added reminiscently, "No father of mine has been looking for me so assiduously."

'The inevitable Tom approached us again. Charlie whispered something. Tom ran away while we waited for him. A moment later he appeared with a cap. Charlie pulled the cap over his eyes, a little at an angle, and, his appearance changed so, he was unrecognizable. With a twist he set his tie a little aside. One of his cuffs was sticking out from his sleeves. His gait changed.

'"Let's go down town to Los Angeles and look around."

'"Much chance you have! You would be spotted everywhere."

'"No, I won't," Charlie answered.

'I turned around to look at him. What a transformation in the man! His trousers were baggy, his shoulders were sagging, a cigarette hung from one corner of his mouth. He looked no different than a hundred other young men passing to and fro from work and loafing around the corners. We walked side by side, Charlie inventing a fantastic tale about a boss who wasn't treating him right.

'"If he ain't giving me a raise next week, I am going to quit! By God, I am going to quit!" He said it several times. "And I told that Union delegate, 'It ain't fair!'"

'He had worked himself up into the mood of

the man whose gait and clothes and speech he was imitating. His voice vibrated with anger. We stopped at a corner to listen to a Socialist soap-box speaker. And no man shouted louder his approval of what the orator was saying than Charlie.

'"Gee, that's right! Every word of it." And talking loudly to me, he attracted the attention of the others. "My boss bought two new cars inside of a month. By God, with everything going up the way it does, something's got to be done!" And he repeated the "something's got to be done" so frequently that a few people who had been noncommittal till then agreed with him, and only when everyone had repeated, "something's got to be done" did Charlie leave the place.

'I wanted to laugh. It was an excellent imitation. The mood had been well-sustained. But the look in Charlie's eyes! I couldn't possibly laugh about a man's misfortunes.

'"It's a shame. Why is it they pay good moving-picture actors thousands of dollars a week when they wouldn't pay a good carpenter the same price? It's a shame the way them moving-picture actors get everything just because they amuse the people. And we who do the work don't get anything or hardly anything."

'"Well, some of them are worth it," I said, following the mood. "Take for instance Charlie Chaplin."

'"Shucks!" Charlie answered. "He ain't worth it! And besides, he is getting so much fun out of his work! What fun do I get out of mine! Gee, if I played like him I wouldn't care whether I got paid or not!"

'When he had dropped out of this mood, while we were sitting in a little coffee house frequented by workmen, Charlie told me the story of how he had gone to San Francisco incognito to try to win a prize offered by a moving picture house to the man best imitating Charlie Chaplin.

'"I did my best," Charlie assured me, "but coudn't even win the booby prize. The man who won the first prize was perfectly awful. If that's what I look like in other people's eyes, well ..."

'And he wouldn't say another word. How-ever, when we walked out he straightened up, put the cap at a different angle, shoved the cuffs in, and was immediately recognized by the passers-by who greeted him and followed us to the next corner.

'I didn't know that Kono, Charlie's driver, had followed us everywhere with the car. We stepped into it as casually as if we had known it was there all the time. Speeding rapidly against all traffic rules (for Charlie's car is recognized by all policemen), we went to see a prize fight. I couldn't hold Charlie down to his seat. The people sitting in the tiers above us were continually yelling, "Sit down!" Charlie was following every movement in the ring. He had picked his favourite and so completely identified himself with him that whenever the man was hit Charlie cried out with pain. When the man was hit in the stomach Charlie bent like a jack-knife. When the man was hit in the jaw Charlie held his face with both hands. When the man was finally knocked out the little comedian literally fell into my arms.

'At the door an old friend of Chaplin's said to me: "He always picks the losers."

'Chaplin looked at him with big childish eyes, watery with pain. "Have you ever been in the ring?" Chaplin asked.

'"No."

'"Well, I have been. And I was always the loser. And do you know why? Because the winner had always eaten better than I had the day before." Then turning to me, he said, "Don't you ever become a successful man."

'"What about yourself?" I asked.

'"I am sorry," Charlie said apologetically. "But it was either that or die."

'"And isn't it the same with the others?"

'"It is," he assented. "But it's terrible."

'Back in town we noticed a young couple looking in the show windows where complete bedrooms for $169 were exhibited. Charlie turned around and said to me: "Suppose I give them a cheque for $169. What would happen?"

'"They would probably buy the set."

'"But then it will only be a bedroom set for them and not an ideal. They would not have anything to talk about. They will eventually get it. It's like my house in Beverly Hills. Now

Special offer from *Family Journal* in 191[

that I have it, it's like everything else."

'Pulling his cap down, he began to invent another fantastic grievance. He was a street-car conductor. The pay was bad. The hours were bad. For three years he had wanted to marry but couldn't. What hope was there for a street-car conductor?

'But he didn't carry this mood as well as he had carried the previous one, for he was soon talking about his next picture. He was even worrying that he wasn't recognized as frequently as he used to be.

'Two young girls marched slowly in front of us as if they wished to be overtaken.

'"Let's give them a good time."

'The four of us stopped in front of a jewellery window. They were two working girls on a lark. It was Saturday evening. We were soon sitting about a round table in an ice cream parlour. The two girls, playing us for easy marks, picked the most expensive things on the bill of fare. They hadn't recognized Charlie. He was boasting to them of his earnings. He told them he was a fencing master. He had taught Valentino to fence. The "wop" wasn't all he was cracked up to be.

'What a look in the eyes of the girls! They didn't believe a word he said. They looked at me appealingly. Finally one girl asked of me: "Are you a fencing master too?"

'"No, I am a locksmith, a fancy locksmith."

'"Why don't you lock him up?" she said. "Don't leave such a thing loose."

'A red-headed, Irish, freckled miss, she appealed tremendously to Charlie's sense of humour. She was sharp, witty, and didn't let an opportunity pass without making some cutting remark. When Charlie had boasted about the tremendous sums of money he was making at his profession and the girl hadn't believed him, he plunged his hands into his rear trousers' pocket and brought out a roll of bills of large denominations.

'"Gee," the other girl said, "maybe all he says is true!"

'But the freckled one had risen from her chair at the sight of so much money.

'"Come on, Maggie, I don't want to be mixed up in any such thing. The cops may be after him any minute."

'We were back in the car, driving towards Hollywood. It was close to midnight by now, yet the streets were as animated as in the daytime. There were fewer persons in costumes, but Hollywood had lost nothing of its fantastic appearance. The outlines and the shadows of the Spanish bungalows and the pagodas, and the strange coloured lights that pierced through the shades of the windows made Film Town appear even less real than in daylight. Though the night was so far advanced, it seemed only like a prolonged twilight.

'"I am hungry," Charlie suggested, and then said something to the driver.

'He was possessed by a new mood – a mood that appeared much more real than before. The race, he said, was to the swiftest. He argued that those who were too weak to stand up, fell. He agreed thoroughly with the superman theory. Christianity had hurt the world by making the humble one and the unsuccessful one appear in a favourable light. It was all against nature, against the trend of history. In a garden one weeded out the strong to give the weak one a chance to live. Life was a stern affair. Doctors maintained the cripple and the weakling. They were against the interest and the welfare of the strong, the only ones who should be protected and encouraged. All other ideas were but sickly sentimentality. He was occasionally overcome by such sentiments, but when he came to his senses he knew better. Other men had started life with him on the same plane. Most of them had had fewer handicaps than he. He succeeded because he was stronger.

'Talking like this, we entered into a rather luxurious Russian cabaret which was totally empty. We were the only guests. The waiters fell one over another in their hurry to serve us. From a side door there appeared a half-dozen Russian women dressed in gypsy costumes and three men in Cossack costume. One of the men went to the piano, the rest began to sing wild Russian songs. The voices were indifferent and there wasn't a single attractive woman in the group.

'When the first song was finished, they sat down to rest but one of the women remained standing to sing a solo. When that number had come to an end one of the men rose to his feet and began to dance the Dagger Dance, throwing and fixing in the floor the points of the daggers as he turned and whirled. By the time the dragging dinner was half through, each member had done his individual turn, and the pianist had rolled out a long sentimental Chopin ballad. I thought they were through. I felt awkward to be entertained by so numerous a troupe. The place was absolutely empty. These were Russian princes, counts, and princesses, trying to make a living. Their Slavic faces and their eager eyes were continually directed at us.

'The whole thing began over again. The choir sang, the Cossack did his dagger dance, one after another the gypsy-costumed girls got up to sing their songs, and the pianist played another sentimental ballad. And still no other guest had come in. We had finished our dinner. We were anxious to go. But it wasn't polite to leave while someone was dancing or singing. And the Russians never left any space open between numbers. The echo of one song was still ringing when another song was begun.

'Charlie looked at me appealingly as if I could do something. It was one o'clock in the morning. It was two o'clock in the morning. Not once was the door opened by a client. And the Cossack was dancing the dagger dance. The girls were singing gypsy songs. The pianist was playing the sentimental ballad – a continually moving circle with not a moment in between or a chance for us to leave. We couldn't possibly offend them and get up while Prince So-and-so or Countess So-and-so was doing a solo. I felt as if in a squirrel cage.

'"Let's go," I said to him.

'He spread out his hands appealingly as if to say, "How can we?"

'A dozen pairs of eyes were fixed on us. The sword man was dancing. The pianist was pounding out another sentimental ballad. I was ready to get up and cry out in pain; ready to commit murder, when the door opened and two ladies, looking a little the worse because of the hour of the night, their white dresses crumpled and in need of the cleaners, and two men perfectly groomed, with their silk hats a little at an angle, entered joyously. Seldom has relief come at a more needed moment.

'"Welcome, welcome!" Charlie cried out, bowing low.

'Before these people had sat down we dashed out. Kono was sleeping, his big dark head rested on his arms upon the steering wheel.

'"What about that strength of the strong?" I mocked Charlie. "What about that relentlessness? Why did you stay longer than you wanted?"

'"I am so sleepy. I am so tired." And crumpling on the seat, Charlie collapsed.

'Kono took charge of him. I walked back to my hotel. On Sunset Boulevard, at every fifty feet or so, I met some man or woman walking in one direction or another – men and women who had come to Hollywood with great hopes and great ambitions, and who were now walking the streets because they had no lodging for the night. A little later a luxurious limousine would take the celebrated dog star out for his morning ride. I looked through the window of the Russian cabaret. The two couples were still there. The Russians were dancing and singing furiously. For a moment I thought of opening the door to save these poor wretches; but I remembered I had already done my good deed, and there was a long day ahead of me.'

Charlie Chaplin
DOES THE PUBLIC KNOW WHAT IT WANTS?

CHAPLIN, NATURALLY, had his own very particular ideas about his art and what his audiences expected from him. Apart from writing, directing and composing the music of his pictures, he also exercised rigorous control of every aspect of their making from building the sets right through to the final editing and presentation. All this merely serves to underline his profound belief in his own skills – skills that by the 1920's were totally proven. In the article here, Charlie expounds his philosophy of film making: it was first published in *The Adelphi* magazine of January 1924, and is here reprinted for the first time.

'IN THE DAYS before the films had become a leading industry and the filming of complicated stories, the building of elaborate sets, the spending of weeks in preparation, and standards of lighting and photography that prevail today were not even dreamed of, I was called upon to make a short comedy between nine in the morning and three in the afternoon. When I reached the studio of the old Keystone Company I was told by the director that a short comedy was needed, and needed that day. I was promised that if I could turn out the sort of picture that was wanted I would receive an extra twenty-five dollars. I had no story, I hadn't even an idea, and I had no actors, but I wanted that twenty-five.

'I dashed about the studio. "I want you for the girl, you for the heavy man, and you," I said to a stunt comedian, "to do just any bit of clowning."

'Then I thought of my story. A beginning came to me, and we rarely had more than a beginning in those days. The character that I play in all my pictures was to be on a bridge, standing on the rail about to jump. A pretty girl passes by, and the would-be suicide changes his mind.

'The resultant picture, which was called

Twenty Minutes of Love, proved to be a fair success. The public was willing to vote it a laugh-maker, but in the filming of that crude little comedy I completely disregarded the public. I had a high regard for the twenty-five dollars, and my job was to please the man who had asked me to make the picture, and not the public.

'In the progress of the screen, which has made careful planning not only possible but neccessary, a great deal of the old spontaneity which made converts to the screen in the early days has disappeared. Naturally, if it is necessary to spend several hundred thousand dollars instead of a few hundred, the business man, the banker, the artist, or whoever he is who puts up the money, wants to be assured in his own mind that he has a good chance of success and that the public will respond.

'And therefore, we all argue about what "they" want – "they", of course, meaning the paying public. But this has created a situation which I firmly believe stultifies imagination and is a barrier to originality. When *The Cabinet of Doctor Caligari* proved a failure, although an artistic success unquestionably, our wiseacres jumped to the conclusion that the public did not want originality. Certainly *Caligari* was original, and surely it failed, but the truth of this does not mean that the public, although it may never like *Caligari* in any guise, is lined up in solid ranks to protest against originality.

'The public may generalize that they do not want a certain type – *Caligari*, if you will; but that does not prove that they have a definite type in mind that they do want.

'The public does not stand at the box-office window and say: "We want a drama after this pattern: Virtue shall be its own reward. Punishment shall be meted out to the wrongdoers, and there must be a happy ending, with the assurance that the boy and girl are to live happily for ever after. And there must be a

85

nice blend of pathos and humour. Give us that, or we will stay away."

'Nor does the public demand that the film comedy shall contain a good deal of slapstick, a certain number of gags – and by "gags" I mean those good old tricks that have always proved successful – three or so dashes of serious situation, and a bit of irony to top off. The public has no such specifications for films. The demands of the public are negative at best. Entertainment is what "they" really want.

'Quite frankly, I do not believe that the public knows what it wants; that is the conclusion that I get from my own career. There was no idea in the public mind that it wanted to see the character that I have played in so many films and through so many situations until the character was revealed. Before I could get that character to the public I met with every discouragement. It would require quiet treatment, and what "they" wanted was robustness. It would be necessary to use make-up, and that was not effective on the screen. The public paid to see real persons as they are.

'In the early days, when I made pictures for the sheer money and vicarious happiness I got out of the work, I had no responsibility, and I turned out genuine comedy. Suddenly, with no thought to that end, it was brought home to me, I may write in all modesty, that I was famous.

'From that time on, at least from the time that I felt I had a reputation to sustain, I had responsibility, and my work became in most ways improved, but in many respects more studied. Finish alone, however, will not count for long. The more I thought and planned, the more I found that I was depending on the mechanism of humour and not the spirit. I was trying to intellectualize myself and to study the demands which the films were creating in the public. I wanted to please the people who were so good as to like me. I must give them what we call the "sure-fire stuff," or the things that are bound to get a laugh and often have nothing to do with the other action or the sheer exuberance of the story.

'Just about this time, when I had decided that I knew what the public wanted and my

87

Charlie causing trouble in a theatre in *A Night in the Snow* (1915)

success encouraged me to that belief, I received a jolt in the form of a letter from a man I have never seen and whose name I don't even know today, though his letter I can write here word for word. He had seen me in *The Fireman* in a large theatre in the Middle West, and wrote:

> I have noticed in your last picture a lack of spontaneity. Although the picture was unfailing as a laugh-getter, the laughter was not so round as at some of your earlier work. I am afraid you are becoming a slave to your public, whereas in most of your pictures the audiences were a slave to you. The public, Charlie, likes to be slaves.

'This letter was a great lesson to me, and I took stock, so to speak. My work could be no good unless I got the right spirit of joy, joy in itself. And since that letter I have tried to avoid what I think the public wants. I prefer my taste as a truer expression of what the public wants of me than anything that I can observe, either in my own work or in that of others that are unmistakably successful. This is obviously not meant as a slap at the public, but rather at those of us who think we can tell just what "they" want, whether we are editors, theatrical managers, or business men who have commodities to sell to the public. In the eternal argument as to what is wrong with the pictures there is the recurring criticism that pictures are always alike. And they are, most of the time! If you are a regular follower of the films, or if you have seen only a few pictures, you will come to but one conclusion, and that is that in naming the best pictures you have seen you will not include five or six that are all in one field. You may like a certain actress and may go and see all of her pictures, but if called upon to select your favourites you will not place all her six pictures in your pet list. Your list will contain variety, and most often you will find that variety in something that is either very different or else is a new way of doing the old.

'It must be certain that the public does not get what it wants, for the first of any new thing, type, or story, or the first appearance of any new or different personality, is almost always an immediate success. When Douglas Fairbanks left the stage and appeared on the screen he was a success at once. He offered something new and different to the conventional type of young American that had come to be known as the screen hero. He had served in the theatre and had from the beginning great seriousness, earnestness, and enthusiasm for the films. But in his succes the producers saw merely athletics, and, one after another, acrobats were brought forward to wrest his laurels from him. But Fairbanks' spirit and ability were missing, and some years afterwards the original was so firmly established in the public mind that no one bothered any longer to try to imitate him.

'When a new personality comes along the producer concludes: "Now that's what 'they' want – new personalities entirely. Let's get rid of the established favourites." But just then the old-time favourite comes back, with a conventional or simple story that rings true, and it gets well-deserved success. But we may complicate the case still further: An old story made into a good film is produced; it made no difference what the cast was in *Over the Hills*; its story, although highly sentimental, had colour, sweep, and universal appeal.

'Now where are we? And they shake their heads. The confusion is more confused, because the very next week one of the new personalites may succeed quickly, as Valentino did in *The Four Horsemen*. I can just imagine how many arguments were made out of this man's success. The natural conclusion of the producer mind would be: "He's a foreigner; they are tired of American faces." In this hastily-arrived-at conclusion it is, of course, forgotten that Valentino is a good actor, handsome, and, what so few actors are either on the stage or on the screen, picturesque and natural in costume, and that his first real success was when he was cast as a young soldier in the extremely well-made film from a popular and highly-advertised novel, *The Four Horsemen*.

'When we had such a run on vamp films, for which I am sure there was no great demand,

Two examples of Charlie's famous walk: in the film *Laughing Gas* (1914) and on a picture postcard

89

one or two met with success, and the deduction was that the public wanted to see such pictures, and one sinful sister followed another in machine-made stories. When four or five of these failed the producer hesitated and pondered just what was the matter with the public. It was getting what it wanted and still stayed away. There might be a sixth attempt, which was by chance a good story, and the producer would be reassured that he was right after all, and then there could be no halting of the procession of chequered careers for women.

'In the early days a few costume pictures were attempted, and because they were untrue, the acting bad, and the costumes the merest apology for correctness, the plays were disastrous to the box-office. It was a stock argument that patrons would look at the billing in front of a picture-house, and if they saw costumes in those advertisements they journeyed across the street and saw some gripping modern drama where there were at least three dress suits. Along came the German film, *Passion*, and it was forthwith certain that the costume picture would be worked to death.

'When Griffith produced *The Birth of a Nation* in many reels, the rival producers who knew to a certainty what the public wanted shook their heads. The effort was beforehand consigned to failure. The two-reel picture was the natural length. But when *The Birth of a Nation* turned out to be a tremendous success the future of spectacular films was certain and many others followed quickly. These did not come up to the mark, so – from the producers' angle – the public was tired of long pictures.

'Thus every time the all-knowing person who can figure to a nicety what the public wants goes wrong. He assumes a wrong psychology to account for success: a big picture – its length; a strange personality – its newness. And when both their dope and their pictures go wrong it is easy for them to blame it all on the public's lack of taste.

'I have heard directors, scenario writers, and others who are directly concerned with the shape that the moving picture shall take, argue under the shadow of this great fear of the public. They begin with a good idea, and then they lose courage and deceive themselves. The consciousness of what the public will want is for them so terrific. If they do something that is a little different because they have forgotten – while filming the episode – that there is such a thing as an audience, they are in doubt about it when they stop to consider. It is difficult to consider the public secondarily, but unless the person making the picture can achieve that state there will be no originality in his work.

'One man, who thinks that the public's taste is bad, will write down to his public, and another man, who appreciates his own sense of inferiority as a creative artist, will write up to the demands of his medium and the public. Both of the types will make mistakes, and there will be just as many mistakes up as down, just as many bad pictures from persons who know their inferiority as from those who condescend in meeting their audiences. In no particular field is this truer than in the so-called artistic attempts, the conscious effort to do something fine.

'I do not know what constitutes the so-called art picture. Very often around film studios it has meant something that the producer and the initiated like but that they fear is too good for the public. Often it is a tragedy or a picture with a tragic ending. Now there can be just as inartistic tragedies – in spite of their accumulation of woe and grief – as comedies, and the unhappy ending, which is so often in plays, stories, and pictures misconstrued for artistry, can be worse than a custard pie. Usually the unhappy ending in films is inartistic because it is jumped at and arrived at through false scenes.

'There haven't been many pictures that could be called "art" pictures – and I quote the word "art"; but then, so far as I know, there are but few perfect works of art in any creative field. Without apologizing for the medium of the films – which all those of us who use it accept as an art – there is more reason for imperfection in the pictures than there is in any other field. We cannot revise as a writer may, nor correct and redraw as a painter may. There is a natural flow to the

Charlie posing as a minister in *The Pilgrim* (1923)

picture when exhibited, but sequences are often taken over many days. Items are forgotten, and even with the elaborate system used to check up, that is employed in the best studios, mistakes are made.

'The films may have their drawbacks from the point of view of the creative artist, but they have, too, their joys; and one of the incidental joys of making pictures is that every now and then the unexpected – and at times even a mistake – triumphs. In the making of a comedy I usually leave the mistakes in, as there is a certain spontaneity, and sometimes the very recorded annoyance that the wrong thing caused may prove funny. In the making of *The Pilgrim* I was wearing a flat-brimmed clerical hat instead of my usual Derby. In walking up and down a station platform, trying to be very dignified, my hat blew off. I was much irritated, for I felt that what we had been doing was fairly good, and now we would have to take the scene over again. We did so, and succeeded in getting the hat to keep in place; but when both sequences were run, we found that we had done the first one better, except for the one mistake.

'When we were showing the first "take", a stranger in the projection room suddenly burst out laughing, and it occurred to me: Why should not my hat blow off? Certainly here was the element of comedy, and I was annoyed at the accident simply because I had approached my work conventionally, as re-hearsed. The camera-man insisted that it held up the action of the scene, but this mistake was retained in the picture and audiences laugh at the incident.

'It seems unreasonable to me to make a picture in six or eight weeks. A fine and authentic picture would take a year to make. Even then there probably wouldn't be much art in it, and I doubt whether the man who made it would care to look at it ten or twelve years afterwards. If there were time, and we had the money, the ideal way would be to take a picture quickly and see what it was like, and then do it all over.

'From the making of pictures I get a good deal of thrill. I get it more as a director and producer than I do as an actor. It is the old satisfaction that one is making something, forming something that has body. There is the photography. There are the angles of the sets. There is the day's work, making individual scenes; whether one acts in them or not, one feels a little elated when they are well done.

'There are the "rushes" or "takes" of the day before to look at, and corrections to be made, and the gradual assembling of the whole in sequence as ultimately it will go before an audience.

'I like making pictures, and I like acting in them; and I suppose that I shall always be a bit of film – that is, just as long as I have the money to buy the raw stock on which to take pictures.'

Joan Jordan
MOTHER O'MINE

ASIDE FROM the pleasure his artistic success gave him, Chaplin was also delighted that his financial security now enabled him to bring his ailing mother from England to Hollywood to spend the rest of her days in peace and comfort. Life had been one long struggle for Hannah Chaplin since she lost her husband to drink in 1894, and then herself suffered periodic bouts of ill-health as she struggled to bring up her two sons, Charles and Sydney. Charlie was quite clearly devoted to his mother and had to undertake a protracted fight with the American authorities to gain her admission to the country – which he finally achieved in 1921. Joan Jordan, an American journalist who became a friend of Mrs Chaplin, wrote this moving account of their reunion for *Photoplay Magazine* in July 1921. Hannah Chaplin died in Glendale Hospital in 1929 with the son she had seen rise from poverty to become a multi-millionaire film star by her side.

'IN THE WIDE, bay window of a charming house on a hill in Hollywood, sits a little, grey-haired woman, with delicate old hands folded upon the open pages of her Bible.

'Every day, just as the sun is setting behind the waving line of hills, a big, expensive motor draws up before the door.

'A slender young man in blue jumps out and runs lightly up the broad, white steps.

'A white-capped maid opens the heavy door.

'Often the little grey-haired woman rises from her seat in the window and takes a few faltering steps to meet the man in the doorway of her drawing room. Almost always, now. . .

'On the evenings when she does not, he slips quietly in and sits down beside her in the window, holding her hand in his.

'Because then he knows that her gentle mind has strangely slipped back to the horrors of a Zeppelin raid, to the shock of bursting

Charlie's mother, Mrs Hannah Chaplin, during her days in Hollywood

93

shells and crashing buildings, death screams and imminent destruction.

'And she does not even know he is there.

'But either way – Charlie Chaplin and his mother are together again.

'Together after nine years of separation – years of war and heartache for the mother, of triumph not unmixed with tragedy for the son. Years that have been filled with unimagined, unequalled success and unforeseen, stupendous catastrophe for them both, but that has altered not one jot the great love they bear each other.

'"It's wonderful to have my mother again," is all Charlie Chaplin says.

'Just the simple story of most mothers and sons, only a bit more dramatic, the story of Charlie Chaplin and his mother, a story as commonplace as life and death and joy and pain.

'Nine years ago an unknown young vaudeville performer named Charlie Chaplin, kissed his erect, smiling little mother an excited goodbye in a London railway station. He was going to America to seek his fortune.

'A few weeks ago, Charlie Chaplin, the world's greatest comedian, the most famous male genius the screen has yet produced stood on a platform in Los Angeles, and with tears running down his cheeks, took into his arms a little grey figure, bent and puzzled, and oh, so changed.

'That is the heart of the story.

'It was seven years ago that Charlie Chaplin just beginning the movie career that led him to what I personally consider the screen's greatest performance (The Kid) began the long struggle to bring his mother to America.

'But England was at war, and war, among other horrors, produced yards of regulations and red tape. Even Americans had difficulty in returning to their own country. Mrs Chaplin, a British subject, would not be permitted to leave England for America.

'So she stayed on in London, until one frightful night when a London air raid crumpled the world about her frightened head. Charlie again renewed his efforts to bring her to safety in America.

'Again he failed. His mother's health, as well as some new rules concerning war stricken patients would not permit it.

'Months then, for her, in a sanitorium where large monthly cheques with the scrawling signature "Charlie Chaplin" brought her every care and comfort; months of red tape and preparation; at last the long journey across the Atlantic with her famous son's secretary and a trained nurse sent over by the screen star to bring her to him.

'Long weeks of weary waiting, while Mr Chaplin made arrangements with the immigration authorities who, because of the shell shock Mrs Chaplin had suffered, could not admit her to the United States without certain precautions and assurances.

'All those things are but steps leading to the accomplishment of the dearest wish of Charlie Chaplin's heart.

'Charlie Chaplin has brought so much sunshine into other lives. He has made so many of us laugh and forget our heartaches. He has showered upon us the priceless gifts of smiles and laughter. In darkened theatres all over the earth, he has filled hearts with a song, smoothed away grief and cares and pain.

'And I think the world that has known the story of that tiny grave out in Hollywood – the world that has whispered and laughed and frowned over the wreck of his marriage – and I think the world when next it sees him on the screen will rejoice because he has his mother again. I think we will be just a little more grateful, a little more appreciative of his gifts.

'But why, for this man, must the laughter always hold a tear? Why is there always a bitter drop in his cup?

'For above the joy of his reunion with his mother hovers the white, faintly menacing cloud of her affliction. He has his mother again – and yet she is not wholly his.

'But he is very hopeful. California is a wonderful place. It is very far from London and the things that happened to her there.

'Already in her beautiful home in the foothills, with her competent staff of servants to relieve her of every step and every worry, with her luxurious limousine and its chauffeur to take her on long, exquisite drives through the mountains and beside the sea, she is losing the actuality of the war. It is a bad dream only.

'Already the lapses of memory and of mind are growing less frequent.

'With tears in his eyes, her son told me that the second night she was here she went to the piano and sang, in her sweet, faint voice, several songs from *Patience*.

'Because you see, little Mrs Hannah Chaplin – she is just fifty-five now – whom we can think of only as the mother of Charlie, was once a personage herself.

'Many years ago, London knew her as Florence Harley, a vocalist with the Gilbert and Sullivan opera company in London who sang "Pinafore" and "Iolanthe" and "Mikado" to enraptured audiences and finally married a young actor named Charles Chaplin.

'He died and left her with two little boys, Charles Jr, and Sydney. Small wonders that the bond between the young mother and her boys was close.

'And small wonder that her new pride in her two sons is helping to lift the veil of her illness.

'Do you remember that little trick Charlie has of covering his mouth with his hand when he laughs? And the well-known, deliciously funny shrug?

'Sydney Chaplin tells me that he inherited both of them from the little grey-haired woman who sits in the window.

'"Mother has – always had – the keenest, most delightful sense of humour," said Charlie, with a tender smile. "I remember it in all my thoughts of the early days. If I have any sense of fun, I owe it all to her."

'Perhaps everybody is not as grateful for laughs as I am. But I feel that we owe Mrs Hannah Chaplin many thanks – those of us who have laughed joyously at the reproductions of her in her son.

'Oddly enough, his mother does not find the great screen idol particularly funny.

'Perhaps that is because, during the years of the war when she lived so close to the seeming wreck of civilization and Christianity, Mrs Chaplin became devoutly, earnestly religious. She reads little now except the Bible. She cares for little that she does not, as she puts it, "tend to teach the world to believe in and live the religion of Christ".

'"You seem a very remarkable young man," she said to her son. "Wherever I go, no matter what the society or the place, I hear you spoken of in terms of love and admiration. I am very glad, my son. But I do not exactly see why."

'She has seen only one of Charlie's pictures, an old one called *Shanghaied*.

'But now that he has so established himself, become so famous, his mother can see but one future for him.

'"My son," she said to him on an evening soon after her arrival, when they all sat together in the drawing room of Sydney's house, and she was at her best, "you must give up the screen and enter the pulpit. Think of the souls you could save!"

'It staggered Charlie a bit.

'And these two – the famous comedian who in real life is so simple, so sincere, so serious a person, and the little spiritual-faced woman who bore him – they had one of those discussions that mothers and sons must always have if the world is to go on at all.

'Charlie tried to show her that in the pulpit he could reach but a few people compared to the vast number he reaches on the screen. He tried to explain to her his philosophy – that in making people laugh cleanly he was helping them to grow kinder, more tolerant, more law-abiding, that he was bringing sweetness into the world.

'We must all be glad that even the well-meaning persuasions of his mother could not shake him from this resolve.'

Thomas Burke
THE TRAGIC COMEDIAN

IN THE SUMMER of 1921, with his mother safely installed in California, Chaplin decided to fulfil a desire to return to his homeland and see once again the places where he had spent his childhood and youth. Naturally enough, his return was destined to be very different from his leaving: and indeed thousands of people thronged his route from the moment he docked in Southampton on 18 September 1921. The month-long trip which followed also took him to France and Germany where he was greeted by equally enthusiastic crowds, and proved a huge success. It also provided Charlie with many nostalgic moments as he revisited his old haunts. He was reunited with a number of his relatives, was deluged with fan mail (over 73,000 letters apparently!) and was courted by admirers from all walks of life. One of the highlights of his stay in London was a quiet wander through the bleak streets of the East End of London in the company of the famous novelist, Thomas Burke who, like him, had grown up in the area. Burke shortly afterwards recorded his impressions in the essay which follows – an essay still widely regarded as one of the most revealing of Chaplin the man. It appeared in *Pearson's Magazine* of March 1922.

'A FRAIL figure, small-footed and with hands as exquisite as those of Madame la Marquise. A mass of brindled grey hair above a face of high colour and nervous features. In conversation the pale hands flash and flutter, and the eyes twinkle; the body sways and swings and the head darts bird-like back and forth, in time with the soft chanting voice.

'His personality is as volatile as his lithe and resilient figure. He has something of Hans Andersen, of Ariel, touched with rumours of far-off fairyland tears. But something more than pathos is here. Almost, I would say, he is a tragic figure.

'Through the universal appeal of the cinematograph, he has achieved universal fame in larger measure than any man of recent years, and he knows the weariness and emptiness that accompany excess. He is the playfellow of the world, and he is the loneliest, saddest man I ever knew.

'When I first heard that Charles Chaplin wished to meet me I was only mildly responsive. I can never assume much interest in the folk of the film and the stage; their hectic motions, their voluble, insubstantial talk, and their abrupt transitions are too exhausting. But I was assured that Charles Chaplin was "different", and finally, a rendezvous was made at a flat in Bloomsbury.

'He *is* different. I was immediately surprised and charmed. A certain transient glamour hung about this young man, to whose doings the front pages of important newspapers were devoted, and for a sight of whom people of all classes were doing vigil: but discounting that, much remained; and the shy, quiet figure that stepped from the shadow of the window was no mere film star, but a character that made an instant appeal. I received an impression of something very warm and bright and vivid. There was radiance, but it was the radiance of fluttering firelight rather than a steady sunlight.

'At first, I think, it was the pathos of his situation that made him so endearing, for he was even then being pursued by the crowd, and had taken this opportunity to get away for a quiet walk through the narrow streets. But the charm remained, and remains still. It is a part of himself that flows through every movement and every gesture. He inspires immediately, not admiration or respect, but affection; and one gives it impulsively.

'At eleven o'clock that night I took him alone for a six-hour ramble through certain districts of East London, whose dim streets made an apt setting for his dark-flamed per-

Charlie off-screen – a photograph from Thomas Burke's article

sonality. I walked him through by-ways of Hoxton, Bethnal Green, Spitalfields, Stepney, Ratcliff, Shadwell, Wapping, Isle of Dogs; and as we walked he opened his heart and I understood. I, too, had spent hard, inhospitable hours of youth in those streets, and knew his feeling about them, and could, in a minor measure, appreciate what he felt in such high degree at coming back to them with his vast treasure of guerdons and fame. The disordered, gipsy-like beauty of this part of London moved him to ecstasy after so many years of the bright, angular, gem-like cities of Western America, and he talked freely and well about it.

'At two o'clock in the morning we rested on the kerb of an alley-way in St George's and he talked of his bitter youth and his loneliness and his struggles, and the ultimate bewildering triumph.

'Always, from the day he left London, he had, at the back of his mind, vague and formless and foolish, the dream of a triumphal Dick Whittington returning to the city whose stones were once so cold to him; for the most philosophic temper, the most aloof from the small human passions, is not wholly free from that attitude of "A time will come when you *shall* hear me."

'Like all men who are born in exile, outside the gracious enclosures of life, he does not forget those early years; and even now that he has made that return, it does not quite satisfy. It is worth having – that rich, hot moment when the scoffers are dumb, and recognition is accorded; the moment of attainment; but a tinge of bitterness must always accompany it. Chaplin knew, as all who have risen know, that the very people who were clamouring and beseeching him to their tables and receptions would not, before, have given him a considered glance, much less a friendly hand or a level greeting. They wanted to see – not himself, but the symbol of success – *le dernier cri*; and he knew it.

'He owes little enough to England. To him it was only a stoney-hearted stepmother – not even the land of his birth. Here, as he told me, he was up against that social barrier that so impedes advancement and achievement – a barrier that only the very great or the very cunning can cross.

'America freely gave him what he could never have wrested from England – recognition and decent society. He spoke in chilly tones of his life in this country as a touring vaudeville artist. Such a life is a succession of squalor and mean things. The company was his social circle, and he lived and moved only in that circle. Although he had not then any achievements to his credit, he had the potentialities. Although he was then a youth with little learning, an undeveloped personality and few graces, he had an instinctive feeling for fine things. Although he had no key by which he might escape, no title to a place among the fresh, easy, cultivated minds where he desired to be, he knew that he did not belong to the rude station of life in which he was placed.

'Had he remained in this country he would have remained in that station. He would never have got out. But in America the questions are: "What do you know?" and "What can you do?" not "Where do you come from?" and "Who are your people?" "Are you public school?"

'Today England is ready to give him all that it formerly denied him. All doors are open to him, and he is beckoned here and there by social leaders. But he does not want them. Well might he quote to them the terms of a famous letter – "The notice which you have been pleased to take of my labours, had it been early had been kind; but it has been delayed till I am indifferent and cannot enjoy it . . . till I am known and do not want it."

'But twice during our ramble – once in Mile End Road and once in Hoxton – he was recognised, and the midnight crowd gathered and surrounded him. There it was the real thing – not the vulgar desire of the hostess to feed the latest lion, but a spontaneous burst of hearty affection, a welcome to an old friend. He has played himself into the hearts of the simple people, and they love him. The film "Charlie" is a figure that appeals to them, for it is a type of thwarted ambitions, of futile strivings, and forlorn makeshifts for better things.

'As I watched the frail, elegant figure struggling against this monstrous burst of enthusiasm, in which voices, hot with emotion, voices of men and women, cried boisterous messages of goodwill to "our Charlie," I was foolishly moved. No Prime Minister could have so fired a crowd. No Prince of the House of Windsor could have commanded that wave of sheer delight. He might have had the crowd and the noise, but not the rich surge of affection. A prince is only a spectacle, a symbol of nationhood, but this was a known friend, one of themselves; and they treated him so. It was no mere instinct of the mob. They did not gather to stare at him. Each member of that crowd wanted privately to touch him, to enfold him, to thank him for cheering them up. And they could do so without reservations or compunctions for they could not have helped him in his early years: they were without the power.

'I do not attempt to explain why this one man, of all other "comics" of stage and film, has so touched the hearts of the people as to arouse this frenzy of adulation. It is beyond me. I could only stand and envy the man who had done it.

'Yet he found little delight in it. Rather, he was bewildered. I think his success staggers or frightens him. Where another might be spoilt he is dazed. The "Charlie," the figure of fun that he created in a casual moment, has grown upon him like a Frankenstein monster. It and its worldwide popularity have become a burden to him. That it has not wholly crushed him, ejected his true self and taken possession of him, is proof of a strong character.

'Your ordinary actor is always an actor "on" and "off"; but as I walked and talked with Chaplin I found myself trying vainly to connect him, by some gesture or attitude, with the world-famous "Charlie". There was no trace of it. When a little later, I saw one of his films, I again tried to see through the make-up the Chaplin I had met, and again I failed. The pathetic, fragile clown of the films is purely a studio creation, having little in common with its creator, for Chaplin is not a funny man. He is a great actor of comic parts. Every second of his pictures is *acted*, and when he is not acting he casts off "Charlie," drops the mask of the

98

world's fool, and his queer, glamorous personality is released again.

'He described to me the first sudden conception of his figure of fun – the poor ludicrous fool, of forlorn attitudes, who would be a gentleman, and never can; who would do fine and beautiful things and always does them in the wrong way and earns kicks in place of acceptance and approval. At every turn the world beats him, and because he cannot fight it he puts his finger to his nose. He rescues fair damsels, and finds that they are not fair. He departs on great enterprises that crumble to rubbish at his first touch. He builds castles in the air and they fall and crush him. He picks up diamonds and they turn to broken glass and at the world's disdain he shrugs his shoulders, and answers its scorn with rude jests and extravagant antics.

'He is sometimes an ignoble Don Quixote, sometimes a gallant Pistol, and in other aspects a sort of battered Pierrot. All other figures of fun in literature and drama have associates or foils. "Charlie," in all his escapades, is alone. He is the outcast, the exile, sometimes getting a foot within the gates, but ultimately being driven out, hopping lamely, with ill-timed nonchalance, on the damaged foot.

'He throws a custard-pie in the world's face as a gesture of protest. He kicks policemen lest himself be kicked. There is no exuberance in the kick; it is no outburst of vitality. It is deliberate and considered. Behind every farcical gesture is a deadly intent. Never do the eyes, in his most strenuous battles with authority, lose their deep-sunken, haunting grief. Always he is the unsatisfied, venting his despair in a heart-broken levity of quips and capers. Chaplin realized that there is nothing more universally funny than the solemn clown, and in "Charlie" he accidentally made a world-fool; though I think certain memories of early youth went to its making.

'But I am more interested in the man than his work. When, at four o'clock in the morning, he came home with me to Highgate, and sat round the fire, I felt still more warmly his charm and still more sharply his essential discontent.

Thomas Burke, standing behind Chaplin, photographed during the star's visit to H.G. Wells in London

'I do not mean that he is miserable: he is indeed one of the merriest of companions; but he is burdened with a deep-rooted disquiet. He is the shadow-friend of millions throughout the world, and he is lonely. He is tired, too, and worn – this young man, whose name and face are known in every habitable part of the world. It is not a temporary fatigue, as of a man who is over-working or running at too high a pitch. His weariness, I think, lies deeper. It is of the spirit. To the quick melancholy of the Latins – for he is Anglo-French, and was born at Fontainebleau – is added that unrest which men miscall the artistic temperament. But even without these he could not, I think, command happiness. He is still an exile, seeking for something that the world cannot give him.

'It has given him much – great abilities, fame, fortune, applause; yet it has given him, for his needs, little. The irony that pursues genius has not let him escape. He is hungry for affection and friendship, and he cannot hold them. With the very charm that draws would-be friends towards him goes a perverse trick of repulsing them. He desires friendship, yet has not the capacity for it. "I am egocentric," he confessed. To children everywhere his name brings gurgles of delight; and children embarrass him. He has added one more to the great gallery of comic figures – Falstaff, Pickwick, Don Quixote, Uncle Toby, Micawber, Touchstone, Tartarin, Punchinello – and he hates "Charlie".

'He sat by the fire, curled up in a corner of a deep armchair, like a tired child, eating shortbread and drinking wine and talking, talking, talking, flashing from theme to theme with the disconcerting leaps of the cinematograph. He talked of the state of Europe, of relativity, of Benedetto Croce, of the possibility of a British Labour Government, of the fluidity of American social life; and he returned again and again to the subject of England.

'"It stifles me," he said. "I'm afraid of it – it's all so set and solid and *arranged*. Groups and classes. If I stayed here I know I should go back to what I was. They told me that the War had changed England – had washed out boundaries and dividing lines. It hasn't. It's left you even more class-conscious than before. The country's still a mass of little regiments – each moving to its own rules. You've still the county people, the 'Varsity sets, the military caste – the governing classes and the working classes. Even your sports are still divided. For one set, there are hunting, racing, yachting, polo, shooting, golf, tennis – and for the other, cricket, football and betting. In America, life is freer, and you can make your own life and find a place among the people who interest you."

'And Chaplin has surrounded himself with quiet, pleasant people.

'He is an unpretentious man, spending his evenings at home with a few friends and books and music. He is deeply read in philosophy, social history and economics. His wants are simple, and although he has a vast income, he lives on a fraction of it, and shares everything with his brother Syd Chaplin. During the day he works, and works furiously, as a man works when seeking distraction or respite from his troubled inner self. What he will do next I do not know. He seems to be a man without aim or hope. What it is he wants, what he is seeking, to ensure a little heart's ease, I do not know.

'I have here tried to present some picture of this strange, gracious, elusive, self-contradictory character; but it is a mere random sketch in outline, and gives nothing of the opulent, glittering, clustering, light and shade of the original.

'The ambition that served and guided him for ten years is satisfied; but he is still unsatisfied. The world has discovered him, but he has not yet found himself. But he has discovered the weariness of repeated emotion, and he is a man who lives on and by his emotions.

'That is why I call him a tragic figure – a tragic comedian.'

An evocative picture of Charlie, the tragic figure, in *City Lights* (1931)

Charlie Chaplin
A MEMORABLE NIGHT IN LONDON

ON HIS RETURN to America in October 1921, Chaplin breathlessly dictated an account of his tour to Elsie Cod, which was published the following Spring under the title, 'My Wonderful Visit'. Light-hearted and rather self-indulgent, it nevertheless proved a success with the public – unlike his earlier fictionalized 'autobiography' – although copies are now extremely hard to find. As a man with an eye for the girls, it is perhaps not surprising that Charlie dwells on a number of encounters with women in Paris and London – including the following rather charming meeting with some young prostitutes! It serves as a rather suitable prelude to the remarkable day that Charlie spent shortly afterwards in New York with the notorious womaniser, Frank Harris, who features next in the book.

'SO WE WANDERED along through South London by Kennington Cross and Kennington Gate, Newington Butts, Lambeth Walk, and the Clapham Road, and all through the neighbourhood. Almost every step brought back memories, most of them of a tender sort. I was right here in the midst of my youth, but somehow I seemed apart from it. I felt as though I was viewing it under a glass. It could be seen all too plainly, but when I reached to touch it it was not there – only the glass could be felt, this glass that had been glazed by the years since I left.

'If I could only get through the glass and touch the real live thing that had called me back to London. But I couldn't.

'A man cannot go back. He thinks he can, but other things have happened to his life. He has new ideas, new friends, new attachments. He doesn't belong to his past, except that the past has, perhaps, made marks on him.

'My friends and I continue our stroll – a stroll so pregnant with interest to me at times that I forget that I have company and wander along alone.

A flashback sequence from *The Face on the Bar-Room Floor* (1914)

'Who is that old derelict, there against the cart? Another landmark. I look at him closely. He is the same – only more so. Well do I remember him, the old tomato man. I was about twelve when I first saw him, and he is still here in the same old spot, plying the same old trade, while I——

'I can picture him as he first appeared to me standing beside his round cart heaped with tomatoes, his greasy clothes shiny in their unkemptness, the rather glassy single eye that had looked from one side of his face staring at nothing in particular, but giving you the feeling that it was seeing all, the bottled nose with the network of veins spelling dissipation.

'I remember how I used to stand around and wait for him to shout his wares. His method never varied. There was a sudden twitching convulsion, and he leaned to one side, trying to straighten out the other as he did so, and then, taking into his one good lung all the air it would stand, he would let forth a clattering, gargling, asthmatic, highpitched wheeze, a series of sounds which defied interpretation.

'Somewhere in the explosion there could be detected "ripe tomatoes". Any other part of his message was lost.

'And he was still here. Through summer suns and winter snows he had stood and was standing. Only a bit more decrepit, a bit older, more dyspeptic, his clothes greasier, his shoulder rounder, his one eye rather filmy and not so all-seeing as it once was. And I waited. But he did not shout his wares any more. Even the good lung was failing. He just stood there inert in his ageing. And somehow the tomatoes did not look so good as they once were.

'We get into a cab and drive back towards Brixton to the Elephant and Castle, where we pull up at a coffee store. The same old London coffee store, with its bad coffee and tea.

'There are a few pink-cheeked roués around and a couple of old derelicts. Then there are a lot of painted ladies, many of them with young men and the rest of them looking for young men. Some of the young fellows are minus arms and many of them carry various ribbons of military honour. They are living and eloquent evidence of the War and its effects.

There are a number of stragglers. The whole scene to me is depressing. What a sad London this is! People with tired, worn faces after four years of War!

'Someone suggests that we go up and see George Fitzmaurice, who lives in Park Lane. There we can get a drink and then go to bed. We jump in a cab and are soon there. What a difference! Park Lane is another world after the Elephant and Castle. Here are the homes of the millionaires and the prosperous.

'Fitzmaurice is quite a successful moving-picture director. We find a lot of friends at his house, and over whiskies-and-sodas we discuss our trip. Our trip through Kennington suggests Limehouse, and conversation turns toward that district and Thomas Burke.

'I get their impressions of Limehouse. It is not as tough as it has been pictured. I rather lost my temper through the discussion.

'One of those in the party, an actor, spoke very sneeringly of that romantic district and its people.

'"Talk about Limehouse nights. I thought they were tough down there. Why, they are like a lot of larks!" said this big-muscled leading man.

'And then he tells of a visit to the Limehouse district – a visit made solely for the purpose of finding trouble. How he had read of the tough characters there and how he had decided to go down to find out how tough they were.

'"I went right down there into their joints," he said, "and told them that I was looking for somebody that was tough, the tougher the better, and I went up to a big mandarin wearing a feather and said: 'Give me the toughest you've got. You fellows are supposed to be tough down here, so let's see how tough you are.' And I couldn't get a rise out of any of them," he concluded.

'This was enough for me. It annoyed me.

'I told him that it was very fine for well-fed, over-paid actors flaunting toughness at these deprived people, who are gentle and nice and, if ever tough, only so because of environment. I asked him just how tough he would be if living the life that some of these unfortunate families must live. How easy for him, with five meals a day beneath that thrust-out chest with

Charlie the caveman in *His Prehistoric Past* (1915)

his muscles trained and perfect, trying to start something with these people. Of course they were not tough, but when it comes to four years of War, when it comes to losing an arm or leg, then they are tough. But they are not going around looking for fights unless there is a reason.

'It rather broke up the party, but I was feeling so disgusted that I did not care.

'We meander along, walking from Park Lane to the Ritz.

'On our way we are stopped by two or three young girls. They are stamped plainly and there is no subtlety about their "Hello boys! You are not going home so early?" They salute us. We wait a moment. They pause and then wave their hands to us and we beckon them.

'"How is it you are up so late?" They are plainly embarrassed at this question. Perhaps it has been a long time since they were given the benefit of the doubt. They are not sure just what to say. We are different. Their usual method of attack or caress does not seem in order, so they just giggle.

'Here is life in its elemental rawness. I feel very kindly disposed toward them, particularly after my bout with the well-fed actor who got his entertainment from the frailties of others. But it is rather hard for us to mix. There is a rather awkward silence.

'Then one of the girls asks if we have a cigarette. Robinson gives them a package, which they share between the three of them. This breaks the ice. They feel easier. The meeting is beginning to run along the parliamentary rules that they know.

'Do we know where they can get a drink?

'"No." This is a temporary setback, but they ask if we mind their walking along a bit with us. We don't, and we walk along towards the Ritz. They are giggling, and before long I am recognized. They are embarrassed.

'They look down at their shabby little feet where ill-fitting shoes run over at the heels. Their cheap little cotton suits class them even low in their profession, though their youth is a big factor toward their potential rise when they have become hardened and their mental faculties have become sharpened in their eternal battles with men. Then men will come to them.

'Knowing my identity, they are on their good behaviour. No longer are we prospects. We are true adventure for them on this night. Their intimacy has left them and in its place there appears a reserve which is attractive even in its awkwardness.

'The conversation becomes somewhat formal. And we are nearing the hotel, where we must leave them. They are very nice and charming now, and are as timid and reserved as though they had just left a convent.

'They talk haltingly of the pictures they have seen, shyly telling how they loved me in *Shoulder Arms*, while one of them told how she wept when she saw *The Kid* and how she had that night sent some money home to a little kid brother who was in school and staying there through her efforts in London.

'The difference in them seems so marked when they call me Mr Chaplin and I recall how they had hailed us as "Hello, boys". Somehow I rather resent the change. I wish they would be more intimate in their conversation. I would like to get their viewpoint. I want to talk to them freely. They are so much more interesting than most of the people I meet.

'But there is a barrier. Their reserve stays. I told them that I was sure they were tired and gave them cab fare.

'One of their number speaks for the trio.

'"Thanks, Mr Chaplin, very much. I could do with this, really. I was broke, honest. Really, this comes in very handy."

'They could not quite understand our being nice and sympathetic.

'They were used to being treated in the jocular way of street comradery. Finer qualities came forward under the respectful attention we gave them, something rather nice that had been buried beneath the veneer of their trade.

'Their thanks are profuse, yet awkward. They are not used to giving thanks. They usually pay, and pay dearly, for anything handed to them. We bid them "good night". They smile and walk away.

'We watch them for a bit as they go on their way. At first they are strolling along, chattering about their adventure. Then, as if on a signal, they straighten up as though bracing themselves, and with quickened steps they move toward Piccadilly, where a haze of light is reflected against the murky sky.

'It is the beacon light from their battle-ground, and as we follow them with our eyes these butterflies of the night make for the lights where there is laughter and gaiety.

'As we go along to the Ritz we are all sobered by the encounter with the three little girls. I think blessed is the ignorance that enables them to go on without the mental torture that would come from knowing the inevitable that awaits them.'

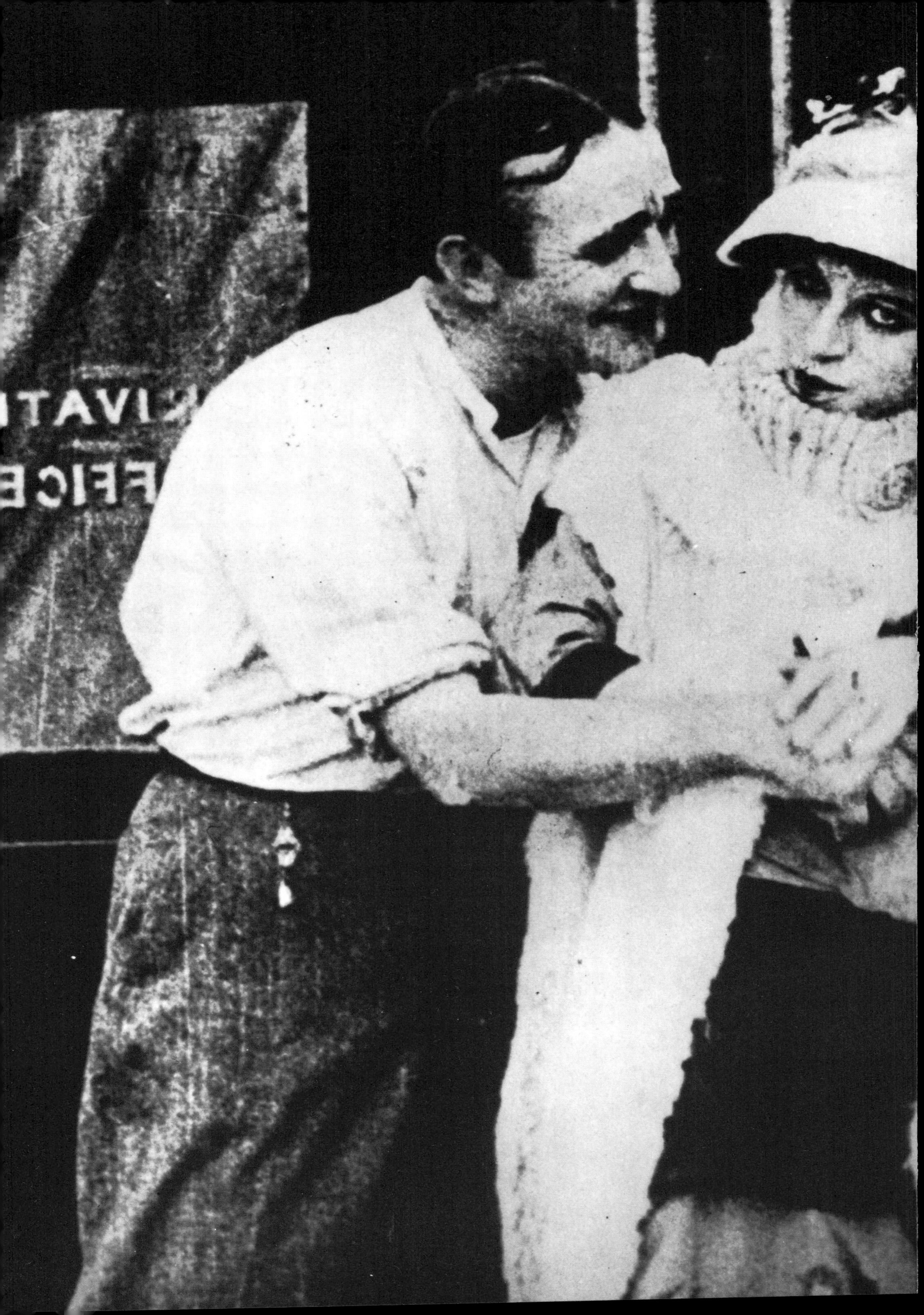

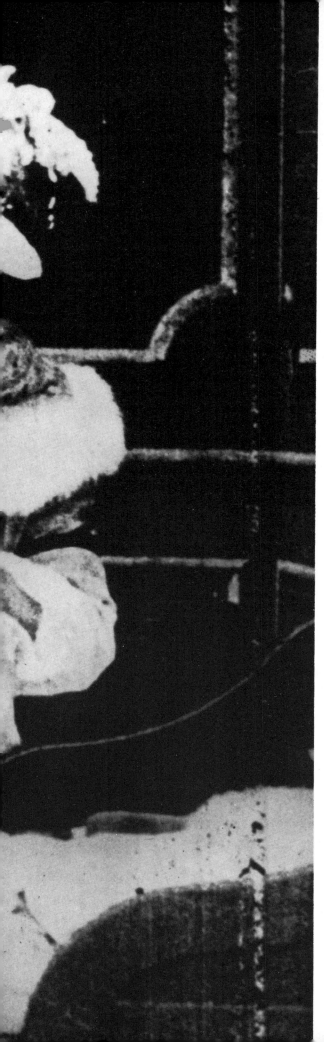

Frank Harris
CHARLIE CHAPLIN AND A VISIT TO SING-SING

ALMOST IMMEDIATELY on his arrival back in New York from London, Chaplin spent some time with Frank Harris, 'the most colourful figure in contemporary journalistic circles' to quote one authority. Although his proclivity for boasting, philandering and adventure was well-known, Harris had ony just begun writing the notorious *My Life and Loves* (1923–1927) and was mainly busy on writing a series of idiosyncratic profiles of famous people. Chaplin tells us in his autobiography that he had read and admired Harris's work and considered him 'my idol'. When Harris invited him to dinner he naturally accepted with alacrity, although Chaplin had to disguise himself as a woman to get past the crowds outside his hotel! The dinner proved the beginning of a friendship between the two men, and a few days later Chaplin and Harris paid a visit to the infamous Sing-Sing prison to visit a man named Jim Larkin. Harris later utilized this strange visit as a part of a highly personal portrait of Chaplin which was published in the magazine he was then editing, *Pearson's Weekly* in April 1922.

'LIKE EVERYONE else in Christendom, I have seen Charlie Chaplin in the "movies" time and again, till he has become for me the chief attraction, and I go to the "movies" always when his pictures are being given. I have been told that he modelled his walk and his big feet from an English public-house wastrel, and that he dates his success from the moment of his imitation.

'I have now had the pleasure of meeting Charlie Chaplin in person. I have talked with him for hours on several occasions; with his brother and his secretary, he came to one of my lectures, and afterwards reduced me to half-hysterical laughter by his brilliant impersonation of my peculiarities. He is, indeed, the greatest mimic I have ever met. When he talked to me of the late Sir Herbert Tree, he

109

Chaplin's famous female impersonation in *A Woman* (1915)

involuntarily assumed Tree's attitudes, favourite gestures, even his hesitating tones and his bursts of bad epigram – a surprising reincarnation.

'Then he told of how Sir Herbert spoke of his daughter, "little Iris", and how he was hoping to take the little child on his knee and lose some of his shy embarrassment at Tree's overwhelming personality; but the next moment the door opened and Iris came into the room – a tall young women, with absolute self-possession; a cigarette in one hand, a cocktail in the other. Charlie imitated Iris and reeled off a line or two of her poetry, so that again I shouted with laughter. A most surprising mimic – a mimic of genius, and therefore a great actor.

'It dawned upon me gradually that Charlie Chaplin was about the best actor I had ever met; astonishingly endowed, indeed. I asked him why he did not go on the ordinary stage. He immediately began quoting *Hamlet* – "The play's the thing" – and I found myself asking him seriously, so impressed was I with his talents, why he did not play Hamlet.

'"I should love to," he confessed. "I think certain sides of the character have never been brought out as they should be. There was a humorous side in him, don't you think?"

'"Of course," I said. "Does not Hamlet himself, even in his disdain of the courtierly, show a sympathetic appreciation of humour, and he praises Yorick at the end as 'a fellow of infinite jest, most excellent fancy'. But how far you can show the humour in him, and yet keep to the character of Hamlet, I don't know. It would be a very interesting experiment. I wish you would try and let me be present. 'God send Rome such another sight, And send me there to see.' He laughed.

'But Charlie Chaplin is something more than a humorist and great actor. He is a man of genius. He is absolutely devoid of pose, and pretends to no scholarship. He tells how he has come from poor people, and yet he has read a great deal of the best, and is a most interesting companion to all sorts and conditions of men.

'One little story his brother told of him should be recorded. The brother is four years older than Charlie, and he said when he was about twelve and Charlie seven or eight, Charlie was very small indeed, but preternaturally precocious. When they came across a barrel organ Charlie would dance and sing, and, as soon as a crowd collected, Charlie would take off his hat and run round collecting the pennies; then he would bolt with the money, to the rage and exasperation of the organ-grinder.

'Surely it speaks volumes for such a man when he keeps his sympathy for the poor and outcast in spite of his most astonishing success. Ten years ago, as he says, he was glad to get two and a half dollars a day; a month after he was worth half a million a year; and yet he is absolutely unspoiled.

'The other night, after talking with us for some hours, he went out and took a taxi – to go back, as I thought, to his hotel. Instead of that, he wandered off from hotel to hotel; none of them could take him in, they were all full. He chummed up with the driver of the taxi, and about four o'clock in the morning the driver proposed to take him home and find a bed for him in his house. The adventure tempted Charlie. He confided to the driver who he was. The driver was delighted, but said: "Don't give your name; my wife wouldn't believe me; she'd think I was trying to make a fool of her, and there would be a row. I shall just say that you are a fare that couldn't get in anywhere; I often have fares like that in New York."

'With all his heart Charlie entered into the fun, and they drove out to the Bronx. He was taken on tiptoe into a very small apartment, and, with his finger on his lips, the driver showed him a hall bedroom where there was already a twelve-year-old boy asleep in a tiny bed. Unceremoniously the father pushed him to one side, and told Charlie he could sleep on the edge of the bed. The millionaire actor chuckled with glee, undressed, and went to bed. In the morning the boy awoke early, peered at his new companion, and vanished. There was loud whispering in the hall; an elder sister came to the door and looked in. "Yes, it is Charlie," she said, and the whispering grew louder. In a few minutes she returned, followed by a cortege of Jewish children eager to see the famous hero, and the children were followed by their elders; and Charlie, the uncrowned king, held impromptu court with such faithful and admiring subjects as surely no monarch possesses.

'And he told the story with a hundred gestures, so that the Jews of the Bronx lived for you as if they had suddenly been brought before your eyes by the waving of a wizard's wand.

'Far away from the din and glare of the make-believe stage, I have come to know the real Charlie Chaplin, a far more interesting personality than the movie star. He does not wear a moustache; his features are well cut; large eyes; large head, too, and excellently shaped; lips astonishingly mobile and well formed; a very handsome face, and a handsome, slight figure, with tiny hands and feet.

'"The feet I understand," I said, "you had to disguise, but why wear that moustache?"

'He shrugged his shoulders. "I had to caricature myself to pin myself in the memory of the public. The moustache and the feet have done it."

'And then he gave us an unforgettable experience. His brother darkened the room in his hotel, put up a sheet, and Charlie's six-film picture, *The Kid*, unrolled itself before our eyes. It was far and away the best thing that Charlie Chaplin had done up to that time; a real story, magnificently rendered. How Charlie finds a little kid, precociously intelligent, and trains him to be a fellow-conspirator, must be seen to be fully appreciated. One scene that I shall never forget is that in which the kid goes and breaks the windows in advance, and Charlie comes afterwards to mend them. How the kid gets caught by policemen, how he gets away, and the various vicissitudes of the street Odyssey are simply enthralling. At the end, Chaplin's view of Heaven, a comic goody-goody Paradise with flashes of intermittent humour, and the final happy consummation.

'A great piece, *The Kid*, and Charlie Chaplin is a great man and a great artist.

'His difficulties with his wife have been told by her in a dozen news sheets, and therefore a true picture of the pair may now be given.

'Every morning in the paper a fresh appeal appeared from Mildred Chaplin: the injured lady wept, protested, cajoled, threatened all in a breath. One morning a change: she published the following:

'"My final statement: Mr Chaplin is not a Socialist. He is a great artist, a very serious personality, and a real intellectual." Yes, those are her very words; and she continues: "The world will be amazed at the intensity of his mind." What can have happened? I ask myself. Has Charlie weakened and paid without counting?

'I read on: "I have no desire to obtain half of his fortune. (No?) I will not hinder the sale of his latest moving picture." (Whew, the wind sets in that quarter, does it?)

'And then: "I am entitled to a settlement. (Eh?) I am too ill, physically and mentally, to work at present, and this notoriety and exposition of my personal affairs is very disagreeable to me." (Really? You needn't indulge in it, madame, unless you want to.)

'Finally: "He is a great artist, a brilliant man, plays the violin, 'cello, piano, and so forth ... I have already filed papers against him." Well, well, and again well.

'Here is Charlie's story of talks with his wife on the phone about their divorce.

'"Is that you, Charlie? It's me Mildred. I'm ill and have no money. Won't you give me $50,000, and settle all this disagreeable law business? You will. You're a dear: I knew a great artist like you couldn't be mean. If you knew how I hate to quarrel and dispute. Let us meet at my lawyer's in an hour, eh? Goodbye, dear. Goodbye till then."

'Quarter of an hour later:

'"Is that you, Charlie? Oh, I'm so sorry, but my lawyer won't let me take $50,000; he says it's ridiculous. Won't you give $100,000, and I can satisfy him? Please: I'm so nervous and ill. You will? Oh, you——! Well, you're just you – the one man in the world. I can't say more. Now for that dreadful lawyer, and then we'll meet and just sign. How are you? Well! Oh, I'm so glad. In half an hour, dear."

'Quarter of an hour later:

'"Charlie! What can I say? I'm just heart-broken, and I've such a headache. That lawyer says I mustn't settle for $100,000. His fee is goodness knows how much. I must have at least $150,000. What am I to do? Mamma says—— You will? Oh, my! I'm so glad. I don't know how to thank you. It's your last word, you say? All right, Charlie. I'm satisfied. In half an hour, then."

'Ten minutes later:

'"It's no good, Charlie. I can't settle for that; it's really too little. You see, Charlie! Charlie! Did you ring off? Or is it that filthy exchange? Oh, dear! Damn! D——n!"

'Charlie Chaplin is a master of comedy in life, as he is on the stage; an artist in refined humour, he can laugh even at himself and his own emotions. On the point of leaving Pasadena for a trip to New York, he rang his wife up.

'"Mildred, it's me, Charlie. Will you take half a million dollars, and settle this ridiculous claim? You will? No, I'm not a darling; but meet me at my lawyer's in an hour, and we can sign."

'Quarter of an hour later:

'"Mildred, dear: I'm so sorry, but my lawyer won't let me give half a million; he says a year's earnings for a week's marriage is too much. He says $100,000 is more than generous. Will I listen to you? Of course, I will. Talk away. . . ."

'A woman's voice, high pitched: "You're no man! Again you've let me down and made a fool of me. You've no character. I'll teach you . . . (Left talking.)

'Charlie Chaplin strolls away from the phone with a smile on his lips and a little sub-acid contempt for human, and especially for feminine, nature.

'One morning, quite unexpectedly, I was called to the phone by Charlie Chaplin's friend and secretary, Tom Harrington: "Charlie wants to know would you go with him to visit Sing-Sing?"

'"When?" I asked.

'"This morning, now! If so, I'll bring the car for you."

'"Come; of course, I'll go."

'"But you're not well enough," warned my secretary; "you said you were dizzy and feeling ill!"

'"I'm going all the same," I replied; "isn't Jim Larkin at Sing-Sing? Besides, I've never seen the inside of an American prison, and with Charlie Chaplin – I'd never forgive myself if I didn't go."

'I profess myself of the rapidly increasing band who believe that Charlie Chaplin is one of the great artists of this time, one who ranks above Dan Leno or even Chevalier, a master of laughter, of comedy, low or high. And to say of a man that he is a great artist ought to imply that you regard him as one of the choice and master spirits of the age, one of those whose judgment is subtly fair because he stands in true relation with this visible world, as well as with the viewless mysteries.

'There are very few men on Manhattan Island with whom I would care to spend a whole day, but Chaplin is one of them.

'In half an hour we set out in the auto; I had so many things to ask him that I started off without preliminary:

'"In your two months on the other side, who was the most interesting man you met?"

'"Oh, Wells," he replied at once. "Wells, certainly.

'"A fine mind and very interesting; with, of course, all sorts of knowledge that I had not got and did not pretend to; taking for granted, too, all sorts of reading in me that I had not done; but lightning quick and kindly.

'"I saw a film of *Kipps* with him. It was very bad, the mechanical part of it astonishingly bad, and I said: 'You mustn't allow this, Wells, you know it; it will never do.' I wanted to help him. The chief actor, a very nice young fellow, came over to us afterwards, and Wells twitched my arm, evidently fearing that I might continue my criticism, and said: 'Say something kind to the boy.'

'"I thought it very sweet of him. Of course, I praised the actor. Very interesting man, Wells, and very kind; his eyes, as you have said, very fine."

'And then the impish spirit came over him, gilding his recollection, and he turned to me, his eyes dancing.

'"Wells introduced me to his son. Oh, such a clever boy, a wonderful boy, 'from Cambridge, Cambridge University, you know', mimicking Wells's voice and manner. I mightn't know, d'ye see? Everyone in the house,'' added Charlie, "seemed to be from Cambridge – Cambridge University dons – the Ark of the Covenant must have been in Cambridge.''

'The imitation was so perfect, the understanding so keen, that I had to smile, for there are many kinds of snobbery – and intellectual snobbery is one of the most whimsical.

'"Who else did you see?" I asked; "that counts, I mean."

'"Oh! I saw Barrie – Sir James Barrie; he is getting old, and takes himself very seriously. He criticized my *Kid*, telling me that all the heavenly part was nonsensical, 'absurd and worthless'. The author of *Peter Pan*," added Charlie, with dancing eyes again, "the inventor of the crocodile with the clock in its stomach, seemed to think my scene in Heaven absurd and therefore worthless, as if the two adjectives were synonyms," and Charlie grinned again.

'Chaplin has got a smile that not only lights up his eyes and mouth, but lights up the man he is talking about with irresistible, kindly mockery. Of course, everybody knows perfectly well that the absurdities of *Peter Pan* have made Barrie a millionaire.

'"You were received by royalty, were you not, Charlie," I went on, "on your way to Berlin?"

'"Yes, yes," he replied, laughing; and then his face grew thoughtful-sad. "Berlin was terrible; the people all working so hard, but an air of gloom over everything as if they were up against it dreadfully. I wanted to see the slums, the real poor, you know; but there were no slums in Berlin, and in the poorest quarters the children were happy and well-dressed. No slums. You attribute that to Bismarck's wise social legislation, don't you?"

'"All of it," I replied. "He thought it the first duty of the State to help workmen to work; but then he was the greatest governor that has yet appeared in Europe. If Harding would only imitate his system of land-banks, he might bring happiness throughout our immense Middle West, and widespread well-being."

'"It's wonderful in Berlin," Charlie went on. "Prices are so low; we got a lunch at the Adlon Hotel, the best hotel in Berlin, where we stayed – and a very good lunch – that cost, I think, nearly twenty-five cents. The Allies, determined to make Germany pay, will probably find it is at the expense of their own poor. The Germans are being forced to undersell everyone."

'Talk like this, witty and wise, and always kindly from Charlie, brought us round a turn to the prison. Oh, it could not be mistaken, even when seen from afar. There it lay in the autumn sunlight, with the beautiful river and the heights beyond, all bathed in glory; there it lay like a vile plague spot; a great bare, yellow exercise yard; a dozen buildings, the nearest a grey stone building with narrow slits of windows for eyes, and bars, bars everywhere. The heart shrank before it.

'The next moment we stopped before the prison steps; went down, down, down to the barred gate, which slowly swung open for us. My heart contracted.

'Everyone was eager to see Charlie; he was acclaimed as a monarch, as indeed he is: a monarch who can make the whole world loyal with a smile, who can bring joyous laughter to the lips of the world-weary.

'After the usual introductions, we were taken in charge by Mr Thomas McInerny, the principal keeper, a big fellow, six feet odd, with a fine, kindly face, who acted as master of ceremonies. Nobody, of course, knew Tom Harrington or me, or paid any attention to us, so I was free to use both my eyes.

'We were taken first into a long room. As the door opened, McInerny announced "Visitors' Room". There they were, perhaps a score of prisoners, with thirty or forty people about them. Here in front a prisoner nursing his baby, who was playing with his hair, while he talked to his wife and apparently a sister; there, another prisoner holding his wife's hands – infinitely pathetic.

'"Wonderful, terrible," was Charlie's comment. "How long do you allow visitors?"

'"An hour," answered the head keeper. "Of course, if it isn't Sunday, we are not particular about a few minutes"; humanity in the jailer, more humanity than in the judge or law-givers – States, like fish, go rotten first at the head.

'In Brixton Prison, in London, prisoners are not allowed to see their wives and children except in the presence of a warder, who listens to every word. In Brixton, too, the visits are limited to half an hour, and are harder to get. In democratic France, worse still. In America, if Sing-Sing be a fair specimen, the treatment is more humane, as good as in the German prisons, where visits from near relatives, wives and mothers, brothers and sisters, are encouraged.

'But we were not to leave the prison with this kindly lifting of the pall. Almost immediately we were taken into a room with heavy muslin curtains; from it you could peep into the bare yard, forty or fifty yards long and perhaps fifteen wide; two men were walking up and down; one a tall warder, the other a short man in grey, with a pipe in his mouth, walking briskly in the sunshine. The head keeper announced shortly: "The next for the Chair".

'How awful! I peered through the curtains. The man's hands were in his pocket; he was looking straight in front of him, coming towards us, nearer and nearer; a puff of smoke from the pipe, and I missed his face as he turned. Charlie put his hand against his heart. "Did you see his face?" he whispered. "As if he were choking down the terrible fear and agony! Tragic, appalling!"

'I had not seen the look, but could well believe it. The mere thought of it wiped out any taste for more horrors.

'Then the head keeper, who was going back, delivered us over to the doctor, Dr Amos Squire, and to the head teacher, Mr Norbert Henzel. The doctor was a man just below middle height, with a keen face and eyes, very business-like, excellently informed. As we followed him, Mr Henzel said to me: "Did I get your name right? Are you Frank Harris?" Charlie and I had spoken on our way to the prison of the fact that they might object to me, so he had just introduced us as "Mr Harris," "Mr Harrington," quite casually. I was at first taken aback by the recognition, and asked Mr Henzel not to tell anyone. "Charlie asked me to go with him," I explained, "and I jumped at the chance."

'Mr Henzel said he was very glad to know me; he had read some of my books and enjoyed them, and said if he could do anything for me he would be glad to; he spoke most cordially.

'"There is one thing you can do for me," I answered. "Find out where Jim Larkin is, and let me have a word with him." He said he would, adding:

'"You know I have to examine all the prisoners, to find out how they are educated, so I asked Larkin where he had been educated and how many years he had gone to school. He replied casually: 'Oh, my schooldays were very short; you can take it that I am unlettered.' That 'unlettered',' said Mr Henzel, "told me a great deal, and I soon found out that, wherever he had got his education, he had got a good deal of it."

'"He is one of God's spies," I cried warmly; "a wonderful man. He has got the manners of a great gentleman; you have no idea how perfectly he bore himself at the trial, though there were insulting interruptions from the judge at every moment – uncalled for and malevolent when they were not stupid. Not only has he manners and reading, but wisdom and kindness to boot – an extraordinary man, a great man. He and Debs both in prison. Could any criticism of American government be more damning!"

'"They were afraid at first," said Henzel, "that he might use radical propaganda on the prisoners. If they only knew, this is a worse place for radical propaganda than even Wall Street. The prisoners all think Larkin a damned fool for having come here just because he would stand up for others. What have the workmen ever done for him, they say, 'the poor boob!' They all think him rather a fool. And you call him one of the noblest."

'"Yes," I said. "We are told pretty early in life to let well alone. It is a good proverb, but no one tells us that it is still more dangerous not to leave ill alone. That's Jim Larkin's fault. He couldn't sit still and see the wrong triumph."

'"Be still, my soul, be still; it is but for a

season;
Let us endure for an hour and see injustice done.''

'I was roused by the doctor's voice.

'"Twenty-seven per cent of all the prisoners are syphilitic,'' he said, "and sixty per cent have venereal disease of some sort or other.''

'"Good God!'' exclaimed Charlie. "How appalling!''

'"Oh, nothing out of the common,'' replied the doctor. "The returns of the officers in the war showed twenty-five per cent syphilitic – one in every four.''

'"You use 606?'' asked Charlie.

'"Oh, yes,'' answered the doctor. "Salvarsan and mercury. We continue it till the Wassermann test shows that there is not a trace of the bacilli in the blood – a great cure.''

'How I wished poor little Ehrlich, the discover of salvarsan, had been alive to hear that. How his fine little Jew face would have glowed. I remember his telling me in 1913 how he hoped we should meet at the International Medical Congress that would be held in Munich in 1917. "By then,'' he cried, "I shall have discovered an absolute cure for consumption, for sleeping sickness, for all the plagues. I have found the way to poison the bacilli of disease.''

'What faith and hope! But in 1917 there was no International Medical Congress in Munich, and if there had been, Ehrlich could not have been there; he had already passed away.

'The doctor went on, evidently interested. "We can cure all the diseased here except the dope fiends, and we can cure them while they are here, but dope long continued seems to break the will power and once they get out again we find that the addicts go back; they are as bad as pickpockets.''

'"Really?'' I cried, "are pickpockets so hard to cure?''

'"Impossible to cure,'' he returned. "Whether it is vanity in the art or not, I don't know, but ninety out of a hundred come back; once a pickpocket always a pickpocket.''

'Of course we had to visit the Death House. It was a plain bare room, perhaps fifty feet by thirty, with a heavily barred iron door at the left. The door was not green, as the reporters say, but plain white, like the whitewashed walls. Three yards from us stood the chair – a plain yellow wooden armchair with a high back; over the back dangled a wire of five or six strands; on the arms of the chair bands to hold the arms down; bands, too, for the feet. The doctor told us how a copper cap is put on the head with a sponge in it filled with salt moistened; the conductivity is improved three-fold by this appliance. To the right of the chair, a wooden partition, concealed from the chair, the lever to turn the death current off or on, and above it indicators showing the exact voltage: the executioner has only to depress the lever handle.

'"As soon as the cap is put on the forehead I try to watch the breath,'' said the doctor, "and give the signal so that the lungs will be as empty as possible. I generally get it right. If I do, death is instantaneous. The man, through the electric current, dies with the stoppage of breath; strangulation practically. From a minute to a minute and a half and all is over. I don't think the man feels any pain from the moment the lever is pulled; the nerve shock is too tremendous.''

'The doctor then led the way into the next room, which looked like an operating chamber, because there was a high long table in the centre.

'"Here we put the body,'' he said; "it is carried in at once; the temperature of the body is 130 degrees; I have tested it by putting a knife and then a thermometer into the stomach – 134 or 135 degrees quite usual – the blood is all boiling. The brain heat must be higher still ... Oh, yes, I have had several in a day.''

'"Five, doctor,'' the keeper added. "Seven was our biggest day,'' returned the doctor casually.

'Seven! I thought of the poor creatures holding on to themselves, trying to go to death bravely; the beautiful sunshine, the joy of life, all blotted out in one dreadful moment. When will another Jesus come and stop it all? Man's inhumanity to man.

'They put Charlie Chaplin in the chair; the doctor showed him just how everything was adjusted, just how his arms and feet were fettered and his head thrown back, but when we came away Charlie said: "Worse even than the chair was that man in the yard – the condemned man – and his face. I shall see that till I die."

'As we passed from building to building, the prisoners gathered and applauded Charlie, twice even cheered him. I could not help admiring the boyish, laughing good-nature he showed in return. Time and again he won all hearts by sheer humanity and tact. You may think this easy: I marvelled at it. He was introduced by the doctor to the barber; he laughed and held out his hand.

'"That's one for me," he cried, "the doctor sees I didn't shave today – I wish I had time to get it done now." Of course the barber was delighted.

'Half an hour later another cried: "Where's your moustache, Charlie?"

'He turned and retorted whimsically: "Are you, too, from the barber's shop?" And again there was a burst of laughter.

'In the more serious cases he was even finer.

'The head keeper showed us a young man in a cell alone: solitary confinement for breaking loose a short time ago. The prisoner scarcely lifted his eyes as we entered. Charlie said, half aloud: "What a pity! What a handsome fellow!" And indeed he was good-looking. The kindliness won an immediate response; the young fellow looked up brightly and said:

'"Nothing serious, Charlie; only for trying to get away. A real movie stunt, eh?"

'The repartee was apt and cemented the good-fellowship.

'Again, when we were shown some automobiles that the prisoners keep in order and are proud of, one said: "1909 is the date of that one, Charlie; rather behind the times, eh? But then, we're behind the bars, so——" (and a shrug). Charlie said: "If we're free, it's only because we've not been found out. Good luck, boys!"

A little later he was stopped by a jovial old coloured man with a profile very like Dante's, hawk-like, hard and keen, who cried: "I'm Black Joe. I'll be out in 1932. Mind you have a new picture ready, Charlie."

'Charlie took his hat in laughing response, and made it twirl in the air – a trick that brought shouts of laughter. Another time he just danced a grotesque step or two, and the crowd applauded wildly, as only those could applaud whose days and nights are monotonous and sad.

'Charlie, true and humorist as he is, never missed the sadness; time and again he stopped: "How dreadful! Look at that cold grey stone building with the narrow slits. How abominable it all is!"

'Never once does he separate himself from the prisoners, and the tragedy of their punishment was always with him.

'He was at his best when they brought us into a great room with a stage at the left, where movies are shown every day. The actors and operators grouped themselves at once about him with laughing, cordial remarks.

'"Give us a spiel, Charlie," cried someone. "A talk," said another.

'Charlie turned. "How can I talk to you? What is there to say except that we are all pals in this life, and if I can make you laugh, by God! you can make me cry."

'With a wave of his hands he went down the steps.

'After a visit to the drug shop, the busy doctor handed us over to Mr Joyce, the superintendent of the industries, who told us that they made stockings, brushes, and all sorts of things, and sold them to institutions; last year goods to the value of $600,000 – the product of 300 men's work.

'Mr Joyce, too, seemed capable and was interesting; he said the men did not work as well as the men outside; their attention flagged in five or six hours. I remembered that the doctor had told me that over fifty per cent of the prisoners were morons; that is, with the brain development of children under twelve years of age. No wonder their attention flagged.

'Mr Henzel came to me. "Larkin is in the boot place; he's there now; it's the next room."

'Into the next room we went, Mr Joyce explaining in advance to Charlie all about the making of boots; I with eyes for only one man, for one figure. Suddenly on the other side of the room I caught sight of him. I went across, and our hands met.

'"Jim," I cried; "I have done my best again and again, but our Government is brutally indifferent!"

'"You never sent me your books," he said.

'"I sent them, Jim," I cried; "but you shall have them again. I have a friend here now. Mr Henzel, the teacher, will pass them on to you; you shall have them within forty-eight hours. We are all still working, you know, for you and Debs."

'"I know," said Jim; "I know!"

'"How are you in health?" I asked.

'"Fine," he said, carelessly, rearing himself to his full six feet two and throwing out his great chest.

'"But you broke your leg?" I questioned again.

'"It's first-rate now," he said; "they patched it up; I'm all right; but (this in a whisper) is there any chance they might deport us? I want to get back to my people."

'"I'll see what can be done," I cried, "you may be sure. We'll all do what we can."

'"I know; I know."

'"I want you to meet Charlie Chaplin," I said, so I brought Charlie across the room, and they shook hands. Jim at once excused himself. "I had better go off," he said; he didn't want to take up the time of the great visitor; he is the most courteous of gentlemen, with the best of manners – heart manners.

'The visit lasted hours; innumerable things in it that I have forgotten, but when we were in the car again I drew Charlie's attention to the fact that they were building another prison on the heights to our right.

'Charlie turned to me. "Someone has said that prisons and graveyards are always in beautiful places"; and indeed the location was beautiful, looking out over the great river three miles across to the opposite shore.

'"What was your deepest emotion, Charlie?" I asked.

'"O!" he said; "the face of the condemned man walking in that yard, with the pipe in his mouth, and the withdrawn eyes – unforgettable, appalling!"'

The debonair womaniser, Frank Harris

Mary Pickford
MY UNPREDICTABLE PARTNER

ALTHOUGH IT was as far back as 1919 that Chaplin decided to take the major step of going into partnership with three other film personalities to form their own production and distribution company, it was not until 1923 when he had completed his nine contracted pictures for First National Films (with whom he had signed after Essanay and a brief, but lucrative stint with Mutual Films) that he was free to involve himself fully in the partnership. The new company was called United Artists, and the other partners were the director, D.W. Griffith, whom Charlie had known since his days with Mack Sennett, and the famous film couple Douglas Fairbanks and Mary Pickford, who were his next-door neighbours in Hollywood. Surprisingly, Charlie's first film was not an obviously bankable comedy about the Little Tramp, but a tragic drama called *A Woman Of Paris* which seemed to indicate he was planning a new direction for his career. Once again he wrote and directed the movie, but did not appear in it. More than one critic has suggested that Charlie got the inspiration for this film from his visit to Sing-Sing, and certainly its portrayel of the good and evil in mankind gives this opinion a good deal of credibility. Perhaps predictably, the picture was not a success at the box office, although it revealed elements of film technique ahead of its time and was undoubtedly influential on the motion picture styles of several later directors, and so Charlie returned to his more familiar role in comedy. In this article, Mary Pickford, a star in her own right as well as one of the partners in UA, writes of the formation of the company and her not always happy relationship with Chaplin. It appeared in *Woman's Home Companion* of November 1955.

'ONE OF THE most successful people in my husband Douglas' group of early friends was Charlie Chaplin. Charlie was also one of the four original members of United Artists,

Chaplin with his partners in United Artists, Douglas Fairbanks, D.W. Griffith and Mary Pickford

which included D.W. Griffith, Douglas, and myself. My relationship with Charlie over the years has been strange and unpredictable, fluctuating between mutual affection and admiration and intense resentment and hostility. And I want to be very fair in my appraisal of him both as an artist and as a human being. I think that the most moving and human memory I have of Charlie is his grief over Douglas' passing in December 1939. I had called him in Los Angeles from Chicago because of urgent United Artists business, never dreaming that he would come to the phone. I thought I might get the butler and have a message relayed to him. Charlie will rarely if ever answer a telephone, no matter how urgent the call may be. Nor does he ever answer letters. In all the years I have known him I have received just one short note from him.

'When I made my call, it was ten o'clock in the morning in Chicago, and eight in Los Angeles. To my great surprise Charlie answered the phone himself. I believe he was then working on his picture *The Great Dictator*. We talked for an hour. Charlie reminisced warmly and volubly about the happy days the three of us had spent together. I realized then, perhaps as I had never before, how very deep the friendship of Charlie and Douglas had been.

'"I've lost the inspiration and incentive to make pictures, Mary," he said.

'"You mustn't say that, Charlie; Douglas would be furious with you."

'"You know how much I depended upon his enthusiasm. You remember how I always showed my pictures first to Douglas."

'"Yes, Charlie, I can still hear Douglas laughing so heartily he couldn't look at the screen. Remember those coughing fits he'd get at that moment?"

'"More than anything else I remember this, Mary: whenever I made a particular scene I would always anticipate the pleasure it would give Douglas."

'It all came back to me how Douglas used to treat Charlie like a younger brother, listening patiently and intently, hours on end, to his repetitive stories, which frankly bored me to

extinction. Charlie had a way of developing his scenarios by repeating them over and over again to his most intimate friends – testing them privately on people he had faith in. Only then would he put them on film ... I heard a catch in Charlie's voice.

'"Mary, I couldn't bear to see them put that heavy stone over Douglas."

'In 1912 I had heard about Charlie Chaplin, but had never seen him, either in person or on the screen. I knew of the furor he had created, but at that time I just thought of him as a pie-throwing comedian. I was at Levy's, one of the two places where we usually dined in Los Angeles, when I saw a dark-eyed figure, with heavy black wavy hair, high starched collar with stock tie, seated alone at a nearby table. My companion leaned toward me.

'"Charlie Chaplin," he whispered.

'I remember how amazed I was. For one thing, I had expected a much older man. Then, I was totally unprepared for the sensitivity of his face and the smallness of his hands. As I looked in Chaplin's direction a waiter came up behind him and opened a transom, unloosing an avalance of dust on Charlie's head and into his plate of soup.

'Charlie just waved him and the bowl of soup away. There was a touching grace and restraint about his gesture. I would never have recognized the slapstick comedian who looked more like a poet or a violinist.

'I didn't meet Charlie until years later. And it wasn't until I married Douglas that the three of us became almost inseparable.

'Charlie once engaged a Hawaiian orchestra to come all the way from the other side of Los Angeles to serenade me at Pickfair in the middle of the night. That was one of the weirdest experiences of my life. Charlie was spending the week end with Douglas and me, as was his habit when we had become virtually one family. No invitation was ever needed. He was always welcome to come and play with us, and we were just as happy to have him as he was to be with us. It was a moonlit night, and I was dreaming, dreaming that I was dying to the accompaniment of celestial music. I awakened and couldn't believe my ears. The music seemed to be real. And those four Hawaiian

A moment from Chaplin's first film for United Artists, in which he did not appear, *A Woman of Paris* with Edna Purviance and Adolphe Menjou (1923)

musicians on the lawn below were very real indeed. The next morning as we were talking about it at breakfast, Charlie said:

'"You'd never guess, Doug, what was going through my mind while those men were playing."

'"Probably a scene from your next picture."

'"No, I had a strange vision that Mary was dying. I saw her in bed with the moonlight falling on her face and her long blonde hair ..."

'I gave a shiver.

'"... And I thought what if Mary were really dying and this music was accompanying her exit——"

'"Charlie," I said, "you've just made that up. You didn't really imagine it last night!"

'"So help me, Mary, it's true!"

'"This is the most frightening coincidence! You see, Charlie, I dreamed the very thing you were thinking. I dreamed I was actually dying."

'Whatever the stunt, whatever the prank or practical joke, so long as Charlie was responsible for it, Douglas thought it was great ... And the two of them would romp all over Pickfair like ten-year-olds. I couldn't count the number of times I stayed behind to entertain one or another of Charlie's wives, while they would go wandering up and down the surrounding hills. Sometimes Charlie's current spouse might not be altogether to my liking, or I to hers; and sometimes there were things I wanted to do around the house – I had such little time away from the studio. But I would dutifully sit with whichever Mrs Chaplin it might be and chat amiably till the wanderers strolled in again.

'Once they climbed up on the water tower and almost fell in. Douglas, of course, was always climbing, and whoever was with him had to be prepared for some sort of ascent. We were visiting Henry Ford in Pasadena one summer. As it was getting late, I asked the butler if Mr Fairbanks was ready to go home.

'"I don't know, madam," he replied. "They're up there."

'I followed the butler's pointing finger and there up on the roof, straddled across the tile and facing each other, were Douglas Fair-banks and Henry Ford. They were engaged in a heated discussion, completely oblivious of where they were. I waited fully an hour before the "boys" clambered down again.

'"How in the world did you have the courage to take Mr Ford up there?" I asked.

'"It's all right, Hipper. I rehearsed it three or four times for him and showed him where the handholds were."

'What Douglas was on the screen he was in real life. Whatever the danger in any of his films, he never used a double or any precautions. To him that just wasn't cricket. Douglas was always exploring, and playing the prankster.

'When the whole motion picture industry was in the doghouse over some new black sheep, Douglas and Charlie would pick up the telephone and ring up the more pompous and self-righteous movie people and pretend they were newspaper reporters.

'"We understand you know a great deal more about this scandal than you've told the police. This story may mean our job; can we quote you to the effect that ..."

'There would be an immediate threat of a lawsuit from the other end of the telephone. Of course I was always listening in on an extension. I would get terrified when I heard those indignant tones. I was certain the police would trace the call and the industry would have a fresh scandal on its hands.

'Not that Douglas and Charlie were always acting like a couple of kids out of Mark Twain. I saw them once watching Professor Einstein demonstrate his theory of relativity with a knife, a fork, a plate, and the edge of our dining room table. I can still see the look of complete concentration and befuddlement on their faces.

'We were having dinner with Dr and Mrs Einstein at Pickfair shortly after they arrived in this country. Professor Einstein's language was then only beginning to take recognizable shape as English, which did not make the theory any clearer. I'm afraid that even if the professor's English had been flawless, we would still have been in the dark, relatively speaking. A brain specialist who was present had at first introduced the subject of thought transference.

'"Was is das?" asked Einstein.

'"I think and concentrate my thinking on you," explained the brain specialist, "and you catch my thought."

'"Nein," said Professor Einstein, "das ist not possible."

'"But wasn't your theory just as incredible – and still is to most people?"

'Professor Einstein insisted it was a very simple theory. To prove his point he slapped the edge of the table as the outer rim of space, used the plate as the world or the sun or universe, I can't recall which, and plied away at the fourth dimension with his silverware.

'I was too awed to ask questions, so I amused myself by studying the open-mouthed attention of Charlie and Douglas.'

'I have read and heard many harsh things about Charlie, and I've said a few myself. Nor have we ever seen eye to eye politically, but I've always maintained that if people knew something about Charlie's childhood, they would be more tolerant of his singular temperament. When Charlie was only seven years old his mother lost her reason. I'll never forget the time Charlie told me how the children stoned both him and her as he led her by the hand to the hospital. Destitute, their father dead, Charlie and his brother Syd were placed in a workhouse. There they remained for three years. Charlie used to describe the terror he felt when he saw other children being caned.

'Charlie had never seen an orange until one bleak, rainy Christmas Day shortly after he was admitted to the workhouse, and oranges were being handed out to the boys. Poor little fellow, he had made a mistake in bed the night before. So when his turn came he reached out for the coveted object, only to be yanked brusquely out of line and told, "You're a nasty little boy, and you don't deserve to have an orange."

'"Do you know," Charlie said to me, "I looked at this golden ball of colour, so beautiful against the drabness of the uniforms and the grey walls of the workhouse, and I didn't even know an orange was something to eat."

'Finally he and his brother ran away, and nearly starved to death on the streets of London. Many a night they spent over the gratings of a bakery, almost driven out of their minds with hunger when they smelled the fresh bread. It was the only warm spot they could find, and they slept with newspapers over them. They managed to earn a few pennies by carving out little toy boats, and they had to filch their food where they could.

'Another singular side of Charlie's temperament, which his childhood explains, was his scornful attitude toward any strong family ties. He knew how much I loved my mother, yet once he said to me, quite seriously:

'"That's nothing but spooks, Mary – loving one's family that way."

'Yet, however much he might deny the slightest filial attachment, he went to great lengths to bring his stricken mother from England to California. The few years remaining the poor woman were passed in ease and comfort, but she died never knowing that the world's greatest comedian was her son.

'This same sense of loyalty Charlie has shown to innumerable friends, and no one has ever known exactly how many helpless people owe their sole maintenance to him. Many are friends from the lean days whom he has never forsaken. Charlie has been very careful to keep this all to himself.

'Wealthy as he is, I believe the spectre of poverty still haunts him. I know, too, that for a long time it was a great sorrow to Charlie that he never grew into the tall, romantic type. Douglas and I were in the living room of Pickfair one day. Charlie was studying himself in the glass, and we both heard him say, more to himself than to us:

'"My head is too big for my body; my arms are too short for my body; and my hands are too small for my arms."

'"What about me?" I said, showing him my reflection beside his. "My head is too big for my body and my arms are too long for it. And I'm a woman, Charlie."

'On another occasion Charlie drew a tattered newspaper article out of his pocket and handed it to us.

'"I want you both to read this," he said.

'Douglas and I expected at the very least to

find some kind words about Charlie's gift for pantomime. Imagine our astonishment when we read the most scathing denunciation of Charlie Chaplin we had ever seen in print. Among other things it said that Charlie was the result of "generations of underfed gutter-snipes". The rest was in that redolent vein.

'"You see," he said as we read the clipping in dismay, "not everyone thinks *as well* of me as you do."

'Douglas let him have it.

'"Charlie," he said, "you've got to throw that disgusting tripe away! Of all the wonderful things people have written about you, why should you treasure that rot?"

'And I added, "Only some mean person suffering from envy and resentment could have written that, Charlie. Why must you hug a viper to your heart? If you must carry a clipping in your pocket, select one that can inspire you."

'Charlie was unshakable. Evidently he found some twisted satisfaction in this vicious attack on everything he stood for in the pantomimic art of the screen.

'"No," he said, "I'm holding on to that article, because it tells the truth, not the whole truth, I admit. That man, unfair as he is, says many things about me that are correct, and I must never forget them."

'With that he put the clipping in his pocket, and Douglas and I knew it was useless to go on arguing with him. Real humility, however, is not part of Charlie's make-up, certainly not as regards his art. I believe he knows he is the world's greatest comedian. I, of course, agree with him.

'Profoundly as I respect Charlie Chaplin's talents and much as I valued his early friendship, nothing in the world would induce me to live over the agonizing years I experienced with Charlie as a business partner. As a co-owner of United Artists, I was convinced we could survive only by continually modernizing our setup. This Charlie would not permit.

'"Charlie," I would say, "we ought to streamline the company and keep with the general trend of the times."

'But there was no moving him. I don't think Charlie knew himself what he wanted. I finally became convinced he just didn't want what I wanted, that, somehow, particularly after Douglas' death, I rubbed him the wrong way. It finally came to this: no matter what I proposed, or how I proposed it, Charlie would automatically, without giving the matter any consideration, flatly turn it down. As we were 50–50 partners I was completely stymied. The inevitable, of course, happened. United Artists faced bankruptcy. I gave power of attorney to Joseph Schenck, whom I trusted implicitly as a friend and businessman. I shall never forget that day I went to Charlie's home to urge him to do the same. I thought I had seen Charlie in a tantrum, but this beat everything.

'"I wouldn't give my power of attorney to my own brother," he shouted. "I'm perfectly capable of voting my own stock."

'"But, Charlie, you know Schenck is a good businessman."

'"I'm as good a businessman as anybody else!"

'Of course poor Charlie was no businessman at all. I appealed to his sense of fair play and sportmanship.

'"Charlie," I said, "I'm not here as your partner today. I'm not even here as someone that's been your friend for so many years. I'm here as the voice of thousands of employees the world over, of the producers and bankers——"

'At that word he cut me short.

'"If you're here as the voice of the bankers the interview is terminated."

'"Very well, Charlie," I said, and without another word from either of us I started for the door.

'I saw that he had no intention of opening it for me, and I prayed not to lose my temper. Of course, as luck would have it, something was wrong with the lock, for the door wouldn't give. So Charlie had to let me out after all.

'At length, after years of continual wrangling, in February 1951 we finally sat down in a conference room one day and signed over the company to six young men who then had the power to put United Artists back on its feet. And that was the last time I saw that obstinate, suspicious, egocentric, maddening, and lovable genius of a problem child, Charlie Chaplin.'

124

Waldo Frank
CHARLES CHAPLIN: A PORTRAIT

AFTER *A Woman Of Paris*, Chaplin restored both his own favour with the general public and the financial expectations of United Artists with one of his undisputed masterpieces, *The Gold Rush* which appeared in 1925 after exhaustive location work in snowbound, Truckee, California. The picture was greeted with universal acclaim – in England one critic called it, "probably the funniest film that anyone has ever seen" and to this day it remains among the best-known and loved of Charlie's pictures. From the Klondyke, he turned to a subject that had always been close to his heart, *The Circus*, and although this movie took three years to appear it was another triumph, keeping Chaplin way ahead of his competitors on the screen. The film was an authentic and hilarious recreation of life in a circus and won Charlie an Academy Award with the citation, "For his versatility and genius in writing, acting, directing and producing, *The Circus*." It must have been a very satisfying moment for Charlie because he had then been in the film business for fifteen years and it truly established him as one of the all-time greats. The little man had long felt that few writers understood him or his work, although he did exclude from the criticism the American essayist, Waldo Frank. Of him he says in his autobiography, "I came to know Waldo Frank through his book of essays, *Our America*, published in 1919. Waldo was the first to write seriously about me. So, naturally, we became very good friends." The article that Charlie probably had in mind when he wrote those words was the following one that Waldo Frank contributed to *Scribner's Magazine* in September 1929. It certainly puts into the clearest perspective the man and his art at that moment in time.

'CHAPLIN'S EYES are a blue so darkly shadowed that they are almost purple. They are sad eyes; from them pity and bitterness look out upon the world. They are veiled: while the man moves forward with irresistible charm, his eyes hold back in a solitude fiercely forbidding. No one who sees the eyes of Chaplin could feel like laughing. They are the one part of the man which does not show in his pictures.

'For fifteen years these eyes have looked out on Hollywood. Much nonsense has been written about this suburb of Los Angeles, which is itself a suburb of the country. America reviles it as an indecent stranger somehow lodged in its midst, or romanticizes it into a scene from the *Arabian Nights*. But, of course, Hollywood is no worse a place than any provincial city of our land; nor better. Hollywood's producers are typical money men; its directors are typical professional men; its actresses and actors are typical girls and boys. Its army of mechanics, craftsmen, engineers, are the usual American sort: grime them up a bit, lower their wages, and they would fit into your town garage. Hollywood's swarms of aspirants buzzing about the lots are typical floating seed that finds no soil to root in, whether it rots near home or blows away. Only in one respect is Hollywood unusual: its girls are really as fair as all girls would like to be.

'Hollywood is the perfect mirror of banal American success. Ordinary souls dream extraordinary dreams – in the way of ordinary souls. And in Hollywood the dreams come true. Here is uncounted money, here is glamour, here is the exact mechanical production of that ideal to which success means a show. And Chaplin, with those frightening eyes of his, which almost no one ever sees, looks out upon this world, his home since he was twenty-four. There is another world which he looks in upon: the grey, grinding London of his childhood. He loves the London slums; for these slums were his and they are in his heart. But on his mother's side the blood of Chaplin is half gypsy. Through her, whom he brought from England to live near him on the coast, yet another world lives in him: a world of meadows and irresponsible laughter.

'In the city of success he carries with him the taste of the London slums. But even there he was not at home: even for that sad past which formed his body and his mind he has a grim, ironical refusal – since there, too, the gypsy in him was a stranger.

'This counterpoint of sympathy and denial is our first clue to the man. The drawing room of his house is packed with bibelots, pictures, bric-à-brac sent him by the admiring splendour of the world. Here are tributes from Chinese mandarins and from the royalty of Europe. And here too, on the wall, hang a few coloured lithographs of Whitechapel and Wapping. Chaplin loves to take these from the wall. They depict streets that are like some cold inferno, in which the people stir slowly like souls stripped of all save the capacity to suffer. Watch his eyes as he looks at this picture of his childhood world. They are at once too soft and too hard. The emotions of understanding and of refusal are separate in them. In this room I once sat with Chaplin while the Comte de Chasseloup exhibited to us what are perhaps the most terrible photographs in the world: close-ups in progressive detail of tortures and executions which he had collected in China. We looked on the deliberate process of a man being carved alive – as a butcher quarters a calf. We saw faces black with the horror of their pain, and then white with the relief of death. And in Chaplin there was the same counterpoint of feeling. His eyes took in the tremendous pity of these portrayals of man's way with man. Suddenly his eyes hardened; he jumped up, and his mouth was cruel. "There's humanity for you! By God, they deserve it. Give it to them! That's man. Cut 'em up. Torture 'em! The bastards!" ... The pity he had felt was intolerable to him. He summoned hardness to wipe it out: to save himself from this danger of being overwhelmed. Chaplin does not wish to give himself to any emotion, to any situation, to any life. Life draws him too terribly for that. Whatever he feels must immediately arouse its opposite; so that Chaplin may remain untouched – immaculate and impervious in himself.

'With this same reserve he moves through Hollywood. He is no recluse. His secret apartness is far subtler than that. He frequents the

Coconut Grove at the Ambassador, where the slightly decayed youth of the coast ferments in dance. He sits for hours in the smoke of his friend Henry Bergman's restaurant on the crowded boulevard. He goes to parties – to those of his friend Marion Davies at her Beach House, to those of William Randolph Hearst at his ranch. And wherever he goes he is the life of the crowd. He acts, he mimics, he plays, he insists on amusing and on being seen. But always there is the same immediate wavering away from the life about him and from the effect he produces. He does not give himself nor does he really take. Above all, he does not aggressively refuse any advance or emotion. He is non-committal.

'*Untactness* – this is the principle that best explains the balance of opposites in feeling, conduct, thought which he sets up. He is like an atom that must journey alone through the world. It moves an intricate course, swerving here and there, myriadly attracted, myriadly repelled, seeming to give, seeming to respond – always remaining free and alone. A direct refusal of the world about him would mean a definite relation with it. This is not his game. If the world draws him, he responds – passive. His course has been swerved, but he is uncommitted. He resolves every force with its opposite. Emotionally this means that he frustrates in himself every impulse of utter giving or of utter taking. He remains unpossessed and ultimately unpossessing. But this deep frustration is the key to his profound success. Do not pity him for it. He is no pitiable creature.

'With sure instinct Chaplin has guided his personal life through channels where he would be always alone. He loves the world he lives in, and despises it. He does not want to change it: no man is farther from the fervour of the prophet, and yet few men have done so much to show it up as ridiculous and worthless. He does not want another world. He uses this one, just as it is, in order to insure his aloneness. But, were he really alone, he would meet in the silence of himself some acceptance which would prove his unity with the world. So he courts the world, and dwells in it, in order to frustrate such a possible self-encounter.

'There was a time when Chaplin seemed to me a kind of fallen angel: an angel cursed by God with all human feelings and with the inability to fulfil them: cursed with the gift of evoking laughter and love and with no power to take laughter and love to himself. But this was a sentimental error. The inordinate tenderness of the man, his gentility and grace, are checked by his native rejection of the self-bestowal to which such qualities must lead. Hardness and ruthless egoism are as primal in him as the generous emotions. He refuses to be lost in any synthesis of love. He must remain the atom of himself. And in his perfect poise *between* the forces of the world – the poise of opposites – this is what he remains. And this is what he wants.

'What he wants Chaplin has infinite resources for getting. The shrewd technique of his art is but a phase of the same art in his life. This is the man who, when he was first approached with an invitation to enter pictures – untried and unknown – jacked up the initial offer of seventy-five dollars a week to twelve times that figure. "I saw they were anxious," he explained to me. "When I said to them, 'I think I'll study philosophy; I don't care for acting,' I saw them go white. That's how I knew what I was worth." And this is the man who, three years later, when Mary Pickford, Fairbanks, Griffith, Hart, and himself were in danger of being shamefully exploited by the business end of the game, gathered them all together into United Artists and preserved a fair portion of the treasure to the men and women who were doing the work. Chaplin is endowed with consummate powers for connecting with the world. "I'd make a great banker," he once told me. He is intelligent, so intelligent that he intuitively grasps the abstruse currents of modern thought, aesthetic, political, even philosophic. He is sensitive, so exquisitely that the gamut of human joy and pain plays endless responses within him. And he is passionate and earthy, a lover of good food and of women and of racy words. All these gifts naturally conspire to make him one with the world. Yet there is in him this dominant need to be one only with himself, to submit to no marriage, to let

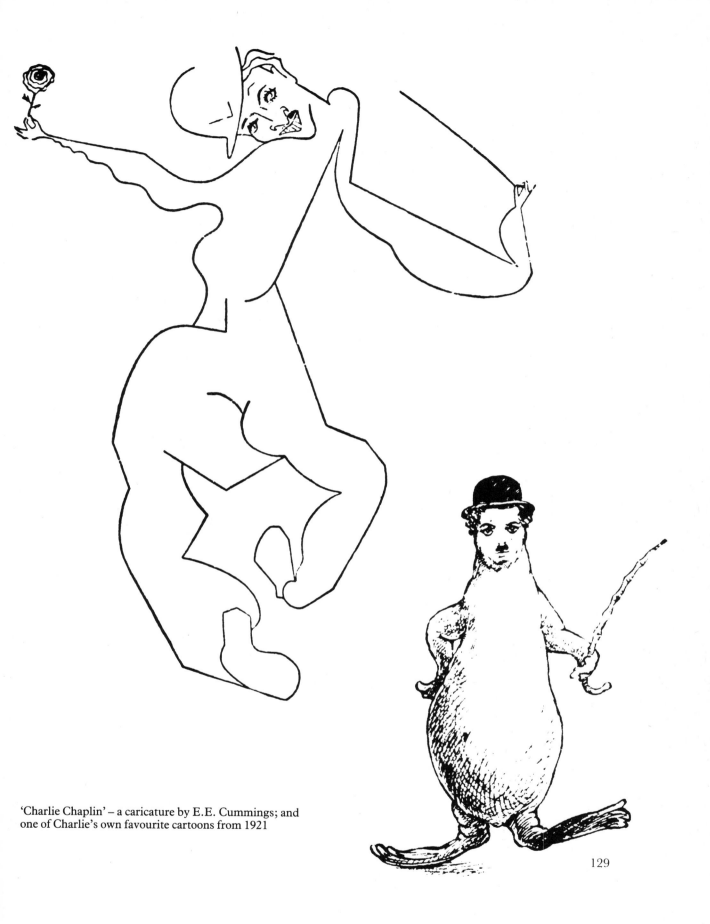

'Charlie Chaplin' – a caricature by E.E. Cummings; and
one of Charlie's own favourite cartoons from 1921

129

himself be lost in no union, to which his mind and sense impel him. What, in this diathesis, can he do? He can keep on moving. He can make his life a constant journey through the inconstancy of impressions which, if he dwelt with them, would bind him. He can make his life an *escape*.'

'The life, then, of this first master of the motion-picture, is motion. His art is the treasured essence of his life. The theme of the Chaplin picture is Chaplin himself, in relation (opposition) to the world. He journeys through it, immeasurably roused, solicited, moved – yet aloof, yet intactly alone. The form of the Chaplin film is his own body, set off by the world: his body made into a mask behind which the man, all intact, goes slyly and painfully on his impervious journey. And the plot of the Chaplin film is merely some sequence of episodes in this constant opposition of himself journeying through life and never fused within it.

'Of course it is not as easy as it sounds. Precisely because his work is the incarnation of his life-mood, of his life-journey, its birth is a delicate issue. In the beginning there is the atomic Chaplin, cast in some rôle that will motivate his passage through the required number of reels. But that passage – as pawnbroker's assistant, circus fool, convict pilgrim, fireman, seeker of gold, tramp, janitor, country bumpkin, etc. – that passage must be blocked out with events. Each foot of the film is an event, an encounter between Chaplin and the world. Since the art is to be the essence of his life, it too, like his life, must be completely *fleshed*; and must breathe! From each encounter, either with another person or with some inanimate object like a brickbat, there must rise visibly and palpably the personality of the entire journey. So each event of the film must be a work of art in itself. And there must be sequence, breathing, flowing, mounting. Each event must rise into the next until the mass of events becomes a plastic music where each episode is a note. The whole tale is a motion of events to represent the journey of the man – his escape, intact, through the myriad mass of life.

'The mood of the tale, being intimately Chaplin's own, is carried within him. What he must wait for is the precise scale of episodes that will form the mood. Even when the events have come to him (the particular stunts of the film) they must be weighed and measured. Where do they fit in? Do they fit in at all?

'This period of gestation is painful and long. Chaplin lies abed an entire morning. He broods, measuring the tentative "body" of his tale by the inner sense of what he wants. This sense is infallible, but it is inarticulate save as the completed picture will be its articulation. Chaplin does not know, he has no words for saying, the exact timbre and gamut of physical actions that will express this particular body of his life-journey. The picture will be his knowing ... Meantime, several miles away, his studio awaits him. It is a charming lot, several acres in size. Here lives Kono, the remarkable Japanese factotum who manages Chaplin's personal journey through life, who serves as a kind of intelligent foil against the inevitable frictions of the inevitable encounters with stranger and friend. Here wait his general staff: Alf Reeves (who has been with him since music-hall days), Harry Crocker, Carl Robinson, Henry Bergman, Henry Clive, Roland Totheroh – possibly the director Harry d'Arrast, who once worked with him in Crocker's present place and who remains his chum. All these men are distinguishably sweet, sensitized, intelligent, aloof in the crass Hollywood world. (That world is full of workers who carry on after they have left him, bearing the stamp he gave them – Menjou is a celebrated instance.)

'The staff all feel the tension of their chief. The strain, indeed, is so great that there are men in the "industry" who could not stand it. At last, possibly around noon, Chaplin arrives. The instant has come when he was ready. He has dropped into his clothes, stepped into the limousine which waits all morning at the door, with the engine throbbing. He is hatless, tie-less, and his vest is open. But the clothes are the most dapper product of the London tailor. He wears them, at work, like a gypsy. Even in this detail there is the meeting of the Chaplin opposites. Gypsy and exquisitely groomed young gentleman delete each

Charlie won an Academy Award for his role in *The Circus* (1928)

other: leaving, as ever, merely Chaplin.

'He joins his crowd in the little bungalow on the lot, where lunch is served and where he has his dressing rooms. Tentative moments of the film are brought up, altered, discarded, readjusted. Chaplin paces, his face hard, his mouth half-open, his eyes far off in himself. Infinitesimal details are studied, rehearsed, discussed: gags, postures, meanings, properties, business. Walking up and down, the little man holds in his head the film's inexorable rhythm, the inner logic of its growth. As the ideas fly back and forth, in words and mimicry, Chaplin brings them to the measure in himself: rejects or accepts.

'There may be months of this. Nothing seems to be going. The corps of workers champ and chafe. Chaplin moves with his preoccupation through his habitual life: parties, dinners, wanderings about town, swift flights with friends, long hours alone. At last certain scenes, having withstood the critical pause, seem certain. Carpenters and plasterers get busy. Sets rise on the lot. Chaplin wanders about among the hammers, alone or with his group: judging, silent, suddenly exasperated, lost in a new angle of vision – giving sharp orders that destroy the work of weeks. A shot that cost a long journey to a location (and $50,000) will be ruthlessly scrapped. Later a scene will be repeated a literal hundred times; and, if the fifty-ninth time was right, each detail of it will be so clear in Chaplin's eye that he will reproduce it for the camera. Finally a thousand feet of photography will be collapsed into a yard so pregnant with the essence of the event that it will move, intact like the man himself, through all the world.

'This perfect consciousness of Chaplin as craftsman would of course be less conspicuous in any other place. (In Paris, for instance, where men work with words and with pigment as Chaplin does with human masses, his *métier* is understood as merely the highest form of a common practice.) But Hollywood is a usual American town – not a capital of artists. And the studios of Hollywood confine their precision and consciousness to problems of mechanics and finance. They are monuments of aesthetic vagueness, intellectual nullity, artis-

tic hit-or-miss. The usual story, to begin with, is an externalized contraption put together by the combined shrewdness of half a dozen wholesalers parading as writers, scenarists, directors, and producers. The actors have no accurate technique. The directors have no conscious control. In such a combination the chance artist is helpless and lost. When a scene is "pretty good" it is shot. And the result is the kind of flat approximation that feeds the dreams of the millions. But by the time Chaplin gets ready to rehearse a scene, its precise place in the architectonic of his tale has been measured, even as the theme itself has been mesured in his life. And as he rehearses he knows what happens. I mean that he knows the interplay of muscle, mass, space, and their focal value as the camera lens will catch it. He is no expert in photography. In his especial choreography he is supreme.

'All organic life has a commanding, individual rhythm: the beat of a heart, the slant of a mind, the indecipherable stir of cells must go with that rhythm. Such an organic rhythm besets the consciousness of Chaplin, incarnating his subjective mood into a story. At the beginning, he knows the rhythm only. He has to grope for the episodes to flesh it. But when he finds his episodes he knows what he wants. And at the moment of shooting a scene he knows how to recall what he wants. And he can do this because, from the twist of a leg to the flicker of an eye, he knows how everything is done.'

'All this, however, has not explained what it is that Chaplin is doing. His work may be the incarnation of his personal escape from those trammels of life to which his sensitivity and capacity for love expose him; his way of escape may be shrewd with all the shrewdness of his cockney-gypsy genius; and the aesthetic expression of that journey of his soul may be done with consummate craft. Yet the inward value of the entire adventure is not yet clear.

'We can best approach the significance of Chaplin's art by considering another constant presence (besides himself) in his meditations on the story, in his conferences with Crocker and d'Arrast, in his rehearsals, in his final prunings, acceptances, and rejections. That other presence he always alludes to by a simple name. He calls it "they". "They" is the public. "They" collaborates unceasingly with Chaplin. "They" has the final veto over even Chaplin himself.

'Of course a similar "they" seems to preside over all the lots of filmland. But in the usual studio there are a number of men pawing over the platitudes of the human race in the deliberate effort to concoct from them a pattern which the public will pay for. Chaplin too is a child of the theatre. And there is no theatre without a "box" in front. But in the studio of Chaplin there is, most really of all, a man of the people – a cockney, a gypsy, a music-hall fellow – who looks into the eyes of the world as in a mirror, in order to see *himself* more objectively and sharply. So it is that, coming to Chaplin's public, we return to the man. By means of this reflection we can see at last, in clarity, how he manages his escape and what it is which, behind the mask of "funny-legs", goes its immortal journey into the heart of the world.

'Chaplin looks upon the world of today. He sees failure: poverty, agony, disease, chaos, fear, pitiful passion, pitiful love. He sees success: deceit, garishness, tinsel, boast, disillusion. He sees his own past in London – his mother in the drab uniform of the poorhouse. He sees his own victorious present. He sees and feels too much. He is afraid of being lost in this world. There is a kernel of him that is neither this success nor this failure: a core in the man that can dance its own life if only it may remain alone. That is why he must escape; why he must look on all the invading world as an enemy and must hate it. Chaplin is a hard and princely fellow: his brow is strong, and his jaw and his mouth. But the modelling about his temples is girlishly tender, and the deepest spirit in his eyes is a retreating terror. He is afraid for that core in him of grace and loveliness and youthful dance. To protect it, he will fight – he will employ all his skill, all his hardness.

'Now consider Chaplin's public, which is the modern world. In each breast live grace and loveliness and wistful dream. But in the common man that personal treasure of each heart cannot remain intact. Family business, law, and war invade it. All civilization becomes a foe, trampling on this secret heart, dispersing its dream, bruising and breaking its love.

'Chaplin, who has striven to keep it whole for himself, has made his fight for the world. Here, in his films, the grace and beauty of the human "atom" are visible once more. Behind the mask of Chaplin – behind the swinging cane, the ambling, painful feet, the tight-drawn coat, the cocky derby hat – marches the common loveliness of man – marches and journeys as it must through a hated modern world – dissociate from social forms, shabby, despised, pitiful, poor; yet miraculously intact and miraculously triumphant.

'Rousseau, I suppose, perfected this tragicomedy of the modern world, with its dualistic conflict between beauty and civilization, between love and man's habitual life. Marvellously gifted, he gave to the world its rationale for the impulse to creep back into a mythic childhood, to worship the self at the expense of the towering forms about it. As Mr Lardner might say: "Jean Jacques started something". Charles Chaplin has finished it. (Even the cut of his comic coat recalls the romantic century – the age of Alfred de Musset.) The cult of loveliness at war with the sobrieties of life could beget no greater art than this journey of Chaplin carrying beauty untouched through an atmosphere of heavy institutions, of brickbats and policemen. French intellectual, London clerk, Chinese coolie, Mexican peon, Park Avenue child, in the common distress of their submission to a world too full of money to leave room for singing and for dancing, can gaze together at this secret triumph which Chaplin has enacted for them. His song explodes their oppressive world. His primitive refusal to "grow up" in the "respectable way" becomes the modern spirit of revolution.'*

'In the old days Charles Chaplin worked not less meticulously but a good deal faster. His theme has always been the exact transcription of the mood of his life. But when his life was simpler the bridge to his work was more immediate. It was easier for the man to remain

* Arturo Mom, the Argentinian writer, tells us that Lenin once said: 'Chaplin is the only man in the world I want to meet.' It is a story readily believed. Chaplin's art expresses the germinal seed of the revolt – tender and ruthless, romantic and realistic – which Lenin's technique attempted to fulfil. Chaplin and Lenin – they are probably the two most potential spirits of our age. Bring them together – pure individualist and pure collectivist – into a single force, and you have a vision of to-morrow.

impervious, intact, virginally himself. The instinctive operation of his will had found no invasion too bruising or too tiring for him to repel. But he has had to pay the toll of his way; and that toll has grown great. It is hard to sustain one's solitude when one is so full of eagerness as Chaplin; and when, precisely because the world loved his aloneness, the world has done everything to destroy it. His recent struggles, not so much against the clamour of the public as against his own human need for that peace and love which can be gained only by some union with another, have made him conscious of himself. Consciousness and weariness have stood between him and his journey – slowing him and slowing his work, which is the expression of that journey. His hair has turned grey, and his beautiful face is lined.

'*The Circus* marks the crisis. The terrible year that separated its first-made scenes from the last brought a new sombreness into his art. The picture on which he is at work at present is the most meditative, the most complex, the darkest story he has ever imagined. A progress like that which distinguishes the end of *Don Quixote* from its rollicking outset is manifest in his work. Chaplin is still alone; still intact. But the fight he has had to wage in order to remain so has worn him. It is the natural destiny of so passionate a man to lose himself. Thus far Chaplin has refused this death. It would mean indeed the death of his old gay art. It might mean the birth of a new tragic artist.

'Meantime the circumstances of his career in Hollywood have conspired to perfect his solitude. Here was an artist whose theme was an essential motion: the pantomimic medium of the motion picture was there to express him. But now the motion picture industry of Hollywood decides to talk. Chaplin, whose excellence made him solitary enough, finds himself almost literally alone.

'A little more entirely than he may have dreamed he is having his way. He is alone in his great house, alone with his few friends, who love him but who cannot really reach him. He is alone among his professional comrades, who, unlike him, have abandoned the silent picture. Chaplin has reached a goal. A goal is an end. An end can be also a beginning.'

Charlie Chaplin
PANTOMIME AND COMEDY

WITH THE advent of talking pictures in the form of *The Jazz Singer* starring Al Jolson in 1927, Chaplin was faced with the greatest dilemma of his career. He knew only too well that the unspoken 'language' of the Little Tramp was universal, that no matter where in the world the pictures were shown there was no barrier to understanding them. Yet would this appeal be the same if he had to speak, he wondered? Chaplin was an astute enough film maker to sense that the talkies were here to stay, but he did not think that necessarily meant the end of the silent movie of which he was such a master. The two could surely co-exist together with the public accepting both on their respective merits, he believed. Despite the pressures on him from several quarters to make his next film, *City Lights*, with a sound track, Chaplin remained firm in his beliefs, and even went so far as to express them in an eloquent article written for the opening of the new picture and published in the prestigeous newspaper, *The New York Times* of 25 January 1931. Despite what has transpired in the intervening years, Chaplin's words still make fascinating reading today.

'BECAUSE THE silent or non-dialogue picture has been temporarily pushed aside in the hysteria attending the introduction of speech by no means indicates that it is extinct or that the motion picture screen has seen the last of it. *City Lights* is evidence of this. In New York it is presented at the George M. Cohan Theatre beginning 6 February. It is a non-dialogue but synchronized film.

'Why did I continue to make non-dialogue films? The silent picture first of all, is a universal means of expression. Talking pictures necessarily have a limited field, they are held down to the particular tongues of particular races. I am confident that the future will see a return of interest in non-talking pro-ductions because there is a constant demand for a medium that is universal in its utility. It is axiomatic that true drama must be universal in its appeal – the word elemental might be better – and I believe the medium of presentation should also be a universal rather than a restricted one.

'Understand. I consider the talking picture a valuable addition to the dramatic art regardless of its limitations, but I regard it only as an addition, not as a substitute. Certainly it could not be a substitute for the motion picture that has advanced as a pantomimic art form so notably during its brief twenty years of story telling. After all, pantomime has always been the universal means of communication. It existed as the universal tool long before language was born. Pantomime serves well where languages are in the conflict of a common ignorance. Primitive folk used the sign language before they were able to form an intelligible word.

'At what point in the world's history pantomime first made it's appearance is speculative. Undoubtedly it greatly antedates the first records of its part in Greek culture. It reached a highly definite development in Rome and was a distinct factor in the medieval mystery plays. Ancient Egypt was adept in its use, and in the sacrificial rites of Druidism and in the war dances of the aborigines of all lands it had a fixed place.

'Pantomime lies at the base of any form of drama. In the silent form of the photoplay it is the keynote. In the vocal form it must always be an essential, because non-visual drama leaves altogether too much to the imagination. If there is any doubt of this, an example is the radio play.

Action vs. Words
'Action is more generally understood than words. The lift of an eyebrow, however faint, may convey more than a hundred words. Like

135

Following page: A delightful scene from *The Circus* (1928) Charlie with one of his oldest friends, Henry Bergman

the Chinese symbolism, it will mean different things, according to its scenic connotation. Listen to a description of some unfamiliar object – an African wart-hog, for example – then describe it; observe a picture of the animal and then note the variety of astonishment.

'We hear a great deal about children not going to the movies any more, and it is undoubtedly true that hundreds of thousands of prospective film patrons, of future filmgoers, young tots who formerly thrilled to the silent screen, do not attend any more because they are unable to follow the dialogue of talking pictures readily. On the other hand, they do follow action unerringly. This is because the eye is better trained than the ear. There is nothing in *City Lights* that a child won't follow easily and understand.

'I am a comedian and I know that pantomime is more important in comedy than it is in pure drama. It may be even more effective in farce than in straight comedy. These two differ in that the former implies the attainment of humour without logical action – in fact, rather the reverse; and the latter achieves this attainment as the outcome of sheer legitimate motivation. Silent comedy is more satisfactory entertainment for the masses than talking comedy, because most comedy depends on swiftness of action, and an event can happen and be laughed at before it can be told in words. Of course, pantomime is invaluable in drama, too, because it serves to effect the gradual transition from farce to pathos or from comedy to tragedy much more smoothly and with less effort than speech can ever do.

The Main Qualifications

'I base this statement on recent observations; the sudden arrival of dialogue in motion pictures is causing many of our actors to forget the elementals of the art of acting. Pantomime, I have always believed and still believe, is the prime qualification of a successful screen player. A truly capable actor must possess a thorough grounding in pantomime. Consider the Irvings, Coquelins, Bernhardts, Duses, Mansfields and Booths, and you will find at the root of their art pantomime.

'My screen character remains speechless from choice, *City Lights* is synchronized and certain sound effects are part of the comedy, but it is a non-dialogue picture because I preferred that it be that, for the reasons I have given.'

In trouble as usual – Charlie resorts to violence in order to escape the law in *Police* (1916)

Virginia Cherrill
A VIEW OF CHAPLIN THE FILM MAKER

Despite the initial reservations of the cinema circuit owners who, in 1931, were besotted with sound films, *City Lights* proved an enormous hit with the public, and several critics even hailed it as a work of genius. Chaplin had certainly created a brilliant mixture of comedy and pathos in telling the story of the Little Tramp embroiled in the harsh realities of life in a big city. The film also made an overnight star of a young actress named Virginia Cherrill. She had been selected from among dozens of starlets for the exacting role of the blind flowerseller whose love Charlie hopes to win through the subterfuge – which she obviously cannot detect because of her blindness – that he is a rich man. Four years after the making of *City Lights*, shortly before the release of Chaplin's next picture, *Modern Times*, Virginia Cherrill wrote the following essay about her experiences with Chaplin. If the piece, from *Picturegoer Magazine* of 9 December 1935, is tinged with a certain nostalgia this is perhaps understandable, for the role of the blind girl was to prove the high point of her career.

'I am waiting as eagerly as any filmgoer to see Chaplin's latest *Modern Times*. Having worked with him for two years during the making of *City Lights* I am sure in my own mind that he is the greatest artist the cinema has given to the world. And I am not the only person who thinks so. There is something strangely unassuming about his studios, twenty years out of date for anyone but him, unaffected by the grandeur of modern Hollywood. And there is something strangely unassuming about the man himself, for one whom the whole world knows. No other person using screen pantomime has so captured the affections of men and women. If the test of time is a true test of genius, then the weathering of twenty years of screen history by the little

baggy-trousered, bowler-hatted figure which the world calls Charlie Chaplin surely shows genius of a lasting quality. For the Chaplin of *Modern Times* is the same tragi-comic little figure of the war-time "shorts". And while Hollywood has pounded on taking sound and colour in its stride, reducing motion picture production to a factory schedule system, creating new techniques and presenting ever new film forms, the Chaplin unit has remained unchanged since its pioneer days. No board of directors control its destiny. No pompous officials plan its daily routine. Just the delicate sensitivity of its artist-owner forms the impulse behind its very activity.

'The Chaplin studios have had the same technicians, the same employees, since film time began. They are on regular pay-roll from Chaplin's own pocket. They work according to his whims and fancy. They play when no duty calls. Imagine this man in his quaint studio, with his quiet voice and manner, his sensitive features and smooth, delicate face. He seems less pompous, less businesslike, than the many technicians, carpenters and electricians going about their work. "Morning, Charlie", mutters a property man as he passes.

'"Good morning, Bill", he quietly, scarcely audibly answers.

'For to each employee his leader is "Charlie", and is always so addressed. Yet, although there exists this genial familiarity, never does "Charlie" lose his workers' respect, nor he their confidence. A state of trust and perfect understanding, built on a bed-rock of life-long acquaintance is the dominant feature of Chaplin and his "colleagues" at work. But Chaplin's merest murmur is invariably and irrevocably law. If something goes wrong, or someone is to blame, Chaplin, though determined, is far too sensitive to create a public showdown. As tactfully as possible he explains his case, and if more persuasion is necessary, that takes place behind closed doors.

Virginia Cherrill with Chaplin on the set of *City Lights* (1931)

Following page: The two drunks encounter the rich man's butler in *City Lights* (1931)

141

'But he is so much the leader, carrying every little responsibility on his own shoulders, supervising every minute detail of work, that there is really little to go wrong.

'He impresses you with his own tremendous sincerity in what he is doing, and makes you feel that he is placing so much faith in you, that you are virtually driven to unusual emotional limits to do your best. Yet, in spite of this, his individual method of working makes it often very hard to understand what he wants. He works from no script, according to no plan, and to no time limit. He is the completely emotional film creator. When he made *City Lights* we had no scenario to work from. I had little knowledge of the story, and no previous experience as an actress either on or off the screen. "But that is exactly why I chose you," said Chaplin to me, "I do not want you to know a lot of things you'd have to unlearn!" So from first principles he made me into the Blind Girl of *City Lights*. He moulded me into a character which only he understood, or saw clearly in his own mind. Patient in the extreme, he would shoot and reshoot scenes day after day, to get the effect just right – the perfect timing, the correct expression. Sometimes his apparently unreasonable persistence on some minute detail which I scarcely understood made me bad tempered and angry. Yet even then it was hard not to reciprocate that gentle kindness and patience he so generously bestowed upon his work.

'For two years, broken occasionally by wet weather (for we made most of the film out of doors) and tennis matches, and other little occupations which caught Charlie's fleeting fancy, we made *City Lights*. Two years is a long time for the actual production of a film. But we were not making a film; we were making a Chaplin film; and there is all the world of difference between the two operations. The regular staff always came to the studio at the same time in the morning, and went out at night, if Charlie did not turn up they played cards, or other things. Once he was away so long that I gave up going to the studio and waited at home until I was called.

'My engagement as his leading lady was strictly a business proposition. I seldom mixed with him or his friends socially. With his real friends he is very intimate. But they are a select few, and almost never find additions. In the studio one never knows what Chaplin is going to do. If he drives up in the morning, huddled and bent up in the car then one can be certain things will not go too well in the day. Generally his gait is quick-stepping and sprightly. That is the sign for a good day's work ahead. He never asks anybody's opinion about anything. About the only regular thing is the seeing of the rushes of the previous day's shots each morning. And when that's over the day's work commences.

'Perhaps his emotional state can be best illustrated by the food he eats. One week he solemnly informs us that he is a vegetarian, that meat is bad for one, and that lettuce and fruit form the ideal food. We all become vegetarian. The next week, he looks up and says: "What I need is a nice big juicy steak. Good meat to build up the body and brain." The following week it becomes cantaloupe filled with ice-cream. "Everybody is eating too much," he says. "One can work much better on light lunches." His favourite dish I remember to be banana nut ice-cream.

'When we made *City Lights* the critics cried, "Chaplin is out of date. His film is silent. It will flop." Yet its release showed that Chaplin, the tragedian, meant as much to the cinema public as ever.

'Chaplin has a fine, soft and mellow speaking voice. Yet I think he is absolutely right in refusing to talk on the screen. The first sound he utters would destroy that grand illusion which he has created.

'His art, furthermore, is international. While he speaks in no tongue it remains international.'

Chaplin with Harry Myers in *City Lights* (1931)

Groucho Marx
HARD
TIMES WITH CHARLIE

FOLLOWING THE launch of *City Lights*, Charlie took a world trip to relax and then began work on a new picture in which he planned to present his ideas on another aspect of the world. The film was called *Modern Times* and its release in 1936 was once again greeted by all the publicity and ballyhoo generated by any new Chaplin movie. The film's portrait of a highly mechanised society and its effect on human beings was both savage and hilarious. It's message was not lost on either cinema audiences or the media – though some sections, as we shall see, took its viewpoint to extreme lengths. When the film opened, a bright young American reporter named Grace Simpson on *Photoplay Magazine* discovered that another of Hollywood's great screen comedians, Groucho Marx, claimed to have known Charlie when both were struggling young comics on the bitterly cold Canadian theatre circuit in the winter of 1911. She went to talk to the ebullient Groucho and came away with an extraordinary story by the 'Maddest Marx' of how he had first 'discovered' Charlie's genius when the young English comedian was on tour with Fred Karno's company.

Groucho Marx

146

'CHARLIE CHAPLIN's latest picture, *Modern Times* strikes a new note in screen humour. Its theme concerns the career of a little tramp caught in the mechanism of factory routine. It's a real treat!

'The country is becoming Chaplin conscious all over again. It's remarkable how Chaplin has lasted, as an actor, all these years. You know him as he is today, but did you know him as he was yesterday? Let us draw aside the curtain of the past and see him as he really was "yesterday", struggling along as best he could, trying desperately to get a foothold on the ladder of success. Let's turn back the clock of time.

'It was snowing in Winnipeg, Canada. In a dusty corner of the depot, a tattered vaudeville troupe huddled around a glowing stove. One hour till train time. And then back on the road. That was the routine.

'With a chilly gust and a flurry of snowflakes, the door rattled on its hinges. The trained animal act shivered. A lifting of eyebrows censored the invader from a frigid world without. The newcomer Groucho Marx, slammed the door shut, stamped his feet, then smiled around at the crowd. Despite the ill protection afforded by a threadbare overcoat, he felt very little cold. Excitement warmed him.

'He flexed the bamboo cane in his hand. A bit of soot from the chimney sufficed for a moustache. He rumpled his hair. He spread his feet fan-wise. Then, with the strange shuffling walk that was later to make millions all over the earth laugh, he put on a hasty little act.

'But no one laughed. As a matter of fact, no one paid any attention. This peeved him a little. "Look," he cried suddenly, "I just saw the greatest fellow I've ever seen on the stage in all my born days!" But who cared what a little known comedian like Groucho Marx thought about actors – or thought about anybody for that matter.

'And who ever heard about the comic that he was talking about. That strange, wistful creature who always wore a big, black, flowing necktie, because his shirt was often dirty, and he only had one.

'His name? Oh, yes, Charlie Chaplin!

'"They evidently thought I was crazy," said Groucho, recently, smiling. "I said then he was the greatest fellow on the stage. I know now there will never be anyone like him. He's in a class all by himself, just as he has always been."

'It's usually pleasant to visit at Groucho's big house, especially if brothers Harpo and Chico are there. You come away with your sides actually strained from laughter! It's a tonic, nothing less.

'But this particular evening was somehow quite different. The lights were very low. A fire crackled cheerily in the hearth. Groucho watched the flickering shadows on the knotty pine walls and spanned unnumbered years to introduce the comedian with the threadbare overcoat. And the comic with the dirty shirt.

'The fire lost its warmth. I shivered, too. Then I heard Groucho's voice breaking the silence, speaking about the first Chaplin show that he'd seen.

'"I was on the Pantages Circuit, the last act on the bill, doing four shows a day, rain or shine," be began. "There was a three-hour lay-over in Winnipeg before jumping to the Coast. As a rule, I made a bee-line for the pool room. It was generally warmer. This particular night, I was feeling rather blue and, besides, I had a headache. I decided on the spur of the moment to take in a show. I had a friend playing on the Sullivan-Considine Circuit. Considine was the father of the present Metro-Goldwyn-Mayer producer, John W. Considine, Jr.

'"Well, sir, at this show, the audience was roaring with laughter. I looked at the stage and saw Chaplin for the first time. I had never heard people laugh quite like that. I began to laugh, too. Soon my polite laughter had turned to an impolite howl! The little comic's act was called 'A Night at the Club'; it was supposed to be an English social club – and what a one, too, I might add! Chaplin sat at a small table and ate soda crackers, one after another. A woman up front was singing all the while, but nobody heard a single note, I'm sure. They were too intent on Chaplin's every move. A fine stream of cracker dust was slowly

147

coming out of his mouth. He kept that up for exactly fifteen minutes.

'"At the table was a large basket of oranges. Finally, he started to pick up the oranges, one by one, and threw them right at the woman. One of them knocked the pianist off his chair. People became hysterical. There never was such continuous laughter. He was the same Chaplin then that he is now." Groucho concluded simply.

'Groucho sought Chaplin out that night. He told him how impressed he was – how the act had him right out of his seat in stitches. They became friends. The two circuits made the same towns.

'Finally, the two actors landed in Los Angeles, land of hopes and dreams.

'"One day, shortly afterwards, Chaplin called me up," continued Groucho. "He had been offered $100 a week to go with Keystone. 'What's the matter,' I said, 'isn't it enough?' Chaplin was then getting about $35 a week. 'You're durned right it's enough,' he replied with a chuckle. 'It's much too much, in fact. I can't be worth $100 a week. I've got it all figured out that these studio guys must be crazy and who wants to work for a bunch of loonies?'

'"O shucks, go ahead and take it!" I told him. "You'll never get another offer as good as that!" How wrong I was! Well, Charlie, finally accepted the motion picture offer. And, shortly thereafter, I had to go East. A couple of years later, Chaplin began to appear with the famed Keystone cops. When I returned to Los Angeles, he was getting $500 a week, I was amazed. He was amazed, too, but seemed remarkably happy.

'"Five years elapsed before I saw him again. I gave him a call and he invited me to his new home. It was gorgeous, magnificent. A stately English butler served. The plates were solid gold!

'"It's an amazing world. When I first met Charlie Chaplin, we often borrowed nickels and dimes from one another. We regularly shot craps together. And the stakes were a penny and the fellow who won as much as fifty cents was considered quite a financier. The loser of such a snug little sum tightened his belt for breakfast. It's a little frightening the way those years, that seem but yesterday, have passed," Groucho added.

'It was only a short time ago that diners in a swank Hollywood cafe enjoyed an unexpected treat. The greatest comic genius of the silent films found himself sitting, back to back, with the equally famous and popular comedian of the screen – the maddest Marx of them all.

'"There we were," said Groucho of Chaplin and himself, "two comedians talking, completely terrified about life and our careers! You would think," he added thoughtfully, "that by this time Charlie would be more or less convinced that he had remarkable talent. But *no!* He was just as frightened as he had been when he first came to me and asked my advice."

'Groucho, with his brothers, Chico and Harpo, recently scored a great screen triumph in the Marx Brothers comedy, *A Night at the Opera* and Chaplin recently released his long-awaited *Modern Times*.

'What a contrast – the life of both of them today and yesterday. And what a commentary on life – the happy-go-lucky comedian with the threadbare overcoat; and the serious-faced little comic with the dirty shirt.'

Serge Eiseinstein
CHAPLIN'S VISION

TWO SIGNIFICANT events occurred with the appearance of *Modern Times*. One, the picture was to prove the last appearance of Charlie the Little Tramp and, secondly, it was to subject Charlie for the first time to accusations that he was a communist sympathiser. Such attacks had already been levelled at a number of Hollywood personalities who had voiced a liberal attitude towards people of other political persuasions – the Russians in particular. Chaplin has commented on this period in his life in his autobiography: 'Before the opening of *Modern Times*, a few columnists wrote that they had heard rumours the picture was communistic. I suppose this was because of a summary of the story that had already appeared in the press. However, the liberal reviewers wrote that it was neither for nor against communism and that metaphorically I had sat on the fence.' In hindsight, it is surprising that any such opinion should have been aired, particularly as in Russia the picture was badly received. (Chaplin himself, though, had been held in high esteem there for years.) One Russian did not share this view – the great director, Serge Eiseinstein, creator of the unforgettable *Ivan the Terrible*. In this article written in 1946 he describes in a far more perceptive way than most of his contemporaries just what Chaplin's vision really was.

'*THE KID*. The name of this most popular of Chaplin's films is fully worthy to stand side by side with his own name: It helps to reveal his character role just as the prefixes: "The Conquerer", "The Lion Heart", or the "Terrible" themselves determine the inner aspect of William who conquered the Islands of Great Britain, of the legendary courageous Richard of the Crusades or the wise Moscovite Tsar Ivan Vasilievitch the Fourth.

'Not Direction. Not Method. Not Tricks. Not the Comic Technique. None of these things move me. I do not wish to delve into these things.

'In thinking about Chaplin, one wants above all to delve into that strange structure of thought which sees Phenomena in such a strange fashion and replies to it with images of equal strangeness. And within that struggle – to see that part which exists as a stage of perception of the outside world, before it becomes a conception of the world.

'In short, we shall not concern ourselves with Chaplin's world outlook (Weltanaschauung) but with his life-perception which gives birth to the inimitable and unrepeatable conceptions of the so-called Chaplin humour.

'The fields of vision of a rabbit's eyes overlap behind the back of its head. He sees behind him. Condemned to run away, rather than to track down, he doesn't complain about that. But these fields of vision do not overlap each other in front. In front of a rabbit is a piece of space it does not see. And a rabbit running forward may bump into an opposing obstacle.

'The rabbit sees the world in another fashion than we.

'A different kind of vision produces accordingly a different kind of picture-image.

'Not to speak of the higher transformation of *vision* into a *look* and then to a *point of view* that takes place the moment we rise from the rabbit to Man, with all his surrounding social factors. Till finally all this is synthesized into a world outlook, a philosophy of life.

'How the eyes are placed – in the given instance the eyes of thought.

'How those eyes see.

'Unusual eyes.

'The eyes of Chaplin.

'Eyes, able to see Dante's Inferno or Goya's Capriccio theme of *Modern Times* in the forms of careless merriment?

'With what eyes does Charlie Chaplin look on life?

Following page: One of the most famous shots in all of Chaplin's films – the finale to *Modern Times* (1936)

'The Secret of his Eyes is undoubtedly revealed in *Modern Times*. As long as he was concerned with the pleiad of the most beautiful of his comedies, of the clash of good and evil, of big and little, his eyes as if accidentally and simultaneously lighting on the poor and the rich – laughed and cried in unison with his theme. But they apparently went contrary to their own theme when in the most modern times of American depression the good and evil "Uncles" turned out to be the real representives of uncompromising social groups, at which the eyes of Chaplin first blinked, then narrowed, but continued obstinately to look at modern times and phenomena in the old way. This led to a break in the style of things. In thematic treatment – to the monstrous and distorted.

'In the inner aspect of Chaplin himself – to a complete revelation of the secret of his eyes.

'In the following deliberation I do not at all wish to say that Chaplin is indifferent to what is happening around him or that Chaplin does not understand it (even maybe partly).

'I am not interested in *what* he understands.

'I am interested in how he perceives. How he looks and sees, when he is lost "in inspiration". When he comes across a series of images of phenomena, which he is laughing at, and when laughter at what he perceives is re-moulded into the forms of comic situations and tricks: and with what eyes one must look at the world, in order to see it as Chaplin see it.

'*A group of delightful Chinese children are laughing.*

'*One shot. Another. Close up. Mid shot. Again close up.*

'*What are they laughing at?*

'*Apparently at a scene taking place in the depths of the room.*

'*What is taking place there?*

'*A man sinks back on a bed. He is apparently drunk.*

'*And a tiny woman – a Chinese slaps him on the face furiously.*

'*The children are overcome with uncontrollable laughter.*

'*Although the man is their father. And the little Chinawoman their mother. And the big man is not*

'*drunk. And it is not for drunkenness the little wife is hitting him on the face.*

'*The man is dead ...*

'*And she is slapping the deceased on the face precisely because he died and left to a hungry death her and the two little children, who laugh so ringingly.*

'That of course, is not from one of Chaplin's films. These are passing strokes from that wonderful novel of Andre Malraux *The Condition of Human Existence*.

'In thinking of Chaplin, I always see him in the image of that merrily laughing little Chinese, seeing how comically the hand-slaps of the little woman make the head of the big man wobble from side to side. It is not important that the Chinese woman is the mother. That the man is the father. And it is not at all important that in general he is dead.

'In that is the secret of Chaplin.

'In that is the secret of his eyes.

'In that is his inimitability.

'In that is his greatness.

'*To see things most terrible, most pitiful, most tragic through the eyes of a laughing child.*

'To see images of these things spontaneously and suddenly – outside their moral-ethical significance outside valuation and outside judgment and condemnation – to see them as a child sees them through a burst of laughter.

'In that Chaplin is outstanding, inimitable and unique.

'The sudden immediacy of his look gives birth to a comic perception. This perception becomes transformed into a conception. Conceptions are of three kinds:

'*A phenomenon genuinely inoffensive.* And Chaplin's perception clothes it with his inimitable Chaplinesque buffoonery.

'*A phenomenon personally dramatic.* And Chaplin's perception gives birth to the humorous melodrama of the finest images of his individual style – the fusion of laughter with tears.

'The blind girl will call forth a smile when, without noticing it, she throws water over Charlie.

'The girl with her sight restored might appear melodramatic when in touching him with her hand she does not fully realize that before her is the one who loves her and gave her back her

The great Russian film director, Serge Eiseinstein

sight. And then within that very incident the melodrama may be comically stood on its head – the blind girl repeats the episodes with the "Bon-vivant", saved by Charlie from suicide: in which the "Bon-vivant" only recognises his saviour and friend when he is "blind"-drunk.

'Finally, *socially-tragic phenomena* – no longer a childish amusement, not a problem for a mind, not a child's plaything – the comical – childish vision gives birth to a series of terrible shots in *Modern Times*.

'The ability to *see as a child* is inimitable, irrepeatable, inherent in Chaplin personally. Only Chaplin sees this way. What astounds is this very quality of Chaplin's sight to see piercingly and immutably through all the workings of professional cunning.

'Always and in everything: From the trifle *A Night at the Show* to the tragedy of contemporary society in *Modern Times*.

'To see the world thus and have the courage to show it thus on the screen is the attribute of Genius alone.

'Incidentally, he doesn't even need courage.

'For that is the way, and the only way, he sees.

'We are grown-ups, and maybe have lost the ability to laugh at the comic without taking into consideration, its tragic significance and content.

'We are grown-ups, who have lost the time of "lawless" childhood, when there were as yet no ethics, morals, higher critical values, etc., etc., etc.

'Chaplin plays up to actuality itself.

'It is the bloody idiocy of war in the film *Shoulder Arms*. The modern era of the most modern times in *Modern Times*. Chaplin's partner is by no means the big, terrible, powerful and ruthless fat man who, when not filming, runs a restaurant in Hollywood.

'Chaplin's partner, throughout his repertoire is another. Still bigger, still more terrible, powerful and ruthless. Chaplin and actuality itself, partners together, a pair in harness, play before us an endless string of circus acts. Actuality is like a serious "white" clown.

'He seems clever and logical. Observant and foresighted. But it is he finally who remains the fool and is laughed at. His simple,

child-like partner Charlie comes out on top. Laughing carelessly, without being aware that his laughter kills his partner.

'Chaplin works "in a pair" with actuality. And that which a satirist is obliged to introduce into the given production by means of two shots, the comedian Chaplin does in one shot. He laughs spontaneously. Satiric indirectness is created by a "mix" of the grimaces of Chaplin back on to the conditions which gave birth to them.

'"You remember the scene in *The Kid* where I scatter food from a box to poor children as if they were chickens?"

'This conversation takes place on board Chaplin's yacht. We have been his guest for three days on the waters near Catarina Island, surrounded by sea-lions, flying fish and undersea gardens, which we look at through the glass bottoms of special little boats.

'"You see I did that because I despise them. I don't like children".

'The creator of *The Kid*, which five-sixths of the world cried over, because of the fate of an orphan child, does not like children. He is a "Beast"!

'But who *normally* does not like children?

'Only children themselves.

'Six months later, on the day I was leaving Mexico, Chaplin showed me the rough cutting copy, as yet without sound, of *City Lights*.

'I sit on Chaplin's own black oilcloth chair. Charlie himself is busy: At the piano, with his lips he fills in the missing sound of editing of the picture. Charlie (in the film) saves the life of a drunken bourgeoise who tries to drown himself. The saved only recognizes his saviour when he is drunk.

'Funny? – tragic.

'That is Saltykov-Schedrin.* That is Dostoyevsky.

'The big one beats the little one. He is beaten up.

'At first – man by man. Then more – man by society.

'Once, long ago, there was a widely popular photograph either in the London *Sketch* or the *Graphic*.

'"Stop for his Highness the Child!" Was the title under it.

156

---

* Michael Saltykov, who wrote under the name of Schedrin, a writer of genius, and one of the world's greatest satirists.

'The photograph depicted an impetuous flood of street traffic, in Bond Street, Strand or Piccadilly Circus, suddenly freezing at the wave of a "Bobby's" hand.

'Across the street goes a child, and the flood of traffic humbly waits, until his Highness the Baby crosses from pavement to pavement.

'"Stop for His Highness the Child!" one wants to shout to oneself, when attempting to approach Chaplin from a social-ethical and moral position in the widest and deepest sense of these words.

"Stop".

'Let's take His Highness as he is!'

Anonymous
HITLER AND CHAPLIN:
THE STORY OF TWO BIRTHDAYS

IN THE YEARS which immediately followed *Modern Times*, Chaplin ignored as best he could the attacks on his sympathies and turned his attention to what he believed to be a much more sinister threat to mankind – Nazi Germany. He was fascinated by the character of Adolf Hitler, whom he saw as a figure at once monstrous and ludicrous: an ideal subject, in fact, for a film. So *The Great Dictator* (initally called just *The Dictator*) began to take shape. 'A Hitler story was an ideal opportunity for burlesque and pantomime,' he wrote later. When news of this picture reached the ears of the press, an anonymous writer in the English magazine, *The Spectator* discovered some remarkable parallels between the film maker Chaplin and the dictator Hitler, and discussed them in the following intriguing article published on 21 April 1939.

'PROVIDENCE WAS in an ironical mood when, fifty years ago this week, it was ordained that Charles Chaplin and Adolf Hitler should make their entry into the world within four days of each other. For most men today the results, in one case, are too alarming for the jest to retain its flavour; but Mr Chaplin at least has appreciated it. Accounts of his new film, *The Dictator*, indicate that he will take the part of a tramp who is mistaken for a Führer – any Führer, is identifiable at will. Hitler's personality today is too intimidating for his prestige to be dissolved by Chaplin's satire, but it would be another proof of the comedian's genius if, by doubling the parts of the clown and the dictator, he recognized that they are but varying manifestations of the same forces. For Chaplin and Hitler, however different their careers and their reputations, have this in common: their success is founded on their understanding of the "little man" of the lower middle class who is perhaps the most

typical product of the fifty years through which both men have lived.

'Each in his own way has expressed the ideas, sentiments, aspirations of the millions of struggling citizens ground between the upper and the lower millstone of society; the date of their birth and the identical little moustache (grotesque intentionally in Mr Chaplin) they wear might have been fixed by nature to betray the common origin of their genius. For genius each of them undeniably possesses. Each has mirrored the same reality – the predicament of the "little man" in modern society. Each is a distorting mirror, the one for good, the other for untold evil. In Chaplin the little man is a clown, timid, incompetent, infinitely resourceful yet bewildered by a world that has no place for him. The apple he bites has a worm in it; his trousers, remnants of gentility, trip him up; his cane pretends to a dignity his position is far from justifying; when he pulls a lever it is the wrong one and disaster follows. He is a heroic figure, but heroic only in the patience and resource with which he receives the blows that fall upon his bowler. In his actions and loves he emulates the angels. But in Herr Hitler the angel has become a devil. The soleless boots have become *Reitstiefeln*; the shapeless trousers, riding breeches; the cane, a riding crop; the bowler, a forage cap. The tramp has become a Storm Trooper; only the moustache is the same.

'Yet both exhibit the anarchism which is their deepest instinct. Two years before their birth, in 1887, Nietzsche wrote: "I describe what is to come, what cannot be otherwise – the rise of Nihilism." The fifty years that followed have fulfilled his prophecy, and most clearly in the work of these two men. For laws, regulations, conventions, rules, the Chaplin of the films has never known respect or regard. To steal a sandwich behind the policeman's back is as instinctive in him as in a child. In the factory, if the foreman's eye is turned, he

WHO IS THIS MAN ?

(WHO LOOKS LIKE CHARLIE CHAPLIN)

Words and Music
by
JOHN WATT and
MAX KESTER.

FEATURED, BROADCAST & RECORDED BY
TOMMY HANDLEY

33, SOHO SQUARE. W.1.

6 D.

seizes the chance of a few moments' dignified leisure and throws the vast machine out of gear. He has no home, no family, no job, except when starvation or pity for some other waif compels him to it. In him anarchism is a claim to human dignity and a resistance to the demand of an infinitely complicated society. In Adolf Hitler, it assumes new and terrible forms. When Charlie throws the machine out of order it is through ignorance, or idleness, or distraction; Hitler deliberately wrecks it. Incompetence becomes a fury of destruction, timidity is converted into truculence, ignorance into mysticism and megalomania. The discipline he has imposed on his people cannot conceal the chaos he has created. In part, it is the means by which anarchy is turned into a weapon against the outside world; in part it is the measure of the violence which is necessary to hold people together after every religious, moral, social and political tie has been destroyed. It was Nietzsche again who predicted, half a century ago, that the modern Nihilist would substitute for the social and cultural ties he destroyed the bare, empty, dogmatic, mystical conception of *das Vaterland*; Hitler has fulfilled the prediction to the letter.

'How is this appalling metamorphosis of the engaging clown into the nightmare figure of the Führer to be explained? The answer can only be found in the changes of the last twenty years. Chaplin's genius, and his puppet, were formed in the years before the war, when society was still firmly based, when the "little man" was assured of some degree of security and prosperity, when he had no thought, no means, and no need of revolt to solve his troubles. But Hitler's little man is post-War, when society was profoundly weakened, when he had endured the War, the inflation, the slump and the years on the bread-line. Chaplin has often shown, for a few moments, the kind of paradise his clown desires – a girl, a hamburger, and four walls, however shaky. It is part of his truthfulness that such moments are always transitory. While they last, he is in heaven; when they are over he shrugs his shoulders, kicks his heels and shuffles jauntily away. Hitler's world was one in which even the hope of such heaven was denied to Germany's millions, and in the end they did not shrug their shoulders; they acquiesced in the fanaticism of their leader, and were ready to torture, murder, persecute, destroy and, if necessary, pull the whole world down in ruins about their heads.

'Thus it is inevitable that men should love Chaplin and hate Hitler. The first still allows them to laugh at their universal predicament, and to see the human condition as a pantomime. And since the comedy is always illuminated by its author's affection, pity and sympathy for his fellow-men, his sometimes intrusive curiosity about their affairs, it is a comedy that inspires hope as well as laughter. For this hope and laughter millions of men and women – white, yellow and black – unite in the tributes and admiration that have greeted him from every quarter of the globe. Hitler's genius, the genius of destruction, is the antithesis of Chaplin's. Germany will pay him honour, part obligatory, part sincere. In the world outside, many as are the millions who bless Chaplin, and bless him rightly, for the wholesome gift of laughter, more millions still, and with even greater justice, execrate the name of the man whose ungoverned ambitions, prostituting right to might, have cast over their lives the chill shadow of fear and impoverishment and bitterness and hate. Even Herr Hitler's power has its limits. It has failed to poison the minds of millions of decent Germans who loathe persecution and hate war as much as any lover of Chaplin's films. But in robbing these of their freedom he has robbed them of their power to veto a policy whose aim is acquisition and whose inevitable end is war. Outside Germany, and in part inside, that reflection must dominate all others which the Führer's birthday exercises inspire.'

Charlie Chaplin
I DECLARE WAR ON HOLLYWOOD

WHEN *The Great Dictator* was released in October 1940, it was greeted with much enthusiasm, particularly in war-torn Britain where one critic called it a masterpiece. Chaplin was naturally delighted at this reception, and also intrigued by a story that Hitler himself had managed to obtain a copy and watched it more than once! Frustratingly, the little star had no way of finding out what the German Führer thought of it! Unfortunately, too, despite the emphatic statement that Chaplin thought he had made about his beliefs through the film, the rumours that he was a communist continued to rumble on through the war years – fuelled, no doubt, by him calling an audience 'comrades' at a Russian War Relief Rally he addressed in 1942.

Despite such personal problems, he also met and fell in love with Oona O'Neill, the teenage daughter of the American writer, Eugene O'Neill. Although there was a considerable difference in their ages, the couple married in June 1943 and, as it transpired, Charlie had at last found the love of his life. Around him the sniping continued, rising to a crescendo when his next picture, *Monsieur Verdoux* appeared in 1947. Although ostensibly about a French 'Bluebeard', the film was more an outcry about the suffering brought on by economic depression and by wars. As Charlie's son was to write later, 'The film served as an outlet . . . for the destructive grief my father had always felt in the presence of the dark undercurrents of the human psyche. It was as though he hoped, with burlesque, to lighten the grimness inherent in life and to project it outside himself.' Certainly, the release of the picture also caused him to exorcise the deep-seated feelings of anger that had been building up inside him about America, and Hollywood in particular. For on 7 December 1947, he brought the whole issue to a head in the following article which appeared in the British newspaper, *Reynolds News*.

'I HAVE MADE UP my mind to declare war, once and for all, on Hollywood and its inhabitants.

'I do not like grumbling – it seems to me to be conceited and futile – but since I have no longer any confidence in Hollywood in general or in the American cinema in particular, I am determined to say so.

'You know of the reception that was given in certain American picture-houses, and more especially in New York, to my latest film, *Monsieur Verdoux*. You know that a few cranks began calling me "communist" and "anti-American".

'That was simply because I cannot and will not think like everybody else; it was because the "big noises" of Hollywood still think they can get away with anything. But soon they will lose their illusions, and begin to perceive certain realities.

'That is what I say: I, Charlie Chaplin, declare that Hollywood is dying. It is no longer concerned with film-making – which is supposed to be an art – but solely with turning out miles of celluloid.

'I may add that it is impossible for anyone to make a success in the art of the cinema if he refuses to conform with the rest, if he shows himself to be an "adventurer" who dares to defy the warnings of cinematographic big business.

'Do not suppose that I am trying to plead my own cause. Let us consider, for instance, the case of Orson Welles. I certainly do not see eye to eye with him on every point concerning the art of the cinema. But he ventured to say *No* to the big business men. And now he is done for in Hollywood.

'Above all, do not imagine that I am a revolutionary – an incendiary, as a Boston journalist put it. But it appears that I have committed a crime. I have repeatedly stated that in my opinion, patriotism has no frontiers. That is as true in regard to the cinema as

Following page: Adenoid Hynkel, alias Charlie, and some of his stormtroopers in *The Great Dictator* (1940)

in regard to politics.

'People often try to catch me out in an argument by saying: "Is it because you remember you were born in England that you talk like that?"

'What idiocy! I am a bit of a philosopher in my own way, and this means that I find a lot to blame in England, as well as in the United States and in the Soviet Union.

'*But, for pity's sake, let us stop mixing up art with the shady political intrigues which go on all over the world!*

'Hollywood is now fighting its last battle, and it will lose that battle unless it decides once and for all, to give up standardizing its films – unless it realizes that masterpieces cannot be mass-produced in the cinema, like tractors in a factory.

'I think, objectively, that it is time to take a new road – so that money shall no longer be the all-powerful god of a decaying community.

'Before long, I shall perhaps leave the United States, although it has given me so many moral and material satisfactions. And in the land where I go to end my days, I shall try to remember that I am a man like other men, and that consequently I have a right to the same respect as other men.'

Another moment from Chaplin's great burlesque of Hitler and Nazi Germany, *The Great Dictator* (1940)

Jean Renoir
CHAPLIN AMONG THE IMMORTALS

THE LAST LINES OF Charlie's article were to prove very prophetic, although in the immediate aftermath of charge and counter-charge between the film star and his critics the only – perhaps inevitable – outcome, was that *Monsieur Verdoux* proved a failure at the box office. Indeed, as a direct result of the controversy surrounding Chaplin the film was actually banned in some states of America, and where it was shown the public were either baffled by the picture or disappointed because Chaplin was playing a role so far removed from those with which he was usually associated. Charlie was not, though, without his defenders, prominent among whom was the French writer and film director, Jean Renoir, who had known the actor for years. The son of the famous painter, Pierre Renoir, he did not reply to the attacks with a paean of admiration, but rather with a carefully measured look at the entrenched attitudes of both sides. Renoir's article, from the *Screen Writer* of July 1947 is an oasis of commonsense among the plethora of ill-chosen and often hasty words that were bandied about in newspapers, magazines and all manner of publications at this time.

'LAST NIGHT, I HAD a strange dream. I was sitting at my dining room table carving a leg-of-mutton. I went at it in the French manner, which is to slice it in length. In that way, you get a great variety of cuts. Those who like it well done are served first. You wait till you get closer to the bone, for those who prefer it rarer. My guests had been lost in a sort of fog, but as I asked each one how he liked his meat, they suddenly came into a very sharp focus, and I recognized them as people I admire and like. The couples of *The Best Years of Our Lives* were right there at my table, smiling amiably at me. I served them, and they ate with evident appetite. Next to them were the priest and the

168

The great French director, Jean Renoir

pregnant woman of *Open City*, a bit more reserved but no less cordial. At the end of the table, the loving pair of *Brief Encounter* were holding hands. This abandon was proof that they felt themselves among friends, and I was gratified by it. As I was about to proceed to the beautiful courtesan of *Children of Paradise*, the door-bell rang.

'I went to open the door and found myself facing a gentleman of distinguished appearance. Off-hand, he reminded me vaguely of someone I knew well, a little old tramp who had made the whole world laugh. But I quickly understood that the resemblance was merely physical. Even under the rich fur coat of a gold-mine owner, the other one had remained a bit of a gutter-snipe. It was obvious that he would never completely get rid of his lowdown ways. Whereas this one, on the other hand, was most certainly the scion of a "good family". His parents had taught him proper table manners, and when and how to kiss a lady's hand. He had breeding. And all of his person gave off that impression of suppressed passions, of hidden secrets, which is the earmark of the bourgeoisie in our old Western civilizations.

'I introduced myself. With exquisite politeness which bespoke his old provincial background and his prep-school education, he told me his name was Verdoux. Then he placed his hat and cane on a chair, flicked a speck of dust from his jacket, adjusted his cuffs, and headed for the dining room. Immediately, the others edged closer together to make room for him. They seemed happy to see him. Obviously, they were all members of the same social world.

'After dinner, we went outdoors. But word of the presence of my famous guests had spread, and the street was crowded with people. When we walked down the porch steps, the public enthusiasm burst out. Everyone wanted to shake their hands, there was a terrific crush, the autograph-seekers were at work. Suddenly, a very dry lady, wearing an aggressive little hat, recognized Monsieur Verdoux and pointed a finger at him. And, strangely, the enthusiasm turned into fury. They rushed at him, raising their fists. I tried

to understand, and kept asking the same question over and over again: "What did he do? What did he do? . . ." But I could not hear the answers, for everyone was speaking at once and the caning the poor man was taking made a deafening racket. So deafening, in fact, that I awoke with a start and had to close my window, which a sudden storm wind was violently banging back and forth.

'I don't believe that the people who attacked Chaplin so sharply over his latest film did so for personal or political reasons. In America we haven't yet reached that stage. I think rather that the trouble is their panic terror before total change, before a particularly long step forward in the evolution of an artist.

'This is not the first time such a thing has happened, nor will it be the last. Molière was a victim of the same kind of misunderstanding. And the Hollywood commentators who have been unable to recognize the qualities of *Monsieur Verdoux* are in very good company, indeed, Molière's detractors had names no less important than La Bruyère, Fénelon, Vauvenargues, Sherer. They said he wrote badly. They criticized him for his barbarism, his jargon, his artificial phrasing, his improper usesage, his incorrect wording, his mountains of metaphors, his boring repetitions, his inorganic style. "Molière," said Sherer, "is as bad a writer as one can be."

'This animosity on the part of certain self-appointed intellectuals is not the only point of resemblance between the careers of Molère and Chaplin.

'In his early stages, the former achieved great success by simply following the traditions of the Italian Comedy. His characters bore the familiar names and costumes, their predicaments were those to which the public was accustomed. Only, beneath Sganarelle's make-up and behind Scapin's somersaults, the author injected a rarer element, a little human truth. But on the surface, there was not too much of an apparent change. When the action slowed down, a solid laying-on with a stick was always good for a laugh. The sentimental side was taken care of with formulae no different, except for the author's masterful

Previous page: Charlie in his 'straight' role as the French mass-murderer in *Monsieur Verdoux* (1947)

touch, from those used elsewhere in the same period: a noble young gentleman falls in love with a scullerymaid and his family will have none of her. But, in the end, it all works out. It is revealed that the ingénue was really a well-born maiden who, as a baby, had been carried off by pirates.

'Chaplin, to begin with, simply followed the traditions of the then most popular form in the world, English farce. His feet foul him up on the stairs and his hands get entangled in flypaper. The sentimental side in his films is represented by babies left on doorsteps, street-girls mistreated by life, or other carryovers from the good old mellers. In spite of that, he never falls into the worst vulgarity of our time, phony, bathetic goodness. And beneath his character's flour-face, as well as behind the fake beards of his companions, we rapidly discern real men of flesh and blood. As he grows, like Molière, he introduces into the conventional framework, which he has made his very own through the vigour of his talent, the elements of a sharper and sharper observation of humanity, of a more and more bitter social satire. Nevertheless, since the appearances remain the same, no one is shocked, no one protests.

'One day, Molière decided to give up the form which had brought him his success, and he wrote *The School for Wives*. Accusations were heaped upon him. He was called a mountebank. People became irritated with him because he was director, actor and writer all at the same time.

'One day, Chaplin wrote *Monsieur Verdoux*. He turned his back on the outward forms to which he had accustomed his public. There was a great hue and cry of indignation, he was dragged through the mud.

'After *The School for Wives*, instead of giving in, Molière went on hitting harder and harder. His next play was *Tartuffe*, which impaled phony religion and bigotry.

'What will Chaplin's next film be?'

'I think it is unnecessary to explain why I like the Chaplin of the old school, since everyone seems to share that taste. It is even probable that some of the attackers of his present film must have written glowing tributes to *The Gold Rush* or *The Kid*. I would like, however, to present a few of the reasons which, to me, made the showing of *Monsieur Verdoux* a pure delight.

'Like everybody else, I have my own ideas about what is conventionally called Art. I firmly believe that since the end of the period in which the great cathedrals were built, since the all-pervading faith which was to bring forth our modern world is no longer present to give artists the strength to lose themselves in an immense paean to the glory of God, there can be quality to human expression only if it is individual. Even in cases of collaboration, the work is valuable only insofar as the personality of each of the authors remains perceptible to the audience. Now, in this film, that presence is, to me, as clear as that of a painter in his canvas or of a composer in his symphony.

'Moreover, every man matures, his knowledge of life increases, and his creations must develop at the same time he does. If we do not admit these truths in our professions, we might as well admit right now that it is an industry no different than the rest, and that we make films like efficiency experts supervise the production of iceboxes or shaving cream. And let's stop priding ourselves on being artists, and claiming that we're carrying forward the grand old traditions.

'It is agreed, some will say, that Chaplin has created a highly personal work, and we admit that he has undergone a natural artistic transformation. We only feel that he has done all this in a wrong direction. And they add that the greatest crime of *Monsieur Verdoux* was the killing-off of the beloved little vagabond who had been such a charmer. His creator should not only have kept him alive but depended on him in his search for a new form of expression. I cannot share this opinion.

'In giving up the rundown shoes, the old derby hat and willowy cane of the raggedy little guy whose pathetic hangdog look used to melt our hearts, Chaplin has gone deliberately into a world that is more dangerous, because it is closer to the one we live in. His new character, with neatly-pressed trousers, impeccably-knotted tie, well-dressed and no longer able to appeal to our pity, does not belong in those good old situations, outlined in strong broad strokes, where the rich trample the poor in so obvious a manner that even the most childish audience can immediately grasp the moral of the story. Before, we could imagine that the adventures of the little tramp took place in some world that belonged exclusively to the movies, that they were a sort of fairy tale.

'With *Monsieur Verdoux*, such misapprehension is no longer possible. This one really takes place in our time, and the problems faced on the screen are really our own. By thus giving up a formula which afforded him full security, and undertaking squarely the critique of the society in which he himself lives, a dangerous job if ever there was one, the author raises our craft to the level of the great classical expressions of the human novel, and strengthens our hope of being able to look upon it more and more as an art.

'Let me add a purely personal note here: Having given up the powerful weapon which was the defencelessness of his old character, Chaplin had to look for another to be used by his latest creation. The weapon he chose is one that appeals particularly to the Frenchman in me, steeped as he is in the 18th Century: psychological logic.

'I understand perfectly the misgivings of certain confused minds before this method which seems to belong to a bygone aristocratic era. I hope they will forgive a devoted reader of the works of Diderot and Voltaire for the pleasure he found in *Monsieur Verdoux*.

'Moreover, even when it is not thus spiced with psychological logic, genius often has something shocking about it, something subversive, some of the characteristics of a Cassandra. That is because it has better vision than ordinary mortals, and the commonsensical truths that it has still strike the rest of us as something akin to madness.

'Another reason for liking *Monsieur Verdoux*: I like to be amused at the movies, and this film made me laugh until my tears flowed like wine.

'I believe I see growing up about me a certain taste for collective accomplishments, the anonymousness of which is a tribute to the adoration of new deities. Let me mention at random some of these false idols: public opinion polls, organization, techniques. These are but the saints of a dangerous god that some are trying to substitute for the God of our childhood. This new divinity is called Scientific Progress. Like any self-respecting God, he tries to attract us with his miracles. For how else can one describe electricity, anaesthesia or atomic fission? But I am very leery of this newcomer. I am afraid that, in exchange for the refrigerators and the television sets that he will distribute so generously, he may try to deprive us of a part of our spiritual heritage.

'In other times, every object was a work of art, in that it was a reflection of the one who made it. The humblest early American sideboard is the creation of one given woodworker, and not of any other. This personal touch was present in everything, in houses, in clothes, in food.

'When I was young, in my village in Burgundy, when we drank a glass of wine, we could say: That comes from the Terre à Pot vineyard up over the hill behind the little pine wood, or from the Sarment Fountain, or from some other specific spot. Some bottles left on your tongue the silex taste of their vines, others were like velvet and you knew they came from a lush green valley with plenty of moisture. Closing your eyes, you could see a certain greyish hill, with its twisted little oaks and the imprints of the boars' feet which had been found there last fall after the harvest. And later the young girls bending under the weight of their baskets full of luscious grapes. Especially, you recalled the wrinkled face of the vintner who had devoted his life to the culture of that difficult soil.

'All the manifestations of life took on a profound meaning, because men had left their mark upon them. You felt that you were in the centre of an immense prayer sent heavenward by all of the workers, with their ploughs, their hammers, their needles, or even simply their brains. Today we live in a desert of anonymity. The wines are blended. The nickel-plated tubing in my bathroom, the hardwood of my floor, the fence around my garden, all bring to mind for me only the uniform purr of the machines that turned them out.

'There are still a few places where we can seek a refuge. A painter can still speak to us of himself in his canvases, as a chef can in his culinary creations. That is probably why we are ready to pay fortunes for a good picture or for a good meal. And then there is also this film craft of ours, which will remain one of the great expressions of human personality if we are able to retain our artisans' spirit, which fortunately is still very much alive. That spirit is Chaplin's, down to the tips of his toenails. One feels it in a certain decent way he has of going into a scene, in the almost peasant-like thriftiness of his sets, in his wariness of technique for technique's sake, in his respect for the personalities of actors, and in that internal richness which makes us feel that each character just has too much to say.

'*Monsieur Verdoux* will some day go into history along with the creations of artists who have contributed to the building of our civilization. He will have his place alongside the pottery of Urbino and the paintings of the French Impressionists, between a tale by Mark Twain and a minuet by Lulli. And during that time, the films which are so highly endowed with money, with technique and with publicity, the ones that enchant his detractors, will find their way God knows where, let us say into oblivion, along with the expensive mahogany chairs mass-produced in the beautiful nickel-plated factories.'

175

Sydney Chaplin
THE TRUTH ABOUT MY FATHER

IN THE FACE OF the simmering hostility which surrounded what were to prove his last years in Hollywood, Chaplin continued to work and indeed devised what he was sure would be counted among his very best films, *Limelight*. As if trying to turn back the clock to a time when his life had been less complicated and unhappy, he created a very personal picture, brilliantly evoking the old-time London music halls as the background to the story of a has-been comedian and the young girl he nurses to stardom. 'When *Limelight* was finished,' Charlie wrote in his autobiography, 'I had fewer qualms about its success than any other picture I had ever made.'

Chaplin intensified the personal character of the movie by starring in it several members of his family; his elder sons, Charles Jr and Sydney (who played the romantic lead) and the younger generation of Geraldine, Michael and Josephine, as well as one of his oldest friends, the comedian Buster Keaton. Shortly before the film was due to open in New York, Charlie and his family decided on taking a trip abroad that would include the premiere of *Limelight* in London. However, no sooner had he left New York than the American Ministry of Justice announced that he would not be allowed to return without an investigation to determine whether or not he was a 'desirable alien resident'. (Despite having lived in America for so many years, Chaplin had never given up his British citizenship.) To Charlie, this action seemed like a curtain falling on part of his life, and he must have wondered whether he would ever again step on the soil that had nurtured his great talent. In truth, twenty years were to pass before he returned: and in the interim he made himself a new home in Switzerland at the Manoir de Ban in Vevey above Lake Geneva. Although *Limelight* was boycotted in America, it became a world-wide success, its haunting theme tune – composed as always by Chaplin – becoming a

bestselling record. On his arrival in London, Charlie was greeted by the following article written by his son Sydney which provided an intensely personal view of his character: it appeared in *The Sunday Chronicle* of 24 September 1952. Although Chaplin was going into exile, he was going surrounded by the love of millions.

'FOR A LONG TIME I have refused to answer any questions about my father. If people have to make a mystery of his private life, that is their affair. It seems no reason for laying it open to inspection.

'But since arriving I have realized that many of these questions are asked, not out of prying curiosity, but out of a genuine love and interest, and for that reason I think it is up to me to answer the ones which seem to be uppermost. I don't know whether my father will forgive me for it, but here goes.

'Is it true that he remains at heart an unhappy man? Does he feel a nagging sense of frustration with his life and his work?

'This is an old romantic invention – the clown who laughs with tears in his eyes.

'Actually, my father is one of the happiest men you could meet. Why shouldn't he be?

'I don't know much about his previous marriages, but the present one is certainly ideal. He has a wonderful wife, Oona, and four wonderful children. He can still enjoy walking along the seafront with his family, munching candied apples among the crowds.

'His new film *Limelight* looks like being a great success, and I don't think he is dissatisfied with the ones he made in the past. In fact, he gets a great kick out of them.

'I remember going to the Silent Film House in Hollywood one evening to see an old Charlie Chaplin film. There was a man with a particularly persistent laugh behind me, and once or twice I was on the point of telling him

176

Sydney Chaplin

Following page: Some of the Chaplin family with their father on the set of *Limelight* (1952)

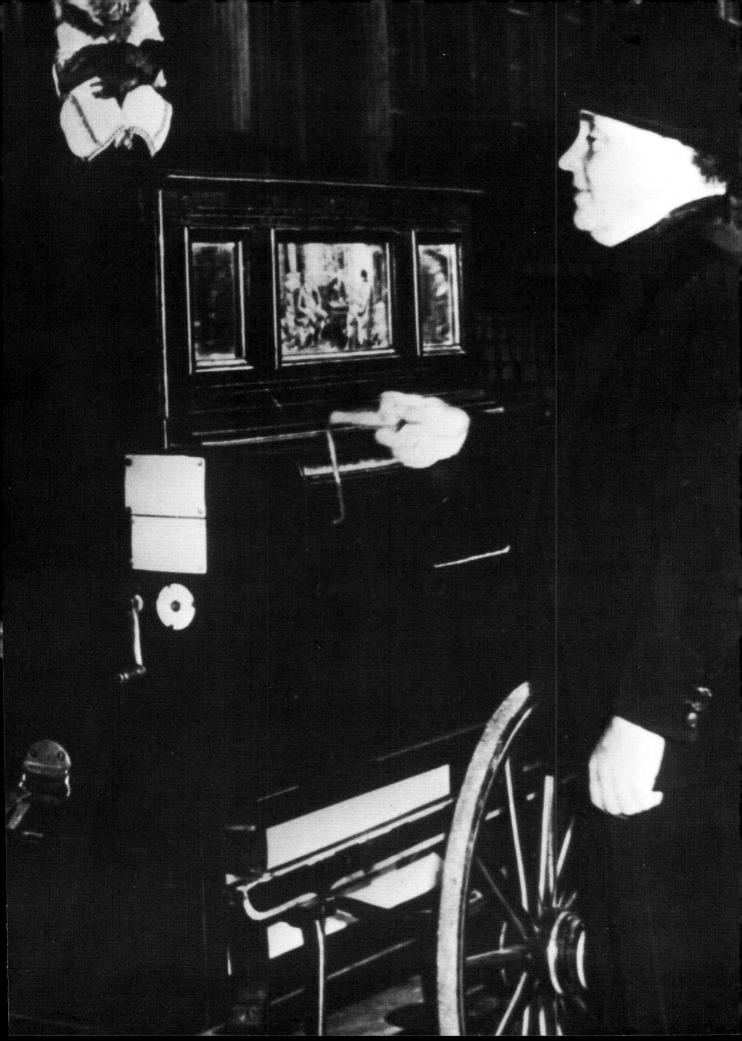

to pipe down. When the lights went up I turned round, and saw it was my father!

'Of course, he is a perfectionist. He has a unique facility for doing the same scene over and over again, without getting bored by it. But he doesn't allow this seeking for perfection to make him miserable.

'*It has long been said over here that he is afraid to leave America in case they would not allow him to re-enter the country. Yesterday's news bears this out. Is it true?*

'I should think the fact that he decided to come over here this week is the best answer to that one. He certainly wasn't expecting any trouble about going back.

'I must confess that this strikes me as being underhanded. He had been granted a re-entry visa some weeks ago and had, in fact, been told by the authorities "to come back real soon".

'The question of him now being banned seems to me to be grossly unfair. Dad is furious – and justifiably so. Not only is he upset and indignant; but everyone else I discussed this with yesterday is shocked by such unethical treatment.

'Each film takes him five years. So if he goes straight from one film to the next, as he has been doing, it means ten years without a holiday abroad.

'*Why has he always refused to adopt American citizenship? Does he often talk about the old country? Why has he not been back to see us since 1931?*

'I think I have already answered the last part of that question – he is too busy.

'Basically, the answer to the citizenship question is that he doesn't regard it as important, because to him it is the man who matters, not the passport. He probably feels that to apply for a passport would be a concession to nationalist ideas; if he were an American earning his living in England, he would stay American.

'But also, taking out citizenship papers would mean studying for an exam and he begrudges time given to such things which to him are not important. It is just the same with his haircuts and driving licences.

'I should tell you about his hair. He cuts it himself with a pair of scissors, hand-clippers and two mirrors. He just snips away until he is satisfied; sometimes it looks all right, sometimes it isn't so good. But he prefers that to the bother of driving into town and waiting for a chair at the barbers.

'For many years he had a driving licence that had turned yellow with age – I think he took it out in 1933. It was only when we all bullied him that he recently went and renewed it.

'His writing really is unreadable. Sometimes he'll walk in with a sheaf of manuscript and say. "I've written some great stuff today. Just listen to this."

'Then it falls flat because he can't read his own writing.

'Tennis is his great relaxation, and he plays it well. When I was a boy he said: "I'll give you a hundred dollars when you beat me at tennis." I won that hundred dollars just before I joined the Army.

'His favourite rest-cure is to take his motor-boat out and anchor off Catalan Island with a few friends.

'They spend two or three days just lazing, resting and diving into the sea. He loves to swim in salt water. When I was a kid I used to think those week-ends boring but now I find them the greatest relaxation ever. No radio, no television, no crowds, no cars for three whole days. It's wonderful!

'Jazz is one thing he can't stand, except now and then when he gets a tune into his head. The last one was "Come on to my House" which William Sarogan composed. The only words he knew were the first line, but he kept singing them all day long.

'He seems to have got his life down to the basic simple things.

'When success was new to him he used to sport a Rolls Royce, but now it is a strictly utilitarian Ford. He used to be a chain smoker but now he has given it up and calls it a disgusting habit. He drinks very little alcohol and has no particular interest in wines.

'*It is said that* Limelight *will be his last picture. What do you think?*

'Every picture is his last! It is a standing joke at home. He says it after finishing every one and then you will hear him say, "Well,

180

The tragic clown with the girl he makes a star – Chaplin and Claire Bloom in *Limelight* (1952)

ek ending October 18, 1952

EVERY THURSDAY 3½ ID.

Picturegoer

THE NATIONAL FILM WEEKLY

this *may* be my last picture."

'It never is.

'When he was finishing *Limelight* he went down with a bad cold and was sent to bed for two days. When I went upstairs I found him sitting up in bed with a pencil and paper and the first words he said to me were, "Sydney, see what you think of this – I've got a great idea for a new film."

'He can't help making films. He'll probably go on making them till he drops!'

'But his affection for Britain is very great. He still prefers British food – kidneys and bacon for breakfast, roast beef and Yorkshire pudding for dinner. He also has afternoon tea, which is a rare thing in Hollywood.

'And there is a constant succession of British visitors. Every British newcomer to Hollywood finds open house; he loves to talk to them about the British theatre, and especially about the old-timers like Tree and Gillette, with whom he once acted in a Sherlock Holmes play.

'The interior of the house is rather English, with a lot of old Staffordshire ware, which he collects.

'*It is said that he makes very few close friends, but plenty of enemies. Is it true?*

'He has literally hundreds of friends, though not many of them are film stars. He rarely mixes with the "star set" in Hollywood. Among his friends are a number of film directors, musicians and writers.

'There are also people without any sort of fame, like Garry Epstein, who started the little Circle Theatre in Hollywood with me, and is nearly always broke. He is regularly up at the house.

'As for enemies, I think the only ones he ever made are newspapermen who are annoyed because he will not allow them to photograph and interview him at home just when they like. I can understand their feelings, because he is different from other movie stars in this respect. He refuses to be photographed for the fan-magazines or to endorse commercial products. But then, why should he lay his private life bare?

'*What is he like in private life, and as a father? How does he spend his time off the set?*

'To me he is just a good dad, and a very normal one. I think he was inclined to spoil me. He hit me only once in his life. I had just dropped my serviette and when he told me to pick it up I pointed to my nanny and said, "Let her pick it up, that's what we pay her for."

'I was only five but it made him hopping mad. Even so, he didn't hit me hard enough to hurt.

'The children (Victoria, Josephine, Michael and Geraldine) adore him – mainly I think because he talks to them like grown-ups. They have only one thing against him – he won't have television in the house, because he thinks this regular feed of canned entertainment spoils their minds. It is especially hard on them because the latest TV children's hero in America is Charlie Chaplin – in his old films.

'When I was posted to Europe in the Army he did something he hardly ever does for anyone – he wrote me a letter, a long one. I couldn't read a line of it, though I thought "Well, it's nice anyway – the old man is thinking about me."'

Graham Greene
THE RETURN OF CHARLIE CHAPLIN

ALSO WAITING FOR Charlie on his arrival in London for the premiere of *Limelight* in 1952 was the following 'Open Letter' from Britain's most distinguished man of letters, Graham Greene, himself one of the star's most ardent fans. The attitude of the American authorities had appalled Greene, but as he reveals in this letter he had a suggestion for Charlie as to how he might turn the events across the Atlantic to his own advantage by utilizing them for a new film! Perhaps not surprisingly, the two men later became firm friends, each sharing a mutual admiration for the other's work.

'DEAR MR CHAPLIN,

'I hope you will forgive an open letter; otherwise I would have added to that great pyramid of friendly letters that must be awaiting you in London. This is a letter of welcome not only to the screen's finest artist (the only man who writes, directs and acts his own pictures and even composes their music), but to one of the greatest liberals of our day. Your films have always been compassionate towards the weak and the under-privileged; they have always punctured the bully. To our pain and astonishment you paid the United States the highest compliment in your power by settling within her borders, and now we feel pain but not astonishment at the response – not from the American people in general, one is sure, but from those authorities who seem to take their orders from such men as McCarthy. When Russia was invaded you spoke out in her defence at a public meeting in San Francisco at the request of your President; it was not the occasion for saving clauses and double meanings, and your words were as plain as Churchill's and Roosevelt's. You even had the impudence, they say, to call your audience your comrades. That is their main accusation against you. I wonder what McCarthy was doing in those days?

'Remembering the days of Titus Oates and the terror in England, I would like to think that the Catholics of the United States, a powerful body, would give you their sympathy and support. Certainly one Catholic weekly in America is unlikely to be silent – I mean the *Commonwealth*. But Cardinal Spellman? And the Hierarchy? I cannot help remembering an American flag that leant against a pulpit in an American Catholic church not far from your home, and I remember too that McCarthy is a Catholic. Have Catholics in the United States not yet suffered enough to stand firmly against this campaign of uncharity?

'When you welcomed me the other day in your home, I suggested that Charlie should make one more appearance on the screen. In this would-be-story Charlie lies neglected and forgotten in a New York attic. Suddenly he is summoned from obscurity to answer for his past before the Un-American Activities Committee at Washington – for that dubious occasion in a boxing ring, on the ice-skating rink, for mistaking that Senator's bald head for an ice pudding, for all the hidden significance of the dance with the bread rolls. Solemnly the members of the Committee watch Charlie's early pictures and take their damaging notes.

'You laughed the suggestion away, and indeed I had thought of no climax. The Attorney-General of the United States has supplied that. For at the close of the hearing Charlie could surely admit to being in truth un-American and produce the passport of another country, a country which, lying rather closer to danger, is free from the ugly manifestations of fear.

'The other day a set of Hollywood figures, some of them rather out-moded (Mr Louis B. Mayer and Mr Adolf Menjou were among the names) set up a fund to support McCarthy's fight in Wisconsin – a form of Danegeld. Now Hollywood uses English stories and English

183

actors, and I would like to see my fellow-countrymen refusing to sell a story or to appear in a film sponsored by any organization that includes these friends of the witch-hunter. Our action would be an expression of opinion only; it would not condemn them to the unemployment and slow starvation to which McCarthy has comdemned some of their colleagues. They will say it is no business of ours. But the disgrace of an ally is our disgrace, and in attacking you the witch-hunters have emphasized that this is no national matter. Intolerance in any country wounds freedom throughout the world.

'Yours with admiration

GRAHAM GREENE'

Cartoon by Vicki to mark Chaplin's return to London; and a special article by Charlie's first biographer and family friend, R.J. Minney, published in 1952

It's Chaplin's Trademark

THE CHAPLIN NOBODY KNOWS: Anyone could dress up as Charlie did. Many tried it — but the law and the public chose the real thing

by R. J. MINNEY

AT the start, when everyone was screaming for more and more Chaplin, there were many imitators. It was so easy to put on baggy trousers, a small derby, a small moustache, twirl a cane and swivel a leg as you hurried round a corner.

Chaplin took action, finally, against one of them, and it was decided in court that the costume and the walk were Chaplin's trademark, not to be infringed. But the public had already given their decision. They wanted Chaplin himself.

Chaplin is essentially a family man. He likes to have his relatives around him. His mother, with whom he and his brother had shared so much poverty, was his first consideration when success came. He had her moved immediately to a comfortable nursing home in London and, in 1918, when the ending of the war made it possible, he built a palatial home for her in Hollywood.

She had a housekeeper, a butler, a cook and a maid. Charlie also bought her a large car and engaged a chauffeur. She wanted for nothing. Charlie and his brother, Syd, often took her out for a drive along the coast. Her last years, at any rate, were extremely happy.

Her death occurred just after the break-up of Charlie's marriage with Lita Grey. It was three years before he made another picture.

After *City Lights*, completed in 1931, Chaplin fled filmdom and came again to London. The crowds were as large as they had been ten years before. Thousands stood in the pouring rain outside the Dominion Theatre on the first night to catch a glimpse of him as he arrived. They missed him, because he had slipped in hours before through the back door, to see to the arrangements for the projection of his picture.

He went to the Continent, joined his brother Sydney in the South of France. Together they went skiing in St. Moritz, and then set out on a world tour, travelling eastward via Malaya, China and Japan.

Everywhere the crowds cluttered up the streets around their hotel. In Tokyo it was impossible for them to get out. For hours they waited in their rooms, then Charlie went to the back of the building, beckoned to Syd and the two together, having done a great deal of tumbling in their Karno days, got out unobserved by sliding down the drainpipes.

The Murder Plot

It was in Tokyo that a plot to murder Charlie was uncovered. Some fanatical Japs, eager for a war with the United States, conceived the idea of killing Chaplin, who was not an American citizen and had not even the protection of an American passport. The men involved confessed their purpose in court.

Had they not been foiled the world would have missed the films that followed — *Modern Times* (inspired by a talk with Gandhi), *The Great Dictator, Monsieur Verdoux* and his latest, *Limelight*.

And there you have in brief the story of a man who did not want to be a comedian and did not want to go into films. Yet as long ago as 1914, when he was only twenty-five, it could be said of him, "He is the first man to be truly world famous." He is known wherever people are able to laugh.

THE END

☆ ☆ ☆ ☆ ☆ ☆ ☆ ☆ ☆ ☆ ☆ ☆

185

Buster Keaton
MY FRIEND CHARLIE

BUSTER KEATON, who appeared in *Limelight* with Chaplin, also shared the abhorrence felt by many people about the way the actor had been treated in America. He had known Charlie since the days when both had been making pictures for Mack Sennett at Keystone, and like him had subsequently earned a world-wide audience as well as respect for his work which resulted in the regular re-showing of his films. Indeed, his mournful face and inevitable collisions with catastrophy, had made him as instantly recognizable to cinema audiences as Chaplin the Little Tramp. In October 1952, while helping to publicize *Limelight*, Keaton gave these recollections of his friend to the French magazine, *Arts*.

'I HAVE KNOWN Charlie since 1912 and our friendship today is as close as ever. This constancy of affection is, perhaps, one of the truest characters of the man who is, to everyone, just Charlie.

'However, so much has been said about his impulsive, unstable chracter; about his pessimism, his sadness and his unkindness. The simple explanation for these quite wrong ideas is that people do not easily forgive a genius for being only a man. Perhaps, too, we want to make him pay the penalty for being so dazzlingly superior.

'Legend requires that clowns – once they have left the arena where they have just given enormous amusement – should return to their sorrow and bitterness in their dressing rooms. It is a great pity for such a touching and romantic image that I have to say that Charlie, in private, is the gayest of companions and the most delightful, kind and brilliant conversationalist I know.

'In truth, it is *at work* that he is least funny, if I may say so! Then, calm, cold, lucid and watchful, he pursues his love of perfection with the same attention to detail as a collector

187

handling the wings of a butterfly.

'There are no minor sequences in a film for Charlie. Each image is prepared with meticulous care. And the so called "classicism" of Chaplin is nothing but his love of work well done.

'Moreover, we can never admire enough his grasp of detail, the clockwork precision which each of his films represents, and which is perhaps the essence of his genius – an element even more important than his art of the gag. For by this perfect precision his comic sense is moulded into an eternal kind of material; into almost human flesh itself. Chaplin was able to put more substance into his walking-stick than there were electrons in the Hiroshima Bomb.

'Charlie knows what he wants, and like all great enthusiasts he creates his own time. That is why his films now take five years to make. He commits himself utterly to each one, and risks his reputation, his talent, his health and his fortune all at once. No price is too high to pay. He is a great artist, always ready to cast aside everything for the sake of his work.

'However, let there be no misunderstanding about Chaplin's passionate attitude. I remember twenty years ago he was asked if he was a Bolshevick. Today he is questioned about communism. To tell the truth, I believe that Charlie does not know what a political party is – only that he has voted to serve Art.

'But he has always been on the side of those who suffer against those who have everything. He is for those who think that everyone should have enough to eat, and can sympathize with anyone who has been hungry and can remember.

'Still, I digress too far from the point. Making *Limelight* with Charlie was a great pleasure for me. Not only because it meant working for an old friend, but because doing anything with him is marvellous.

'He had prepared and written everything in advance. But once in the studio he improvized within the framework he had drawn.

'To my mind he is the greatest director of comic actors there is. Roscoe Arbuckle, who worked with Charlie, was perhaps the only other great director of comedians.

'I recall that on many occasions I was summoned to the studio by Charlie, only to be told when I got there to come back the next day as he had changed his plan of work and was engrossed in something else. His is the only studio in Hollywood where work is done like that. The rest are just factories!

'Finally, I must just mention the "Chaplin Affair". Why shouldn't he be allowed to return to the United States? He has done nothing illegal. There is nothing he can be blamed for. He pays his taxes and keeps the peace.

'Surely he has the right to make a six-month visit to Europe? Isn't he an English subject, after all?

'No, the arguments against him do not hold good! Let him return, I say, no one has the right to do what these people are doing to Charlie Chaplin!'

Charlie with another of Hollywood's tragic funny-men, Fatty Arbuckle, together in *The Funniest Man in the World* (1967)

Following page: Chaplin, the grand old man of films, still busy as a director on *A Countess from Hong Kong* with Marlon Brando, in 1966

189

Charlie Chaplin
ROLES I WOULD LIKE TO PLAY

AFTER SETTLING IN Switzerland,* Chaplin made only two more films and, truth to say, neither of them bear comparison with his best work. *A King In New York* (1957), was a rather unsuccessful satire on the country which had exiled him and in which he co-starred with Dawn Addams while *A Countess From Hong Kong* was an undistinguished farce in which he only had a cameo role with the stars, Marlon Brando and Sophia Loren. Although Charlie, as always, wrote and directed both pictures, they were far removed from the style of films that had made him famous, and neither enjoyed much success at the box office. To the end of his life, Charlie nursed several other ideas that he wanted to bring to the screen. He worked for a time on a script called *The Freak* about an angel coming to earth – in which his daughter Josephine was to star – and the scenario of a black comedy about a condemned man in a Kansas jail which he was tailoring for his older son, Sydney. Of all his unfulfilled desires, however, his greatest ambition was to bring the characters of Napoleon and Jesus Christ to the screen. How he planned two such daunting projects he explained in the following article which he wrote as far back as 1930 for the magazine *Bravo*.

'THE TWO characters I most want to play in films are Napoleon and Jesus Christ.

'For years now, everyone knows that I have been dying to play the part of Napoleon. Long before I had finished *The Circus*, the newspapers were already announcing that my next film would be devoted to Napoleon, and the same thing had already been said after the presentation of *The Gold Rush*. It will certainly happen one day!

'I have very definite ideas about how I would play the Emperor of the French. In fact I want to erase from the minds of countless people the traditional and absolutely false

portrait of him which custom has made them accept.

'I would not portray Napoleon as a powerful general, but as a sickly, taciturn, almost morose man, constantly plagued by the members of his family. For, you see, it was these people, and especially his mother, Laetitia Ramolino, who played a considerable part in shaping the manner of his existence. It has always amused me to think of his efforts to marry off his brothers and sisters, and also his in-laws, in order to remain on good terms with his mother and his wife. And at the same time go about winning wars! What a lot of dramatic situations could be created out of all that!

'Naturally, I would not make him a burlesque character, but I should like to show the domestic difficulties which preoccupied him, and all the trouble he took to try to keep the peace in his family.

'One particular period of his life which interests me is the time of his break with Josephine. I can see that very clear. First, the Emperor summoning her in order to beg her to go away. This, the woman who had helped him, had believed in him, and had driven him on. Then, secondly, a switch to her last night in the palace as she slowly counts off the hours, trying to retain a memory of all that has been familiar to her. When the moment comes for her to leave, I see her wrapping herself in her cloak, getting into her carriage, and disappearing slowly into the darkness.

'In another scene, she would learn from the roar of cannons of the birth of Napoleon's child. And she would count the shots, impatient to know whether it was a boy.

'The dramatic possibilities of the story of Napoleon cannot be denied even by those who detest the man. Think of the return from the island of Elba, the mustering of an army. The march on Paris, the old guard rushing enthusiastically towards their former leader. Flags unfurling, ovations ringing out and the

* A neighbour of Chaplin's in Vevey was the famous novelist, A.J. Cronin, who told Bob Tanner the interesting fact that although Charlie was little involved in village life, whenever a circus visited the place he would appear in his tramp's outfit and lead the parade through the streets! Cronin also revealed that Chaplin had built a miniature operating theatre in the Manoir de Ban in case of emergencies.

Opposite: Charlie in fancy dress as Napoleon – one of the parts he most wanted to portray on the screen

Following page: Chaplin's satire on the country which had exiled him, *A King in New York* (1957), with co-star, Dawn Addams

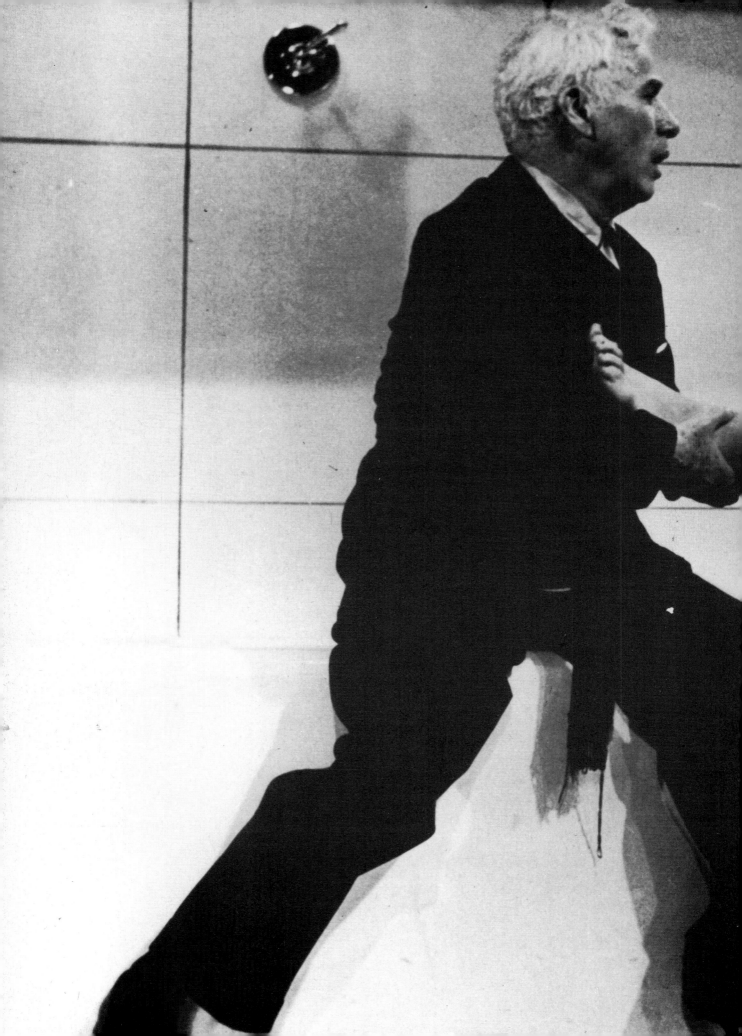

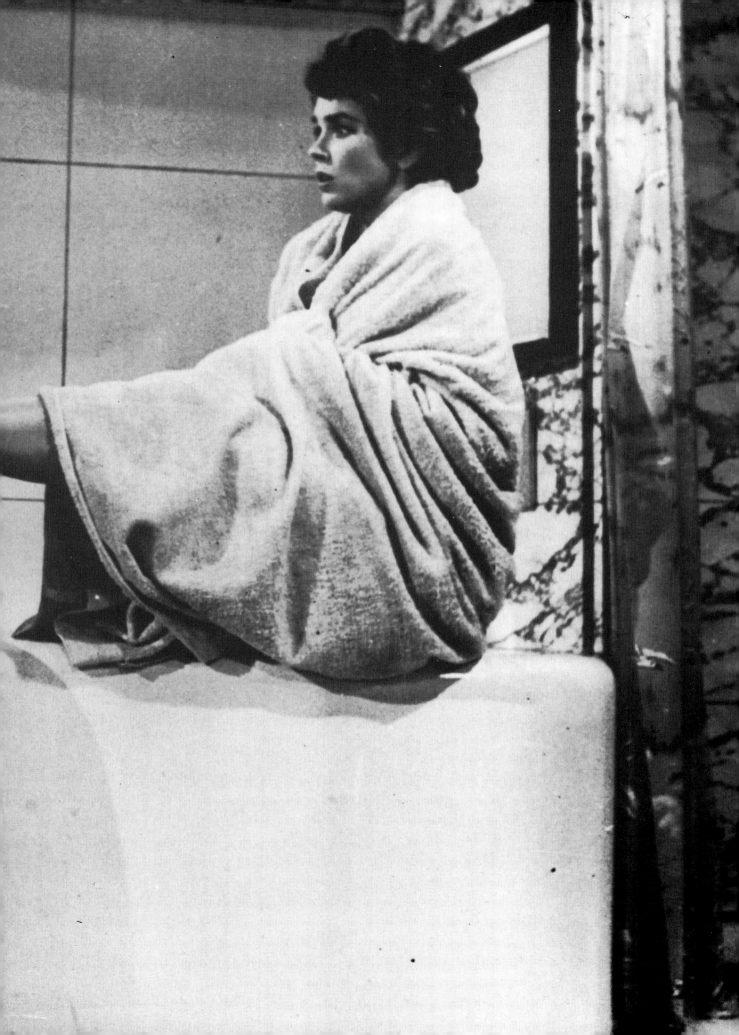

awakening of the war-like spirit.

'If I can give one example, I would show a one-eyed veteran with a wooden leg and an arm missing, dashing out into the road and shouting, "The emperor is coming back! Napoleon is marching on Paris! Stop him! Kill him before he spills more rivers of blood." Then I would show the growing army appearing, with the little Corsican at its head, the band playing the Marseillaise, and Napoleon as he passes saluting the wounded veteran. At this the old warrior would be seized with emotion, throw his hat in the air and shedding tears of joy, join the ranks and march on Paris with the rest.

'I have a pile of notes of this kind on Napoleon for a film. But the scenario is not written and when will I find the time to make it?

'The other figure from history who I should like to portray on the screen in a different light is Jesus Christ. I have long studied the Bible and many works on the Christian religion. Moreover, I know almost all the Faiths. And I consider that the most powerful, most dynamic, and most imposing character ever to live, has been terribly distorted by tradition. He was not just a man with long hair, wearing a white robe, speaking in a sepulchral voice, and looking exceptionally tired and distressed. Some people would also have us believe he was a tortured, depressing figure, seeking to instil fear into the hearts of everyone.

'My view is that he was a splendid, virile, red-blooded man. I would make him real and human, strength personified, as well as being a powerful intellect. He was a man who ate well, and drank well, and loved the company of his fellows. His appearance at any gathering was enough to create an immediate atmosphere of good humour and happiness. I see him in a meeting telling the assembled company, "Let us eat, drink and be merry."

'He was simply a man who was stronger than his contemporaries, full of life, having the power to dominate everybody and everything in any circumstance.

'I do not believe that Pontius Pilate ever intended to put Christ to death. Pilate heard the accusation against him and then asked, "What shall we do with this man?" And some idiot in the crowd shouted, "Crucify him!"

'The cry was then taken up by others and soon the assembly had made its verdict on no more than that. Mass psychology had triumphed and Jesus was sacrificed for no apparent reason.

'If I could produce a film about the story of Christ I would also show him greeted deliriously by men, women and children, swarming towards him to feel his magnetism.

'But somehow I do not foresee myself making such a film about the life of Christ. You can imagine what a storm it would raise in the United States!

'I shall be enormously sorry if it is *never* made, but the Christian religion should be even more sorry. For I believe the picture would do a tremendous service to religion if it taught that Jesus truly deserves to be loved for the beauty of his character and personality.

'I did once see Christ depicted in a film. He appeared to be suffering from stomach-ache. It was awful and ridiculous. I was so angry I walked out.'

Charlie with Oona walking in the streets of London where he had grown up

Candice Bergen
THE HOMECOMING

As HAS SO often proved the case, time heals all wounds, and the last years of Charlie Chaplin's life were crowned with honours and awards – in particular from a shamefaced America. In 1971 he was accorded a special award for his work at the 25th Cannes Film Festival – as well as being given the rank of Commander of the Legion of Honour. A year later, the Academy of Motion Picture Arts and Sciences and the Film Society of the Lincoln Centre invited him to return to America and receive an honourary Oscar in recognition of his services to film making. Momentarily, there was speculation as to whether Charlie would go back to the country that had so cruelly misused him. But the grand old man accepted – and without hesitation. Wildly cheering crowds greeted him on his 'homecoming' and he could only just fight back the tears as he declared, 'This is my renaissance. I am born again.' It was a triumphant return for a man who had done as much as anyone to put the name Hollywood on the world scene. Although he had another five years to live (Chaplin died on Christmas Day 1977), and during the intervening years was knighted by Queen Elizabeth (on 2 January 1975), this return to America was probably the greatest thrill of his last years. It would surely have been a tragedy almost without parallel if the Little Tramp had died unhonoured in the land he had made his own. Among the many accounts of this unique occasion, perhaps the most appropriate for this book – as well as being one of the most warmly felt – was the following item by the beautiful Hollywood actress Candice Bergen, which appeared in *Life* magazine of 21 April 1972. Not yet born when Chaplin was already a legend, Candice symbolizes the continuing delight each new generation shows – and will doubtless continue to show – to a man who was arguably the greatest of all film stars. And can there be any doubt now that his appeal is truly immortal?

'IT IS TIRING for Charlie to stand in the receiving line at a black-tie New York dinner and he is helped to a chair: the scene is like one he staged for *The Idle Class*, a late short of his that will be shown at Lincoln Center the following night. Guests hang round him in busy clusters, jewels and teeth flashing, speaking in that nasal monotone that sounds as though everybody's jaws are wired. And they jostle for position, waiting to be received.

'Being eighty-three years old and on the end of the receiving line, Charlie begins, after a blur of outstretched arms, to operate on conditioned reflex. A little hand rises quickly, almost mechanically, to shake whenever anyone approaches, going out even to Oona till he sees who it is, and once to a waiter serving him a drink. His eyes grow wide and he begins to look uneasy, struggling to stay afloat in the stream of people flowing by him.

'Unlike most people in that unnatural context, Chaplin never assumes an attitude of holding court. He is shy and it exhausts him to meet so many people so fast. He is always interested, polite, almost ingenuous about "so many famous people" – far more interested and enthusiastic, usually, than the people who come to meet him: Gloria Vanderbilt Cooper looking like a white swan in a rhinestone bib, Truman Capote in a pastel sweater set, Johnny Carson (of whom he had never heard) in a crushed-velvet tuxedo, George Plimpton, etc.

'The Chaplin's were conspicuous in their simplicity, their absence of props, the lack of pre-occupation with fashion. With his small hands and feet and ample middle, Charlie looks the same no matter what he wears: padded – a silhouette forsaken for the love of vanilla ice cream.'

'An old family friend took the Chaplins to lunch at "21". As Charlie entered, the dining room burst into warm applause. He was thrilled, almost giddy, with the affection he received wherever he went.

'As he was being seated, the first person to practically assault him was George Jessel – wearing a toupee and medals certifying service to his country, a pillar of its right wing.

'The next one approached more timidly. "Mr Chaplin," he said respectfully, his hands trembling, "my name is Jack Gilford and I'm an actor and I just wanted to thank you for all you've given us. I was blacklisted, and now I'm alive and well in New York and we've all lived for the day when you'd come back."

'"Thank you," Charlie said sweetly. "Someone once wrote me a letter telling me that when I was eighty I should keep warm, so I'm keeping warm."

'It was an interesting rejoinder. He didn't know who Gilford was.

'"I didn't know many actors in California. I was mostly alone there. It was always hard for me to make friends. I was shy and inarticulate. Doug Fairbanks was my only real friend, and I was a showpiece for him at parties."

'At the table, the talk turned to penal systems. "It's horrible the way they put men in cages," Charlie said. "Put men in prison and you make them abnormal.

'"You know they tried to convict me for twenty years [in 1944 on a Mann Act charge that was proven groundless], and all the jurors were for me but one – a musician, a pianist, a girl with a very pretty face, but she was against me," he said wistfully, fondling the napkin tucked in his shirt like a bib, smoothing it over the dinner jacket he had worn by mistake instead of his suit.

'"She said . . ." And he was unable to finish, his eyes filmy. "I can't talk about it," whispered the old man of eighty-three, with the soft pink face and the snow-white hair.'

Commemorative stamp issued by India in 1977

Opposite: Sir Ralph Richardson unveils the statue of Charlie Chaplin by John Doubleday in London's Leicester Square in 1981

'Later, he gave a wonderful imitation of Truman Capote, who had visited them in Vevey. He had everyone roaring, and was clearly delighted when asked to do it again. Which he did – almost immediately.

'He was the last to finish eating – which he did slowly, precisely, like a child who has just mastered a knife and a fork. A waiter helped him up from his chair, confiding. "Mr Chaplin, I was your waiter in '52 when you were here the last time – it's wonderful to have you back."

'"Well, thank you," Charlie replied. "I didn't think I'd ever be back, you know."

'"They all love you, Charlie," someone said.

'"Yes, but they loved Kennedy too," he said softly.

'In their suite at the Plaza, Oona walks by, gently smoothing his hair. It is good to see them together, impossible to imagine them otherwise. They are each other's best friends. It would be hard to find better. Being around them, the institution of marriage seems less obsolete.

'She suggests that he go in and rest, and he grasps the arms of the chair with fine, small hands and tries to propel himself upward. He lets out a tiny "oof!" as he misses and falls back into the chair. "Whoops!" he exclaims weakly, giving himself another hoist and remaining vertical this time.

'He boarded the plane to Los Angeles with great ambivalence. After agreeing in January to come for the Academy Awards, he felt – as the time grew closer – that he could not go through with it. The memories of what he was put through there were too painful. The thought of returning terrified him.

'During the flight, he crossed to the other side of the plane to see the Grand Canyon. His face lit up. "Oh, yes, this is the place where Doug Fairbanks did a handstand on the precipice. He told me about it."

'As they got nearer Los Angeles, he grew more and more nervous, sure he shouldn't have come. He looked fearful and trapped but made a brave attempt to fight it. "Oh well," he sighed, "it wasn't so bad. After all, I met Oona there."

'Driving through the city he found nothing familiar and muttered, "It's nothing but banks, banks, banks." By the time he arrived at the hotel he had relaxed and was fine. He wanted two bedrooms in his bungalow. One had a red bedspread. "Oh no," he said, "it's too much like a bullfight." And chose the other.

'Charlie and Oona watched the Oscar show on TV backstage in a dressing room pointing excitedly to friends in the huge audience. He was relieved. He had been afraid nobody would come.

'Afterward, as he talked about the ceremony, his eyes were bright and childlike, wide with wonder, round with glee. "It almost made me cry – and *this* one," he cocked his head at a beaming Oona, "this one kept saying, '*Oh, don't snivel.*'

'"It was *so emotional* and the *audience – their* emotion. I thought some of them might hiss, but they were so *sweet* – all those famous people, all those artists. You know, they haven't done this to me before. It surpasses everything."

'He looked around for his Oscar and couldn't see it. "*Oh no*" he wailed, "all those sweet people and I've *lost* it." It was retrieved and put back serenely.

'More and more he began to look like an English schoolboy, grinning impishly, rolling is eyes up innocently, pointing a freckled hand to himself, announcing playfully, "The genius . . ."

'Suddenly summoning that old agility, he flew from his chair. Eyes twinkling, he said with mock impatience, "Let's go and celebrate, for God's sake!"

'And happily humming his song, "Smile", he took Oona's arm and stepped out grandly through the door.'

An Annotated Filmography by Denis Gifford
CHARLIE CHAPLIN: THE FILMS

1: MAKING A LIVING
(1030 ft). 2 February 1914. Keystone

Producer, Mack Sennett; Director, Henry Lehrman; Screenplay, Reed Heustis; Photography, E.J. Vallejo. With Charles Chaplin (The Sharper), Virginia Kirtley (The Girl), Henry Lehrman (The Reporter), Alice Davenport (The Mother), Chester Conklin (The Cop), Minta Durfee (The Flirt).

In his first film Charlie plays a con-man in top-hat, monocle and walrus moustache. As a newspaper photographer he steals his rival's scoop, but is chased, caught, and trounced. Said his first film critic: 'The clever player who takes the role of the nervy and very nifty sharper is a comedian of the first water.' (*Moving Picture World*)

2: KID AUTO RACES AT VENICE
(572 ft). 7 February 1914. Keystone

Producer, Mack Sennett; Director/Screenplay, Henry Lehrman; Photography, Frank D. Williams. With Charles Chaplin (The Tramp), Henry Lehrman (The Director), Frank D. Williams (The Cameraman), Gordon Griffith (Boy), Paul Jacobs (Boy), Charlotte Fitzpatrick (Girl), Thelma Salter (Girl).

Asked to improvise some comedy scenes around a children's soap-box car race at a nearby seaside resort, Chaplin donned his classic tramp outfit for the first time, assembling it from fellow actors' clothes around the dressing room. Said *Exhibitors World*: 'We do not think we are taking a great risk in prophesying that in six months Chaplin will rank as one of the most popular screen comedians in the world.'

3: MABEL'S STRANGE PREDICAMENT
(1016 ft). 9 February 1914. Keystone

Producer, Mack Sennett; Directors, Henry Lehrman, Mack Sennett; Screenplay, Reed Heustis; Photography, Frank D. Williams. With Mabel Normand (Mabel), Charles Chaplin (The Drunk), Chester Conklin (The Husband), Alice Davenport (The Wife), Harry McCoy (The Admirer), Hank Mann (A Boarder), Al StJohn (A Man).

Chaplin, wearing his new tramp costume, portrays his classic stage drunk on film for the first time. His persistence in pursuing the pajama-clad Mabel through a hotel's corridors, bedrooms, and lobby, offended many but delighted more: 'The best farce released for many months' (*Bioscope*).

4: BETWEEN SHOWERS
(1020 ft). 28 February 1914. Keystone

Producer, Mack Sennett; Director/Screenplay, Henry Lehrman; Photography, Frank D. Williams. With Ford Sterling (The Masher), Charles Chaplin (A Masher), Emma Clifton (The Girl), Chester Conklin (The Cop), Sadie Lampe (A Girl).

Chaplin teamed with Keystone's top comedy star, Ford Sterling, for the first time. As rivals for a girl and her umbrella, they endeavour to outdo each other in both the film, and in their partly-improvised comedy techniques.

5: A FILM JOHNNIE
(1020 ft). 2 March 1914. Keystone

Producer, Mack Sennett; Director, George Nichols; Screenplay, Craig Hutchinson; Photography, Frank D. Williams. With Charles Chaplin (The Johnnie), Roscoe Arbuckle (Fatty), Virginia Kirtley (Keystone Girl), Minta Durfee (Actress), Mabel Normand (Herself), Ford Sterling (Himself), Mack Sennett (Himself).

Charlie as a film fan crashes Mack Sennett's Keystone Studio to woo the star he loves. There is trouble on the set, and at a local fire, whither the film-makers rush to improvise a rescue scene. A treasure for its glimpses of a 1914 silent movie studio in action, with its producer and stars playing themselves.

6: TANGO TANGLES
(734 ft). 9 March 1914. Keystone

Producer/Director/Screenplay, Mack Sennett. With Ford Sterling (The Bandleader), Charles Chaplin (The Drunk), Roscoe Arbuckle (The Clarinettist), Minta Durfee (Cloakroom Girl), Chester Conklin (A Dancer).

Love triangle improvised in a local dance-hall, with Keystone's top comedy stars in conflict for the cloakroom girl. Chaplin appears as his neat, dapper self, *sans* costume but tipsy.

7: HIS FAVOURITE PASTIME
(1009 ft). 16 March 1914. Keystone

Producer, Mack Sennett; Director, George Nichols; Screenplay, Craig Hutchinson; Photography, Frank D. Williams. With Charles Chaplin (The Drunk), Roscoe Arbuckle (Drunk), Peggy Pearce (The Wife).

Charlie has two favourite pastimes: drink and girls. Having caused a riot in a bar, he pursues a lady home only to be ultimately ousted by her irate husband. Chaplin is expertly acrobatic but outrageously tasteless.

8: CRUEL, CRUEL LOVE
(1035 ft). 26 March 1914. Keystone

Producer, Mack Sennett; Director, George Nichols; Screenplay, Craig Hutchinson; Photography, Frank D. Williams. With Charles Chaplin (Mr Dovey), Minta Durfee (The Girl), Chester Conklin (Butler), Alice Davenport (Maid).

Chaplin plays a wealthy lothario known variously as Mr Dovey and Lord Helpus, according to the print. When his new love arouses the wrath of his jealous maid, Chaplin decides upon suicide. Fortunately his manservant exchanges a glass of poison for one of water.

9: THE STAR BOARDER
(1020 ft). 4 April 1914. Keystone

Producer, Mack Sennett; Director, George Nichols; Screenplay, Craig Hutchinson; Photography, Frank D. Williams. With Charles Chaplin (The Lodger), Minta Durfee (The Landlady), Edgar Kennedy (The Landlord), Gordon Griffith (The Son), Alice Davenport (The Friend).

Charlie is the landlady's favourite, much to the annoyance of his fellow boarders. They get their revenge when the son of the house takes compromising snapshots and projects them to the assembled company.

10: MABEL AT THE WHEEL
(1900 ft). 18 April 1914. Keystone

Producer, Mack Sennett; Directors, Mack Sennett, Mabel Normand; Screenplay, Craig Hutchinson; Photography, Frank D. Williams. With Mabel Normand (Mabel), Charles Chaplin (The Villain), Harry McCoy (The Driver), Chester Conklin (The Father), Mack Sennett (The Rube), Al St John (Henchman), William A. Seiter (Henchman).

Chaplin as a top-hatted cad who abducts his racing-driver rival. Mabel takes his place and drives to victory in the Vanderbilt Cup, despite Chaplin's machinations. Chafing under Miss Normand's direction, Chaplin threatened to quit Keystone, causing Mack Sennett to take over as director.

11: TWENTY MINUTES OF LOVE
(1009 ft). 20 April 1914. Keystone

Producer, Mack Sennett; Director, Joseph Maddern; Screenplay, Charles Chaplin; Photography, Frank D. Williams. With Charles Chaplin (The Tramp), Minta Durfee (The Girl), Edgar Kennedy (The Beau), Gordon Griffith (The Boy), Chester Conklin (The Thief), Joseph Swickard (The Victim), Hank Mann (The Sleeper), Emma Clifton (A Girl).

Chaplin's first original screenplay, an improvised comedy set in Westland Park involving lovers, a stolen watch, and a cop. It ends with everybody in the water except Charlie and his girl.

12: CAUGHT IN A CABARET
(2053 ft). 27 April 1914. Keystone

Producer, Mack Sennett; Directors, Mabel Normand, Charles Chaplin; Screenplay, Charles Chaplin; Photography, Frank D. Williams. With Charles Chaplin (The Waiter), Mabel Normand (The Girl), Edgar Kennedy (The Proprietor), Alice Davenport (The Mother), Minta Durfee (The Waitress), Harry McCoy (The Fiancé), Chester Conklin (The Waiter), Phyllis Allen (The Entertainer), Joseph Swickard (The Father), Gordon Griffith (The Boy), Hank Mann (Customer), Wallace MacDonald (Customer), Alice Howell (Woman).

Charlie, a waiter in a cheap café, is airing his dog when he saves Mabel from a crook. He poses as the Premier of Greenland but is exposed by her vengeful fiancé who takes Mabel and family on a slumming party to Charlie's café. Chaplin and Mabel Normand, having made up their differences, co-directed this co-starring picture.

13: CAUGHT IN THE RAIN
(1015 ft). 4 May 1914. Keystone

Producer, Mack Sennett; Director/Screenplay, Charles Chaplin. With Charles Chaplin (The Flirt), Alice Davenport (The Wife), Mack Swain (The Husband), Alice Howell (The Girl).

Chaplin's first 'one man' film: he wrote, directed and starred as a drunken masher whose fancy sleep-walks into his hotel bedroom. The arrival of her irate hubby forces pajama-clad Charlie to cower on a rainswept balcony. Then the cops arrive!

14: A BUSY DAY
(441 ft). 7 May 1914. Keystone

Producer, Mack Sennett; Director/Screenplay, Charles Chaplin. With Charles Chaplin (The Wife), Mack Swain (The Husband).

An improvised slapstick comedy shot in one day around the opening of the San Pedro Harbour. Chaplin appears 'in drag' as a virulent virago lambasting her flirtatious hubby, the cameraman, the cops, and everyone else in range.

15: THE FATAL MALLET
(1120 ft). 1 June 1914. Keystone

Producer/Director, Mack Sennett. With Mabel Normand (The Girl), Charles Chaplin (The Rival), Mack Sennett (The Adored One), Mack Swain (The Third Man).

Chaplin and Sennett, rivals for Mabel, combine forces when she prefers a third man. A well-placed mallet soon settles things, and Charlie wins Mabel with a swift kick in the panties!

16: HER FRIEND THE BANDIT
(1000 ft). 4 June 1914. Keystone

Producer, Mack Sennett; Directors, Mabel Normand, Charles Chaplin. With Mabel Normand (Miss De Rock), Charles Chaplin (The Bandit), Charles Murray (Count De Beans).

Charlie waylays the Count De Beans and, using his dress suit and invitation card, poses as him at Mabel's posh reception. His disgraceful behaviour at the party brings on the Keystone Cops.

17: THE KNOCKOUT
(1960 ft). 11 June 1914. Keystone

Producer, Mack Sennett; Director, Charles Avery. With Roscoe Arbuckle (Fatty), Minta Durfee (The Girl), Edgar Kennedy (Cyclone Flynn), Charles Chaplin (The Referee), Mack Swain (Spectator), Alice Howell (Spectator), Hank Mann (Boxer), Mack Sennett (Spectator). Al St John; George 'Slim' Summerville; Charley Parrott; Joe Bordeaux; Edward Cline

Chaplin is a 'Guest Star' in this Fatty Arbuckle comedy, appearing briefly as the referee in a boxing-match sequence.

18: MABEL'S BUSY DAY
(998 ft). 13 June 1914. Keystone

Producer, Mack Sennett; Directors, Mabel Normand, Charles Chaplin. With Mabel Normand (Mabel), Charles Chaplin (The Knut), Billie Bennett (A Girl), Chester Conklin (The Sergeant), Harry McCoy (Man), Wallace MacDonald (Cop), George Summerville (Cop).

Charlie looks dapper but is not above swiping Mabel's hot dogs, leading to strife with the girl and the police. Improvised at a local racetrack.

19: MABEL'S MARRIED LIFE
(1015 ft). 20 June 1914. Keystone

Producer, Mack Sennett; Directors, Mabel Normand, Charles Chaplin; Screenplay, Charles Chaplin. With Mabel Normand (Mabel), Charles Chaplin (Her Husband), Mack Swain (Mr Wellington), Alice Howell (Mrs Wellington), Charles Murray (Man at Bar), Harry McCoy (Man at Bar), Hank Mann (Friend), Alice Davenport (Neighbour), Al St John (Delivery Man), Wallace MacDonald (Delivery Man).

Top-hatted Charlie gets drunk when a prize-fighter flirts with his wife, Mabel. She buys a boxing dummy for him to train on, but the tipsy Charlie mistakes it for his rival. Chaplin built this plot around a time-honoured Music Hall routine.

20: LAUGHING GAS
(1020 ft). 9 July 1914. Keystone

Producer, Mack Sennett; Director/Screenplay, Charles Chaplin. With Charles Chaplin (The Assistant), Fritz Schade (Dr Pain), Alice Howell (Mrs Pain), Mack Swain (Bystander), George Summerville (Patient), Joseph Swickard (Patient), Edward Sutherland (Assistant).

Charlie as a dentist's assistant takes over the surgery much to the discomfort of the patients, especially the pretty ones. Elaboration of a familiar Music Hall sketch.

21: THE PROPERTY MAN
(2118 ft). 1 August 1914. Keystone

Producer, Mack Sennett; Director/Screenplay, Charles Chaplin. With Charles Chaplin (Props), Fritz Schade (Garlico), Phyllis Allen (Hamlena Fat), Alice Davenport (Actress), Charles Bennett (Actor), Mack Sennett (Spectator), Norma Nichols (Actress), Joe Bordeaux (Baggage Man), Harry McCoy (Actor), Lee Morris (Actor).

Charlie as the property man in a small vaudeville theatre, disrupting acts and audience alike, ultimately soaking all with a fire-hose. Some brutal humour led *Moving Picture World* to ask 'What human being can see an old man kicked in the face and count it fun?'

22: THE FACE ON THE BAR-ROOM FLOOR
(1020 ft). 10 August 1914. Keystone

Producer, Mack Sennett; Director/Screenplay, Charles Chaplin. Based on the poem by Hugh Antoine D'Arcy. With Charles Chaplin (The Artist), Cecile Arnold (Madeleine), Fritz Schade (The Client), Chester Conklin (Man), Vivian Edwards (Model), Harry McCoy (Drinker), Hank Mann (Drinker), Wallace MacDonald (Drinker).

Burlesque version of the once-popular monologue, in which Charlie is the drunken hobo who describes his artistic past to an audience of barflies, illustrated by flash-back scenes.

23: RECREATION
(462 ft). 13 August 1914. Keystone

Producer, Mack Sennett; Director/Screenplay, Charles Chaplin. With Charles Chaplin (The Tramp), Alice Davenport (The Woman), Rhea Mitchell (The Girl).

Improvised film built around Chaplin's oft-quoted dictum: 'All I need is a park, a bench, and a girl'. To this he added a sailor, a cop, and some brickbats!

24: THE MASQUERADER
(1030 ft). 27 August 1914. Keystone

Producer, Mack Sennett; Director/Screenplay, Charles Chaplin. With Charles Chaplin (Himself), Roscoe Arbuckle (Himself), Chester Conklin (Himself), Charles Murray (The Director), Fritz Schade (The Villain), Minta Durfee (The Heroine), Cecile Arnold (Actress), Vivian Edwards (Actress), Harry McCoy (Actor), Charles Parrott (Actor).

Chaplin appears as himself, the film star, putting on his tramp make-up and spoiling a scene in a Keystone film. Sacked, he dresses up as an attractive young lady and returns to be hired by the director who fired him!

25: HIS NEW PROFESSION
(1015 ft). 31 August 1914. Keystone

Producer, Mack Sennett; Director/Screenplay, Charles Chaplin. With Charles Chaplin (Charlie), Minta Durfee (The Girl), Fritz Schade (The Uncle), Charles Parrott (The Nephew), Cecile Arnold (A Girl), Harry McCoy (The Cop).

Charlie tries to earn a dishonest living by pushing an ancient uncle in a bath-chair, labelling him 'Cripple', and spending the proceeds on drink. The old boy ends up in the water and is arrested for disturbing the peace.

26: THE ROUNDERS
(1010 ft). 5 September 1914. Keystone

Producer, Mack Sennett; Director/Screenplay, Charles Chaplin. With Charles Chaplin (Mr Full), Roscoe Arbuckle (Mr Fuller), Phyllis Allen (Mrs Full), Minta Durfee (Mrs Fuller), Fritz Schade (Diner), Al St John (Bellhop), Charles Parrott (Diner), Wallace MacDonald (Diner).

Two tipsy swells return from a night on the town, and escape their angry wives by going out to continue their bender. They find sleep in a rowing-boat which slowly sinks beneath the water. 'It's a rough picture for rough people.' (*Moving Picture World*)

27: THE NEW JANITOR
(1020 ft). 24 September 1914. Keystone

Producer, Mack Sennett; Director/Screenplay, Charles Chaplin. With Charles Chaplin (The Janitor), Fritz Schade (The President), Minta Durfee (The Stenographer), Jack Dillon (The Clerk), Al St John (Liftboy).

Charlie is the janitor who, sacked for soaking the boss, saves the secretary from assault and the company safe from robbery. Chaplin's first appearance as a hero, down-trodden but triumphant.

28: THOSE LOVE PANGS
(1010 ft). 10 October 1914. Keystone

Producer, Mack Sennett; Director/Screenplay, Charles Chaplin. With Charles Chaplin (The Flirt), Chester Conklin (The Rival), Cecile Arnold (The Girl), Vivian Edwards (Her Friend), Edgar Kennedy (A Suitor), Norma Nichols (The Landlady), Harry McCoy (The Cop).

Charlie has trouble in wooing the ladies: first with his landlady, then with girls in the park, and finally in a cinema. He ends up being thrown through the screen.

29: DOUGH AND DYNAMITE
(2000 ft). 26 October 1914. Keystone

Producer, Mack Sennett; Director/Screenplay, Charles Chaplin. With Charles Chaplin (Pierre), Chester Conklin (Jacques), Fritz Schade (M. La Vie), Cecile Arnold (Waitress), Vivian Edwards (Waitress), Phyllis Allen (Customer), Edgar Kennedy (Baker), Charles Parrott (Baker), George Summerville (Baker), Norma Nichols (Mme. La Vie), Wallace MacDonald (Baker), Jack Dillon (Customer).

Charlie and Chester Conklin are teamed again as rivals, this time working as waiters in a bakery specialising in 'French Tarts'. When the staff strikes, Charlie and Chester become bakers, but the strikers hide dynamite in the dough . . .

30: GENTLEMEN OF NERVE
(1030 ft). 29 October 1914. Keystone

Producer, Mack Sennett; Director/Screenplay, Charles Chaplin. With Charles Chaplin (Mr Wow-Wow), Mabel Normand (Mabel), Mack Swain (Ambrose), Chester Conklin (Walrus), Phyllis Allen (Wife), Edgar Kennedy (The Cop), Charles Parrott (Spectator), George Summerville (Spectator), Alice Davenport (Waitress).

An all-star improvisation built around a day at the auto-races. Charlie is the usual penniless flirt, stealing drinks and squirting soda syphons.

31: HIS MUSICAL CAREER
(1025 ft). 7 November 1914. Keystone

Producer, Mack Sennett; Director/Screenplay, Charles Chaplin. With Charles Chaplin (Tom), Mack Swain (Ambrose), Fritz Schade (Mr Rich), Alice Howell (Mrs Rich), Charles Parrott (Manager), Joe Bordeaux (Mr Poor), Norma Nichols (Mrs Poor).

Chaplin and Swain, removal men, get their orders mixed. As a result they deliver a new piano to a poor pair and take away a rich man's for non-payment. The body of the film consists in the comic complications of piano-shifting, a time-honoured theme in Music Hall sketches.

32: HIS TRYSTING PLACE
(2000 ft). 9 November 1914. Keystone

Producer, Mack Sennett; Director/Screenplay, Charles Chaplin. With Charles Chaplin (Clarence), Mabel Normand (Mabel), Mack Swain (Ambrose), Phyllis Allen (Mrs Ambrose).

Chaplin and Swain as two henpecked husbands who get their jackets mixed in a restaurant. One wife finds a love note, the other a baby's bottle, leading to much misunderstanding and violence.

33: TILLIE'S PUNCTURED ROMANCE
(6000 ft). 14 November 1914. Keystone

Producer/Director, Mack Sennett; Screenplay, Hampton Del Ruth. Based on the play Tillie's Nightmare *by Edgar Smith. With Marie Dressler (Tillie Banks), Charles Chaplin (Charlie), Mabel Normand (Mabel), Mack Swain (John Banks), Charles Murray (Detective), Charles Bennett (Douglas Banks), Chester Conklin (Mr Whoozis), Charles Parrott (Detective), Edgar Kennedy (Proprietor), Harry McCoy (Pianist), Minta Durfee (Maid), Phyllis Allen (Prison Wardress), Alice Davenport (Guest), Alice Howell (Guest), Billie Bennett (Guest), Gordon Griffith (Newsboy), George Summerville (Cop), Al St John (Cop), Wallace MacDonald (Cop), Hank Mann (Cop), Edward Sutherland (Cop), Joe Bordeaux (Cop), G.G. Ligon (Cop), Rev. D. Simpson (Himself).*

Chaplin is a city slicker who gets country girl Tillie to steal her father's money, deserts her, then weds her on learning she is an heiress. Unfortunately her rich uncle turns up alive; so do the Keystone Cops! Famous as the first feature-length comedy, filmed in the summer (note only one Chaplin short released in July) and delayed through the leading lady's lawsuit. 'It is the *Cabiria* of comedy.' (*Photography*).

34: GETTING ACQUAINTED
(1025 ft). 5 December 1915. Keystone

Producer, Mack Sennett; Director/Screenplay, Charles Chaplin. With Charles Chaplin (Mr Sniffles), Mabel Normand (Mrs Ambrose), Mack Swain (Mr Ambrose), Phyllis Allen (Mrs Sniffles), Harry McCoy (Cop), Edgar Kennedy (The Turk), Cecile Arnold (A Girl).

Chaplin's last 'park' film for Keystone: a complicated, improvised love-tangle between two married couples, a cop and a Turk.

35: HIS PREHISTORIC PAST
(2000 ft). 7 December 1915. Keystone

Producer, Mack Sennett; Director/Screenplay, Charles Chaplin. With Charles Chaplin (Weakchin), Mack Swain (King Lowbrow), Fritz Schade (Cleo), Gene Marsh (Favorite Wife), Cecile Arnold (Cave Girl), Al StJohn (Cave Man).

Chaplin's burlesques D.W. Griffith's *Man's Genesis*: as a tramp he dreams he is in prehistoric times, wearing bearskin and bowler. He falls for the King's favourite wife, and usurps the throne by shoving the King over a cliff. Chaplin's final film for Keystone: his 35th in 52 weeks.

36: HIS NEW JOB
(2000 ft). 1 February 1915. Essanay

Producer, Jesse J. Robbins; Director/Screenplay, Charles Chaplin; Photography, Roland Totheroh. With Charles Chaplin (Himself), Ben Turpin (Himself), Charlotte Mineau (Actress), Charles Insley (The Director), Leo White (Actor), Frank J. Coleman (The Manager), Gloria Swanson (Stenographer), Agnes Ayres (Stenographer), Bud Jamison (Actor), Billy Armstrong (Man).

'His new job' was as star of the Essanay Film Manufacturing Co of Chicago, at a salary of $1250 a week – so he burlesqued it in his first film by playing a clumsy carpenter at the Lockstone Studios, totally ruining the costume

208

209

drama supposedly in production. Gloria Swanson's part was so brief she later denied playing it!

37: A NIGHT OUT
(2000 ft). 10 February 1915. Essanay

Producer, Jesse J. Robbins; Director/Screenplay, Charles Chaplin; Photography, Roland Totheroh. With Charles Chaplin (Drunk), Ben Turpin (Drunk), Edna Purviance (The Wife), Bud Jamison (The Waiter), Leo White (The Count), Fred Goodwins (Man).

Charlie, drunk again, returns to his hotel and gets into bed with another man's wife! She is Edna Purviance, in a movie debut that led to a lifetime's contract with Chaplin.

38: THE CHAMPION
(2000 ft). 5 March 1915. Essanay

Producer, Jesse J. Robbins; Director/Screenplay, Charles Chaplin; Photography, Roland Totheroh, Harry Ensign; Assistant Director, Ernest Van Pelt. With Charles Chaplin (The Tramp), Edna Purviance (The Girl), Bud Jamison (Young Hippo), Leo White (The Count), Billy Armstrong (Sparring Partner), Lloyd Bacon (Spike Dugan), Paddy McGuire (Sparring Partner), Carl Stockdale (Sparring Partner), Ben Turpin (Salesman), G.M. Anderson (Spectator).

Charlie the tramp fights his way to the championship, thanks to a lucky horseshoe – in his boxing glove! G.M. Anderson, one of the founders of Essanay and the movies' Bronco Billy, is a guest star in the audience.

39: IN THE PARK
(1000 ft). 12 March 1915. Essanay

Producer, Jesse J. Robbins; Director/Screenplay, Charles Chaplin; Photography, Roland Totheroh, Harry Ensign; Assistant Director, Ernest Van Pelt. With Charles Chaplin (The Flirt), Edna Purviance (The Nursemaid), Leo White (The Count), Bud Jamison (The Beau), Lloyd Bacon (The Tramp), Billy Armstrong (The Man), Margie Reiger (The Girl), Ernest Van Pelt (The Cop).

Another impromptu in the park involving two pairs of courting couples, a hot dog salesman, a purse thief, and a tramp (Charlie).

40: A JITNEY ELOPEMENT
(2000 ft). 23 March 1915. Essanay

Producer, Jesse J. Robbins; Director/Screenplay, Charles Chaplin; Photography, Roland Totheroh, Harry Ensign; Assistant Director, Ernest Van Pelt. With Charles Chaplin (The Tramp), Edna Purviance (The Girl), Leo White (Count De Haha), Fred Goodwins (Father), Paddy McGuire (Old Butler), Lloyd Bacon (Footman), Bud Jamison (Cop), Ernest Van Pelt (Cop).

Charlie poses as a French Count to save a millionaire's daughter from an enforced marriage, falls in love with her, and elopes in a jitney (a slot-meter taxi). The cops-and-car chase climax is pure Keystone.

41: THE TRAMP
(2000 ft). 7 April 1915. Essanay

Producer, Jesse J. Robbins; Director/Screenplay, Charles Chaplin; Photography, Roland Totheroh, Harry Ensign; Assistant Director, Ernest Van Pelt. With Charles Chaplin (The Tramp), Edna Purviance (The Girl), Leo White (Tramp), Bud Jamison (Tramp), Fred Goodwins (Farmer), Paddy McGuire (Farmhand), Lloyd Bacon (The Sweetheart), Billy Armstrong (The Poet), Ernest Van Pelt (Tramp).

Charlie's first definitive 'Chaplin film': the tramp, a loner, wanders into a situation, brings things to a climax, and after a touch of pathos, wanders on. Here he saves a farmer's daughter from fellow tramps, is rewarded with a job (which, of course, he makes a hash of), saves her father in a struggle which leaves him injured, falls in love with the girl, discovers she loves another, bids her a broken-hearted farewell, and shuffles down the road towards a hopeful future.

42: BY THE SEA
(1000 ft). 26 April 1915. Essanay

Producer, Jesse J. Robbins; Director/Screenplay, Charles Chaplin; Photography, Roland Totheroh, Harry Ensign; Assistant Director, Ernest Van Pelt. With Charles Chaplin (The Man), Edna Purviance (The Girl), Bud Jamison (The Dandy), Billy Armstrong (The Other Man), Margie Reiger (The Other Girl), Paddy McGuire (The Cop).

This extemporised slapstick scene involving wind-blown hats, ice-cream cornets, and girls marks Chaplin's return to California from Essanay's Chicago studios. This was made around Crystal Pier. *Bioscope* said: 'Chaplin is the Dan Leno of the screen.'

43: HIS REGENERATION
(963 ft). 3 May 1915. Essanay

Chaplin returned the favour for his employer G.M. Anderson's guest appearance in *The Champion* by playing an unbilled role in a saloon scene.

44: WORK
(2000 ft). 2 June 1915. Essanay

Producer, Jesse J. Robbins; Director/Screenplay, Charles Chaplin; Photography, Roland Totheroh, Harry Ensign; Assistant Director, Ernest Van Pelt; Scenic Artist, E.T. Mazy. With Charles Chaplin (The Assistant), Edna Purviance (The Maid), Charles Insley (The Paperhanger), Billy Armstrong (The Husband), Marta Golden (The Wife), Leo White (The Lover), Paddy McGuire (Hod Carrier).

A slapstick saga of paste and paper as Charlie and his boss attempt to redecorate a house containing an errant wife and an exploding gas-stove. 'Disgusting at many points' said a shocked *Variety*. Based on Chaplin's old Fred Karno sketch, *Repairs*.

45: A WOMAN
(2000 ft). 7 July 1915. Essanay

Producer, Jesse J. Robbins; Director/Screenplay, Charles Chaplin; Photography, Roland Totheroh, Harry Ensign; Assistant Director, Ernest Van Pelt; Scenic Artist, E.T. Mazy. With Charles Chaplin (The Tramp), Edna Purviance (The Girl), Billy Armstrong (The Suitor), Charles Insley (The Father), Marta Golden (The Mother), Margie Reiger (The Flirt), Leo White (The Gentleman).

Contrived around his famous female impersonation, Charlie poses as a flirtatious lady to set a married man and his daughter's fiance against one another. 'Chaplin needs a scenario writer very, very badly,' said *Variety*.

46: THE BANK
(2000 ft). 9 August 1915. Essanay

Producer, Jesse J. Robbins; Director/Screenplay, Charles Chaplin; Photography, Roland Totheroh, Harry Ensign; Assistant Director, Ernest Van Pelt; Scenic Artist, E.T. Mazy. With Charles Chaplin (The Janitor), Edna Purviance (The Typist), Carl Stockdale (The Cashier), Billy Armstrong (The Janitor), Charles Insley (The Manager), Bud Jamison (Client), Leo White (Officer), John Rand (Salesman), Fred Goodwins (Thief), Frank J. Coleman (Thief), Wesley Ruggles (Thief),

Carrie Clarke Ward (Woman), Paddy McGuire (Man), Lloyd Bacon (Man).

Even *Variety* liked this one ('The most legitimate comedy film Chaplin has played in') which told how Charlie, a janitor mistaken in his love for the stenographer, saves the bank from burglars only to find it was all a dream!

47: SHANGHAIED
(2000 ft). 27 September 1915. Essanay

Producer, Jesse J. Robbins; Director/Screenplay, Charles Chaplin; Photography, Roland Totheroh, Harry Ensign; Assistant Director, Ernest Van Pelt; Scenic Artist, E.T. Mazy. With Charles Chaplin (The Tramp), Edna Purviance (Edna), Wesley Ruggles (The Owner), John Rand (The Captain), Bud Jamison (Other Man), Billy Armstrong (Seaman), Leo White (Seaman), Paddy McGuire (The Cook), Fred Goodwins (Seaman), Lawrence A. Bowes (Seaman).

Charlie, hired to shanghai a crew with his mallet, is shanghaied himself. As the cook's assistant, he saves the owner's daughter from the Captain's plot to blow up the ship for insurance. Filmed aboard an old tramp steamer, the *Vaquero*, rough seas caused danger and distress to the Essanay actors and crew.

48: A NIGHT IN THE SNOW
(2000 ft). 15 November 1915. Essanay

Producer, Jesse J. Robbins; Director/Screenplay, Charles Chaplin; Photography, Roland Totheroh, Harry Ensign; Assistant Director, Ernest Van Pelt; Scenic Artist, E.T. Mazy. With Charles Chaplin (Mr Pest/Mr Rowdy), Edna Purviance (The Lady), Leo White (The Count/Prof. Nix), Bud Jamison (The Husband/Dot), James T. Kelly (Dash), John Rand (Conductor), Dee Lampton (Fat Boy), May White (La Belle Wienerwurst), Paddy McGuire (Trombonist), Fred Goodwins (Tuba Player), Wesley Ruggles (Man), Charles Insley (Man), Carrie Clarke Ward (Woman).

Chaplin plays two roles, the drunken dude in the front row and the noisy galleryite who both disrupt a vaudeville entertainment and the theatre audience, finally turning the fire hose on everyone. A cinematic reworking of the famous Fred Karno sketch *Mumming Birds*, which took Chaplin to the USA some years before.

49: CHARLIE CHAPLIN'S BURLESQUE ON CARMEN
(4000 ft). 5 April 1916. Essanay

Producer, Jesse J. Robbins; Director/Screenplay, Charles Chaplin. Based on the story and opera Carmen *by Prosper Merimee, H. Meilhac, L. Halevy, Georges Bizet. Photography, Roland Totheroh, Harry Ensign; Assistant Director, Ernest Van Pelt; Scenic Artist, E.T. Mazy. With Charles Chaplin (Darn Hosiery), Edna Purviance (Carmen), Ben Turpin (Don Remendado), Leo White (Morales), John Rand (Escamillo), Jack Henderson (Lilias Pasta), May White (Frasquita), Bud Jamison (Soldier), Wesley Ruggles (Tramp), Lawrence A. Bowles, Frank J. Coleman.*

Although based on the classic opera, Chaplin's burlesque is actually of two rival movie versions released late 1915, the DeMille epic with Geraldine Farrar and the William Fox production with the original vamp, Theda Bara. Chaplin sued Essanay to prevent them from releasing a four-reel version of what he intended to be a two-reel film, but lost.

50: POLICE
(2000 ft). 20 May 1916. Essanay

Producer, Jesse J. Robbins; Director/Screenplay, Charles Chaplin; Story. Charles Chaplin, Vincent Bryan; Photography, Roland Totheroh, Harry Ensign; Assistant Director, Ernest Van Pelt; Scenic Artist, E.T. Mazy. With Charles Chaplin (Convict 999), Edna Purviance (The Girl), Wesley Ruggles (The Thief), Leo White (Proprietor/Vendor/Cop), James T. Kelly (Drunk/Tramp), Fred Goodwins (Cop/Preacher), Bud Jamison (Cop), Billy Armstrong (Crook), John Rand (Cop), Frank J. Coleman (Cop).

Charlie is an escaped convict who, having lost his last coins to a phoney preacher, falls in with an ex-convict's plot to burglarise a house. Smitten by the charms of the pretty householder, he repents but is soon on the run from the cops once more.

51: THE FLOORWALKER
(1734 ft). 15 May 1916. Lone Star-Mutual

Producer/Director/Screenplay, Charles Chaplin; Story, Charles Chaplin, Vincent Bryan; Photography, William C. Foster, Roland Totheroh; Scenic Artist, E.T. Mazy. With Charles Chaplin (The Tramp), Edna Purviance (The Secretary), Eric Campbell (George Brush), Lloyd Bacon (The Floorwalker), Albert Austin (Assistant), Leo White (The Count), Charlotte Mineau (The Detective), Tom Nelson (Detective), Henry Berg-

man (Old Man), James T. Kelly (Liftboy), Bud Jamison (Cop), Stanley Sanford (Cop), Frank J. Coleman.

Chaplin's first film for release by Mutual under his new and historic contract: $10,000 a week plus $150,000 bonus! It was shot in Hollywood at the Climax Studio, renamed for Chaplin 'The Lone Star', and contrived around an electrical escalator he had seen at a Los Angeles department store. The complex chase involves Charlie, his crooked look-a-like, an embezzling manager, a lady detective, and the cops.

52: THE FIREMAN
(1921 ft). 12 June 1916. Lone Star-Mutual

Producer/Director/Screenplay, Charles Chaplin; Story, Charles Chaplin, Vincent Bryan; Photography, William C. Foster, Roland Totheroh; Scenic Artist, E.T. Mazy. With Charles Chaplin (The Fireman), Edna Purviance (Edna), Eric Campbell (The Captain), Lloyd Bacon (The Father), Leo White (The Householder), Charlotte Mineau (The Mother), Albert Austin (Fireman), John Rand (Fireman), James T. Kelly (Fireman), Frank J. Coleman (Fireman).

Chaplin filmed his burlesque with the cooperation of the Los Angeles Fire Department, purchasing and burning down two old houses in the process. His slapstick fireman redeems himself by rescuing Edna from her father's arson.

53: THE VAGABOND
(1956 ft). 10 July 1916. Lone Star-Mutual

Producer/Director/Screenplay, Charles Chaplin; Story, Charles Chaplin, Vincent Bryan; Photography, William C. Foster, Roland Totheroh. With Charles Chaplin (The Vagabond), Edna Purviance (The Girl), Eric Campbell (Gypsy Chief), Leo White (Gypsy/Jew), Lloyd Bacon (The Artist), Charlotte Mineau (The Mother), Phyllis Allen (Woman), John Rand (Trumpeter), Albert Austin (Trombonist), James T. Kelly (Bandsman), Frank J. Coleman (Bandsman).

Chaplin's first dramatic story: as a wandering fiddle-player he saves a girl from gypsy brutality, cares for her but loses her to a handsome young artist. His painting of her reveals by a birthmark her noble parentage, but the pathetic ending suddenly switches to a happy one when the girl realises her love for the tramp.

54: ONE A.M.
(2000 ft). 7 August 1916. Lone Star-Mutual

Producer/Director/Screenplay, Charles Chaplin; Photography, William C. Foster, Roland Totheroh; Scenic Artist, E.T. Mazy. With Charles Chaplin (The Drunk), Albert Austin (The Driver).

A solo tour-de-force with Chaplin in his 'drunken swell' role returning to his home and entangling with tigerskin rugs, staircases, a pendulum clock and a collapsible wall-bed with a will of its own.

55: THE COUNT
(2000 ft). 4 September 1916. Lone Star-Mutual

Producer/Director/Screenplay, Charles Chaplin; Photography, William C. Foster, Roland Totheroh. With Charles Chaplin (The Apprentice), Edna Purviance (Edna Moneybags), Eric Campbell (Buttinsky), Leo White (Count Broko), Charlotte Mineau (Mrs Moneybags), James T. Kelly (The Butler), Albert Austin (A Guest), May White (Ima Pipp), Eva Thatcher (Flirtitia Doughbelle), Leota Bryan (Girl), Frank J. Coleman (Cop), John Rand (Guest), Stanley Sanford (Guest), Loyal Underwood (Small Man).

Charlie, a tailor's apprentice clumsy with the lady customers, gets the sack. Visiting his girl, a cook at a rich household, he unmasks his late employer who is taking advantage of a stolen ticket to pose as a foreign count. Charlie promptly poses as the Count, making his ex-boss play his secretary, and becomes the star of the party.

56: THE PAWN SHOP
(1940 ft). 2 October 1916. Lone Star-Mutual

Producer/Director/Screenplay, Charles Chaplin; Photography, William C. Foster, Roland Totheroh. With Charles Chaplin (The Assistant), Edna Purviance (The Daughter), Henry Bergman (The Pawnbroker), John Rand (The Clerk), Eric Campbell (The Thief), Albert Austin (Customer), James T. Kelly (Woman), Frank J. Coleman (Cop), Wesley Ruggles (Customer).

Charlie, a somewhat slapstick assistant to a pawnbroker, saves the shop from an armed robber and wins the pretty daughter. Famous set-piece: Charlie's examination of and ultimate destruction of a hopeful client's alarm-clock.

57: THE ESSANAY-CHAPLIN REVUE OF 1916
(5000 ft). 21 October 1916. Essanay

Producer, Jesse J. Robbins

77-minute feature compiled from *The Tramp, His New Job,* and *A Night Out,* claiming to tell a complete, unified story 'guaranteed to supply more laughs in five acts than anything ever attempted!'

58: BEHIND THE SCREEN
(1796 ft). 13 November 1916. Lone Star-Mutual

Producer/Director/Screenplay, Charles Chaplin; Photography, William C. Foster, Roland Totheroh. With Charles Chaplin (David), Edna Purviance (Country Girl), Eric Campbell (Goliath), Henry Bergman (Director (dramas)), Lloyd Bacon (Director (comedies)), Albert Austin (Stage Hand), Charlotte Mineau (Actress), Leota Bryan (Actress), Wesley Ruggles (Actor), Tom Wood (Actor), Frank J. Coleman (Assistant Director), John Rand (Stage Hand), James T. Kelly (Cameraman).

Charlie is David to a head carpenter's Goliath in this film studio comedy, in which he helps a girl disguised as a boy to get a job, causes a custard-pie fight, and gets involved in a studio strike.

59: THE RINK
(1881 ft). 11 December 1916. Lone Star-Mutual

Producer/Director/Screenplay, Charles Chaplin; Photography, William C. Foster, Roland Totheroh. With Charles Chaplin (The Waiter), Edna Purviance (Edna Loneleigh), Eric Campbell (Mr Stout), Henry Bergman (Mrs Stout/Diner), Charlotte Mineau (Friend), Leota Bryan (Friend), Albert Austin (Cook/Skater), Frank J. Coleman (Mr Loneleigh), James T. Kelly (Cook), John Rand (Fritz), Lloyd Bacon (Customer).

Charlie, a clumsy waiter, poses as Sir Cecil Seltzer when he goes roller-skating in his lunch break and saves Edna from the advances of heavyweight Mr Stout. Based on *Skating,* one of the Fred Karno stage sketches in which Chaplin appeared.

60: EASY STREET
(1757 ft). 22 January 1917. Lone Star-Mutual

Producer/Director/Screenplay, Charles Chaplin; Photography, William C. Foster, Roland Thotheroh. With Charles Chaplin (The Tramp), Edna Purviance (The Missioner), Eric Campbell (Big Eric), Henry Bergman (The Anarchist), Albert Austin (Minister/Cop), James T. Kelly (Missioner/Cop), John Rand (Tramp/Cop), Loyal Underwood (Police Chief/Father), Charlotte Mineau (The Wife), Lloyd Bacon (The Addict), Leota Bryan (The Mother), Frank J. Coleman (Cop), Leo White (Cop), Tom Wood (Cop), Janet Miller Sully (Woman).

Charlie the tramp, lured into a Street Mission by the hymns, reforms for love of Edna and becomes a policeman. He gasses the local bully with a bent lamp-post and becomes a hero. A true classic, with autobiographical trimmings: the set was designed by Chaplin to recreate the Kennington slums of his childhood.

61: THE CURE
(1834 ft). 16 April 1917. Lone Star-Mutual

Producer/Director/Screenplay, Charles Chaplin; Photography, William C. Foster, Roland Totheroh. With Charles Chaplin (The Drunk), Edna Purviance (The Girl), Eric Campbell (The Gentleman), Henry Bergman (The Masseur), Albert Austin (Attendant), John Rand (Attendant), Frank J. Coleman (Proprietor), James T. Kelly (Bellhop), Leota Bryan (The Nurse), Loyal Underwood (Patient), Tom Wood (Patient), Janet Miller Sully (Woman).

Charlie, permanently drunk, visits a health resort to take the water cure, making sure to bring his own liquor supply with him. Chaos ensures when this gets dumped in the spa pool and all the patients imbibe freely!

62: THE IMMIGRANT
(1809 ft). 17 June 1917. Lone Star-Mutual

Producer/Director/Screenplay, Charles Chaplin; Photography, William C. Foster, Roland Totheroh. With Charles Chaplin (The Immigrant), Edna Purviance (The Girl), Eric Campbell (The Headwaiter), Kitty Bradbury (The Mother), Albert Austin (Immigrant/Diner), Henry Bergman (Woman/Artist), James T. Kelly (Tramp/Immigrant), Frank J. Coleman (Proprietor/Official), Stanley Sanford (Gambler), John Rand (Diner), Loyal Underwood (Immigrant).

The first hint of social satire in a Chaplin film: Charlie and his fellow immigrants arrive by boat in the Land of Liberty, spot the famous Statue, and are instantly roped in like cattle by officials.

63: CHASE ME CHARLIE
(4500 ft). April 1917. Essanay-Film Booking Offices

Director/Screenplay, Langford Reed; Editor, H.G. Doncaster.

Feature-length compilation of extracts from Chaplin's Essanay comedies, woven into a new continuous storyline with additional scenes enacted by Graham Douglas, a Chaplin impersonator. Charlie the Tramp comes from the country to London, where he ultimately makes good and marries a millionaire's daughter.

64: THE ADVENTURE
(1845 ft). 22 October 1917. Lone Star-Mutual

Producer/Director/Screenplay, Charles Chaplin; Photography, William C. Foster, Roland Totheroh. With Charles Chaplin (The Convict), Edna Purviance (The Girl), Eric Campbell (The Suitor), Henry Bergman (The Father/Workman), Marta Golden (The Mother), Albert Austin (The Butler), Phyllis Allen (Governess), James T. Kelly (Old Man), Frank J. Coleman (Warder), Toraichi Kono (Chauffeur), John Rand (Guest), May White (Guest), Loyal Underwood (Guest), Janet Miller Sully (Marie), Monta Bell (Man).

Charlie is an escaped convict who saves Edna from drowning and becomes a guest in her house. He causes a riot at her posh party, is recognised, and is on the run once more. Chaplin now departed from Mutual, too, having concluded his contract.

65: A DOG'S LIFE
(2674 ft). 12 April 1918. Chaplin-First National

Producer/Director/Screenplay, Charles Chaplin; Photography, Roland Totheroh; Assistant Director, Charles Reisner. With Charles Chaplin (The Tramp), Edna Purviance (The Singer), Sydney Chaplin (Proprietor), Tom Wilson (Policeman), Albert Austin (Thief), Henry Bergman (Tramp/Woman), James T. Kelly (Thief), Charles Reisner (Clerk), Billy White (Cafe Owner), Janet Miller Sully (Singer), Bud Jamison (Client), Loyal Underwood (Client), Park Jones (Waiter), Scraps (The Dog).

Chaplin's first film under his new contract with First National: one million dollars for eight films over eighteen months, plus a $75,000 bonus. With the money Chaplin built

214

his own studio on La Brea Avenue in Hollywood. Charlie the Tramp is in partnership with Scraps, a clever mongrel, who finds Edna's stolen wallet. Syd Chaplin, Charlie's comedian half-brother, appears with him for the first time, in the role of a lunch-wagon proprietor.

66: TRIPLE TROUBLE
(2000 ft). 23 July 1918. Essanay

Producer, Jesse J. Robbins; Director/Screenplay, Charles Chaplin, Leo White; Photography, Roland Totheroh, Harry Ensign; Assistant Director, Ernest Van Pelt. With Charles Chaplin (The Janitor), Edna Purviance (The Maid), Leo White (The Anarchist), Billy Armstrong (Cook/Thief), James T. Kelly (The Singer), Bud Jamison (The Tramp), Wesley Ruggles (A Crook), Albert Austin (Man).

Charlie gets the sack from an inventor's employ and is hired to help steal the man's new explosive device. Fortunately for the civilised world, the police prevent this. A remarkable film, cobbled together from various Essanay sources, including a feature-length comedy, *Life*, which Chaplin never completed.

67: CHARLES CHAPLIN IN A LIBERTY LOAN APPEAL: THE BOND
(500 ft). 4 October 1918. Chaplin-Liberty Loan Committee

Producer/Director/Screenplay, Charles Chaplin; Photography, Roland Totheroh. With Charles Chaplin (Charlie), Sydney Chaplin (The Kaiser), Edna Purviance (The Girl), Albert Austin (The Friend).

Half-reel short made to stimulate Americans into buying Liberty Bonds, in which Charlie ko's the Kaiser.

68: SHOULDER ARMS
(3142 ft). 20 October 1918. Chaplin-First National

Producer/Director/Screenplay, Charles Chaplin; Photography, Roland Totheroh; Assistant Director, Charles Reisner. With Charles Chaplin (The Rookie), Edna Purviance (The French Girl), Sydney Chaplin (Kaiser Wilhelm/Sergeant), Henry Bergman (Hindenberg/Bartender/Officer), Jack Wilson (Crown Prince/Soldier), Albert Austin (Officer/Driver/Rookie), Tom

Wilson (Sergeant), John Rand (Soldier), Park Jones (Soldier), Loyal Underwood (Captain).

Charlie is a rookie in the US Army who wins the war single-handed by posing as the Kaiser's chauffeur and driving the German High Command into captivity. Unfortunately it is only a dream! This was to have been Chaplin's first feature-length comedy, but he shortened it from five reels to three, perhaps because the Great War ended only a few weeks after its premiere.

69: SUNNYSIDE
(2769 ft). 4 June 1919. Chaplin-First National

Producer/Director/Screenplay, Charles Chaplin; Photography, Roland Totheroh. With Charles Chaplin (The Handyman), Edna Purviance (The Girl), Tom Wilson (The Boss), Henry Bergman (The Father), Albert Austin (City Slicker), Tom Terriss (City Man), Loyal Underwood (Old Man), Park Jones (Fat Man), Tom Wood (Peasant).

Charlie works as a handyman in a rustic smalltown hotel. In love with a local girl, he tries to emulate the city gent who temporarily dazzles her during an enforced stopover. He makes a fool of himself, but wins her back when the gent goes back to the city. Famous for a dream sequence in which Charlie dances a ballet with wood-nymphs.

70: A DAY'S PLEASURE
(1714 ft). 26 November 1919. Chaplin-First National

Producer/Director/Screenplay, Charles Chaplin; Photography, Roland Totheroh. With Charles Chaplin (Father), Edna Purviance (Mother), Sydney Chaplin (Husband), Babe London (Wife), Tom Wilson (Cop), Henry Bergman (Captain), Albert Austin (Trombonist), Loyal Underwood (Musician), Jackie Coogan (Boy), Raymond Lee (Boy).

Charlie is a family man, father of two mischievous boys. One of them was played by the son of vaudevillian Jack Cooper. Little Jackie so impressed Chaplin that he built his next film around him, making the boy an international star. Otherwise this film is little more than a Keystone improvisation around the theme of a boat trip.

71: THE KID
(5300 ft). 17 January 1921. Chaplin-First National

Producer/Director/Screenplay, Charles Chaplin; Photography, Roland Totheroh; Assistant Director, Charles Reisner. With Charles Chaplin (The Tramp), Edna Purviance (The Woman), Jackie Coogan (The Kid), Carl Miller (The Artist), Tom Wilson (The Policeman), Charles Reisner (The Bully), Henry Bergman (Proprietor), Albert Austin (Crook), Phyllis Allen (Woman), Nelly Bly Baker (Neighbour), Jack Coogan (Man), Monta Bell (Man), Raymond Lee (Boy), Lolita McMurray (Angel).

Subtitled 'A Picture with a Smile and Perhaps a Tear', this is Chaplin's masterpiece and one of the greatest silent films of all time. Semi-biographical, the relationship between Charlie the itinerant glazier and his adopted waif is brilliantly and movingly portrayed, the film ranging expertly between slapstick and heartbreak.

72: THE NUT
(6000 ft). 3 March 1921. Fairbanks-United Artists

Chaplin appears as himself in a 'guest star' spot in this Douglas Fairbanks comedy, made for the new company in which they were partners: United Artists.

73: THE IDLE CLASS
(1916 ft). 6 September 1921. Chaplin-First National

Producer/Director/Screenplay, Charles Chaplin; Photography, Roland Totheroh. With Charles Chaplin (Tramp/Husband), Edna Purviance (Wife), Mack Swain (Father), Henry Bergman (Tramp/Cop), Rex Storey (Pickpocket/Guest), Allan Garcia (Golfer/Guest), John Rand (Tramp/Guest), Loyal Underwood (Guest), Lillian McMurray (Maid), Lolita McMurray (Maid).

Chaplin appears as Edna's drunken husband and the tramp, his double, who is mistaken for the husband at a posh masquerade ball. A return to Keystone basics. Both Lita Grey, the future Mrs Chaplin, and her mother, appeared in small roles as Edna's maids.

74: PAY DAY
(1892 ft). 13 March 1922. Chaplin-First National

Producer/Director/Screenplay, Charles Chaplin; Photography, Roland Totheroh. With Charles Chaplin (Workman), Edna Purviance (The Girl), Mack Swain (The Foreman), Phyllis Allen (The Wife), Sydney Chaplin (Friend/Proprietor), Henry Bergman (Drinker), Albert Austin (Workman), Allan Garcia (Drinker), John Rand (Workman), Loyal Underwood (Workman).

Charlie is a bricklayer who flirts with the foreman's daughter, gets his pay and goes on a drinking spree.

75: NICE AND FRIENDLY
1922. Chaplin-Accidental Film Corporation

Producer/Director/Screenplay, Charles Chaplin.

'Home movie' production featuring Chaplin and his guests, Lord and Lady Mountbatten.

76: THE PILGRIM
(4300 ft). 24 January 1923. Chaplin-First National

Producer/Director/Screenplay, Charles Chaplin; Photography, Roland Totheroh. With Charles Chaplin (The Pilgrim), Edna Purviance (Edna Brown), Mack Swain (The Deacon), Kitty Bradbury (Mrs Brown), Sydney Chaplin (Father), Dean Reisner (The Boy), Mai Wells (The Mother), Charles Reisner (The Thief), Loyal Underwood (Elder), Tom Murray (Sheriff), Monta Bell (Cop), Henry Bergman (Traveller), Raymond Lee (Pastor), Phyllis Allen (Woman), Edith Bostwick (Woman), Florence Latimer (Woman).

Charlie, a convict on the run, steals the clothes of a swimming minister and poses as a parson in a wild west town. Here he delivers a classic routine: a mime of the story of David and Goliath.

77: SOULS FOR SALE
(7864 ft). 27 March 1923. Goldwyn Productions

Chaplin plays himself in an All Star Cast.

78: A WOMAN OF PARIS
(7577 ft). 1 October 1923. Regent Films-United Artists

THE PEAK OF ENTERTAINMENT

The laughs of a lifetime—in one great picture! Chaplin at his greatest—bringing you masterful comedy, told to the strains of music that will tug at your heart, told through words that will convulse you with laughter . . .

The World's Great Laughing Picture

CHARLIE CHAPLIN
THE GOLD RUSH

with MUSIC and WORDS

n and Directed by CHARLES CHAPLIN

Distributed by

UNITED ARTISTS

LONDON TRADE SHOW
LONDON PAVILION
WEDNESDAY
8th JULY AT 10.30 A.M.

Producer/Director/Screenplay, Charles Chaplin; Assistant Director, Edward Sutherland; Photography, Roland Totheroh; Cameraman, Jack Wilson; Script Editor, Monta Bell; Art Director, Arthur Stibolt; Researchers, Jean de Limur, Henri d'Arrast. With Edna Purviance (Marie StClair), Adolphe Menjou (Pierre Revel), Carl Miller (Jean Millet), Lydia Knott (Mme Millet), Charles French (M. Millet), Clarence Geldert (M. StClair), Betty Morrissey (Fifi), Mavlina Polo (Paulette), Karl Gutman (Conductor), Henry Bergman (Maitre d'Hotel), Harry Northrup (Valet), Nellie Bly Baker (Masseuse), Charles Chaplin (Porter).

Chaplin appeared briefly as a railway porter in this film which he created to make a star of Edna Purviance. He failed in this, but created a uniquely sophisticated romantic tragedy, light-years away from his personal *oeuvre*.

79: THE GOLD RUSH
(8498 ft). 16 August 1925. Chaplin-United Artists

Producer/Director/Screenplay, Charles Chaplin; Technical Director, Charles D. Hall; Associate Director, Charles Reisner; Assistant Director, Henri d'Arrast; Photography, Roland Totheroh; Cameraman, Jack Wilson; Production Manager, Alfred Reeves. With Charles Chaplin (The Lone Prospector), Georgia Hale (Georgia), Mack Swain (Big Jim McKay), Tom Murray (Black Larsen), Malcolm White (Jack Cameron), Henry Bergman (Hank Curtis), Betty Morrissey (Betty), John Rand (Prospector), Albert Austin (Prospector), Heinie Conklin (Prospector), Allan Garcia (Prospector), Tom Wood (Prospector).

Chaplin's most successful silent comedy, just as successful when he reissued it with his own narration and music soundtrack in 1942. Charlie is a lone prospector in the Alaskan gold rush who becomes the reluctant partner of a crazed gold-hunter and loses his heart to a dance-hall girl. Many classic sequences, including the scene where a starving Charlie cooks and eats his boot.

80: A WOMAN OF THE SEA
1926. Chaplin

Producer/Story, Charles Chaplin; Director/Screenpay, Josef Von Sternberg; Photography, Paul Ivano; Art Director, Charles D. Hall. With Edna Purviance (The Woman), Gayne Whitman, Eve Southern.

The famous 'lost' Chaplin film: another dramatic feature for Edna Purviance, but this time Chaplin refused to show it publicly.

81: THE CIRCUS
(6700 ft). 6 January 1928. Chaplin-United Artists

Producer/Director/Screenplay, Charles Chaplin; Assistant Director, Harry Crocker; Photography, Roland Totheroh; Cameramen, Jack Wilson, Mark Marklatt; Art Director, Charles D. Hall; Editor, Charles Chaplin. With Charles Chaplin (The Tramp), Merna Kennedy (Merna), Harry Crocker (Rex), Betty Morrissey (Vanishing Lady), Henry Bergman (Merry Clown), Allan Garcia (Proprietor), Stanley Sanford (Property Man), George Davis (Professor Rosco), John Rand (Property Man), Steve Murphy (Pickpocket), Doc Stone (Boxer), Albert Austin (Man), Heinie Conklin (Man).

Charlie, a tramp pursued by police, accidentally makes good in a circus ring and becomes a clown, then a wire-walker. He loves the cruel proprietor's daughter, but sacrifices her to the wire-walker she loves. Although by no means his best feature, it won Chaplin an Academy Award at the first ever Oscar ceremonies.

82: SHOW PEOPLE
(7453 ft). 20 October 1928. Metro-Goldwyn-Mayer

Chaplin is one of several guest stars in this Marion Davies feature.

83: CITY LIGHTS
(87 mins). 1 February 1931. Chaplin-United Artists

Producer/Director/Screenplay/Music, Charles Chaplin; Photography, Roland Totheroh; Cameramen, Gordon Pollock, Mark Marklatt; Assistant Directors, Harry Crocker, Henry Bergman, Albert Austin; Art Director, Charles D. Hall; Production Manager, Alfred Reeves; Music Director, Alfred Newman. With Charles Chaplin (The Tramp), Virginia Cherrill (The Blind Girl), Harry Myers (The Millionaire), Hank Mann (The Boxer), Allan Garcia (The Butler), Florence Lee (Grandmother), Henry Bergman (Mayor/Janitor), Albert Austin (Sweeper/Crook), John Rand (Tramp), James Donnelly (Foreman), Robert Parrish (Newsboy), Stanhope Wheatcroft (Diner), Eddie Baker (Referee), Jean Harlow (Guest).

Chaplin's first talkie: made with a soundtrack of original music and effects, but without dialogue. The romance and drama of the tramp's love for the blind flower-seller went far beyond mechanical pathos, and added a deep dimension to the surface slapstick comedy.

84: MODERN TIMES
(85 mins). 5 February 1936. Chaplin-United Artists

Producer/Director/Screenplay/Music, Charles Chaplin; Assistant Directors, Carter De Haven, Henry Bergman; Photography, Roland Totheroh; Cameraman, Ira Morgan; Art Director, Charles D. Hall; Music Director, Alfred Newman; Production Managers, Alfred Reeves, Jack Wilson. With Charles Chaplin (A Worker), Paulette Goddard (A Gamin), Allan Garcia (The President), Henry Bergman (The Proprietor), Stanley Sanford (Big Bill), Chester Conklin (A Mechanic), Hank Mann (The Burglar), Stanley Blystone (Sheriff Couler), Richard Alexander (A Convict), Cecil Reynolds (The Chaplain), Myra McKinney (Chaplain's Wife), Lloyd Ingraham (The Governor), Louis Natheaux (The Addict), Heinie Conklin (A Workman), Frank Moran (A Convict), John Rand (Crook).

Charlie is a worker on a production line who has a breakdown when the moving belt goes berserk. Mistaken for a communist agitator, he is jailed and thwarts a prison break. Later, seeking work, he adopts a slum waif. Both make good in a cabaret, but forced to flee authority they set off up the road, hand in hand, in a twist on the familiar Charlie finale. Again Chaplin refused to make a full talkie, but did permit his voice to be heard for the first time, singing a nonsense song.

85: THE GREAT DICTATOR
(126 mins). 15 October 1940. Chaplin-United Artists

Producer/Director/Screenplay/Music, Charles Chaplin; Assistant Directors, Daniel James, Wheeler Dryden, Robert Meltzer; Photography, Roland Totheroh, Karl Struss; Art Director, J. Russell Spencer; Editor, Willard Nico; Production Coordinator, Henry Bergman; Music Director, Meredith Willson. With Charles Chaplin (The Barber/Adenoid Hynkel), Paulette Goddard (Hannah), Jack Oakie (Benzino Napaloni), Henry Daniell (Garbitsch), Reginald Gardiner (Schultz), Billy Gilbert (Herring), Maurice Moskovitch (Jaeckel), Emma Dunn (Mrs Jaeckel), Bernard Gorcey (Mann), Paul Weigel (Agar), Grace Hayle (Mme Napaloni), Carter De Haven (Ambassador), Chester Conklin (Customer), Eddie Gribbon (Stormtrooper), Hank Mann (Stormtrooper), Leo White (Barber), Lucien Prival (Officer), Richard Alexander (Stormtrooper), John Davidson (Superintendent), Stanley Stanford (Man).

Chaplin's war effort: a broad burlesque in which he played an amnesiac Jewish barber and his double, the Dictator of Tomania. Chaplin's first proper talkie, he proved it by climaxing the comedy with a six-minute speech, a heartfelt plea for peace.

86: THE CHAPLIN FESTIVAL
1943.
Compilation of excepts from *The Immigrant, The Adventurer, The Cure, The Count* and *Easy Street*.

87: MONSIEUR VERDOUX
(122 mins). 11 April 1947. Chaplin-United Artists

Producer/Director/Screenplay/Music, Charles Chaplin; from an idea by Orson Wells; Photography, Roland Totheroh, Wallace Chewing; Associate Director, Robert Florey; Assistant Directors, Rex Bailey, Wheeler Dryden; Artistic Supervisor, Curt Courant; Art Director, John Beckman; Editor, Willard Nico; Music Director, Rudolph Schrager. With Charles Chaplin (Henri Verdoux), Martha Raye (Annabella Bonheur), Isobel Elson (Marie Grosnay), Marilyn Nash (The Girl), Robert Lewis (Maurice Bottello), Mady Correll (Mona Verdoux), Allison Roddell (Peter Verdoux), Audrey Betz (Martha Bottello), Ada-May (Annette), Marjorie Bennett (Maid), Helene Haigh (Yvonne), Margaret Hoffman (Lydia Floray), Irving Bacon (Pierre Couvais), Virginia Brissac (Carlotta Couvais), Almira Sessions (Lena Couvais), Edwin Mills (Jean Couvais), Eula Morgan (Phoebe Couvais), Bernard Nedell (Prefect of Police), Charles Evans (Detective Morron), Arthur Hohl (Estate Agent), John Harmon (Joe Darwin), Vera Marshe (Mrs Darwin), William Frawley (Jean La Salle), Fritz Leiber (Priest), Barbara Slater (Florist), Barry Norton (Guest), Pierre Watkin (Official), Cyril Delevanti (Postman), Charles Wagenheim (Friend), Addison Richards (Manager), James Craven (Friend), Franklin Farnum (Victim), Joseph Crehan (Broker), Frank Reicher (Doctor), Lester Matthews (Prosecutor), Wheeler Dryden (Captain Brunel).

Chaplin cut himself off from his old 'Little Fellow/Tramp' persona for all time with this portrayal of a French mass-murderer, which some saw as a social satire. A 'black comedy' ahead of its time. His former co-star Edna Purviance was an extra.

88: CHASE ME CHARLIE
(60 mins). 2 September 1948. Essanay Capital Pictures

Supervisor, Nathan Braunstein; Commentary, Hi Alexander; Music, Elias Breeskin; Narrator, Teddy Bergman.

Compilation of Essanay comedies, the British release (by Exclusive Films) had a new commentary by radio comedian Michael Howard.

A NEW MASTERPIECE OF LAUGHTER—
THE BIGGEST WINNER
OF THEM ALL!

Charles Chaplin's

HUMAN DRAMA

LIMELIGHT

co-starring

CLAIRE BLOOM
SYDNEY CHAPLIN

with

Nigel Bruce, Norman Lloyd, Buster Keaton, Marjorie Bennett

Produced, written and directed by Charles Chaplin

UNITED ARTISTS

89: LIMELIGHT
(143 mins). 23 October 1952. Celebrated Films-United Artists

Producer/Director/Screenplay/Music, Charles Chaplin; Assistant Director, Robert Aldrich; Assistant Producers, Jerome Epstein, Wheeler Dryden, Photography, Karl Struss, Roland Totheroh; Art Director, Eugene Lourie; Editor, Joseph Inge; Choreography, Andre Eglevsky, Melissa Hayden; Music Director, Keith Williams; Production Manager, Lonnie D'Orsa. With Charles Chaplin (Calvero), Claire Bloom (Thereza), Nigel Bruce (Ambrose Postant), Buster Keaton (Partner), Sydney Chaplin (Neville), Norman Lloyd (Bodalink), Andre Eglevsky (Harlequin), Melissa Hayden (Columbine), Marjorie Bennett (Mrs Alsop), Wheeler Dryden (Doctor/Pantaloon), Barry Bernard (John Redfern), Leonard Mudie (Dr Blake), Snub Pollard (Organist), Loyal Underwood (Clarinettist), Stapleton Kent (Claudius), Mollie Glessing (Maid), Charles Chaplin Jr (Clown), Geraldine Chaplin (Child), Michael Chaplin (Child), Josephine Chaplin (Child), Carmelita Maracci Corps de Ballet.

Chaplin is a has-been comedian who saves a young dancer from gassing herself and encourages her to become a ballerina. In turn she arranges for him to make a come-back appearance, but the effort kills him. Slow, sentimental, nevertheless a sincere evocation of the old London music-halls. Chaplin's last American film.

90: A KING IN NEW YORK
(109 mins). 12 September 1957. Attica Films-Archway

Producer/Director/Screenplay/Music, Charles Chaplin; Photography, Georges Perinal; Art Director, Alan Harris; Editor, John Seabourne. With Charles Chaplin (King Shadov), Dawn Addams (Ann Kay), Oliver Johnston (Jaume), Maxine Audley (Queen Irene), Jerry Desmonde (Prime Minister), Michael Chaplin (Rupert McAbee), Harry Green (Lawyer Green), Phil Brown (Headmaster), John McLaren (Mr McAbee), Alan Gifford (Superintendent), Shani Wallis (Singer), Joy Nichols (Singer), Joan Ingram (Mona Cromwell), Sidney James (Johnson), Robert Arden (Liftboy), Nicholas Tanner (Butler), Macdonald Parke (American), Lauri Lupino Lane and George Truzzi.

Chaplin's first film to be made in his home country and a satire on the country he had made his home, but which had exiled him. As a king deposed by revolution he becomes a star of television commercials.

91: THE CHAPLIN REVUE
(117 mins). 25 September 1959. Roy Films-United Artists

Producer/Director/Screenplay/Music, Charles Chaplin.

Chaplin takes a leaf out of the other get-rich-quick merchants by making his own compilation of past hits. With new music and narration by himself, he brought *A Dog's Life*, *The Pilgrim* and *Shoulder Arms* back for a new generation.

92: A COUNTESS FROM HONG KONG
(120 mins). November 1966. Universal Pictures

Producer, Jerome Epstein; Director/Screenplay/Music, Charles Chaplin; Production Supervisor, Denis Johnson; Photography, Arthur Ibbetson; Production Design, Don Ashton; Art Director, Robert Cartwright; Editor, Gordon Hales; Assistant Director, Jack Causey; Music Director, Lambert Williamson; Processes, Technicolor/Cinemascope. With Marlon Brando (Ogden Mears), Sophia Loren (Natascha Alexandroff), Sydney Chaplin (Harvey Crothers), Tippi Hedren (Martha Mears), Patrick Cargill (Hudson), Margaret Rutherford (Miss Gaulswallow), Michael Medwin (John Felix), Oliver Johnston (Clark), John Paul (Captain), Angela Scoular (Society Girl), Peter Bartlett (Steward), Bill Nagy (Crawford), Dilys Laye (Saleswoman), Angela Pringle (Baroness), Jenny Bridges (Countess), Balbina (Maid), Geraldine Chaplin (Girl), Josephine Chaplin (Girl), Victoria Chaplin (Girl), Marianne Stone (Reporter), Larry Cross (Reporter), Carol Cleveland (Nurse), Charles Chaplin (Steward).

Chaplin's last film, made in England, in technicolour, and cinemascope, with two international stars, was supposed to be a featherweight farce but instead was a heavyweight flop. Chaplin's personal farewell to the screen was a cameo role as a seasick steward.

93: CHAPLIN'S ART OF COMEDY
(64 mins). 1966. Pizor-Sherman Productions

Producers, Irwin Pizor, Samuel Sherman; Narrator, Dave Anderson; Music, Elias Breeskin.

Compilation of Essanay shorts: *The Tramp*, *The Bank*, *The Champion*, *His New Job*, *A Night in the Show*, *A Woman*.

94: THE FUNNIEST MAN IN THE WORLD
(102 mins). 1967. Funnyman Films

Producers, Vernon Becker, Mel May; Screenplay, Vernon Becker; Editor, William Dalzell; Music, Albert Hague; Narrator, Douglas Fairbanks Jr.

Compilation of Keystone and Essanay shorts, plus rare footage from Chaplin animated cartoons by Pat Sullivan, and Chaplin impersonators Billy Ritchie and Billie West.

95: THE GENTLEMAN TRAMP
(78 mins). DeDam-Audjeff-RBC Films

Producer, Bert Schneider; Director/Screenplay/Editor, Richard Patterson; Music, Charles Chaplin; Narrators, Walter Matthau, Jack Lemmon, Laurence Olivier.

Compilation of excerpts from Chaplin films together with newsreel footage, photographs, and home movies by Chaplin and Oona Chaplin.

ACKNOWLEDGEMENTS

The compiler is grateful to the following individuals, organisations and publishers for their help in the production of this book: Denis Gifford, W.O.G. Lofts, Kevin Brownlow, Roland Totheroh, Raymond Lee, Joan Jordan, Virginia Cherrill, Groucho Marx, Jean Renoir, Sydney Chaplin, Graham Greene, Candice Bergen and John Doubleday. Also The British Museum, The British Newspaper Library, The British Film Institute, The Press Association, the New York Public Library and The Hollywood Film Archives. Los Angeles, Fleetway Publications, *Photoplay* magazines, Newnes-Pearson Ltd, *Classic Film Collector*, *Punch*, *Harper's Magazine*, *The New York Times*, *Picturegoer* magazine, *Sight & Sound*, *The Spectator*, *Screen Writer*, *The Sunday Chronicle*, *Arts Magazine* and *Life* magazine. And, most especially, the spirit of Charlie Chaplin which inspired this tribute from its inception: he is now truly one among the immortals.

PETER HAINING